IMAGES
of America

MARCY

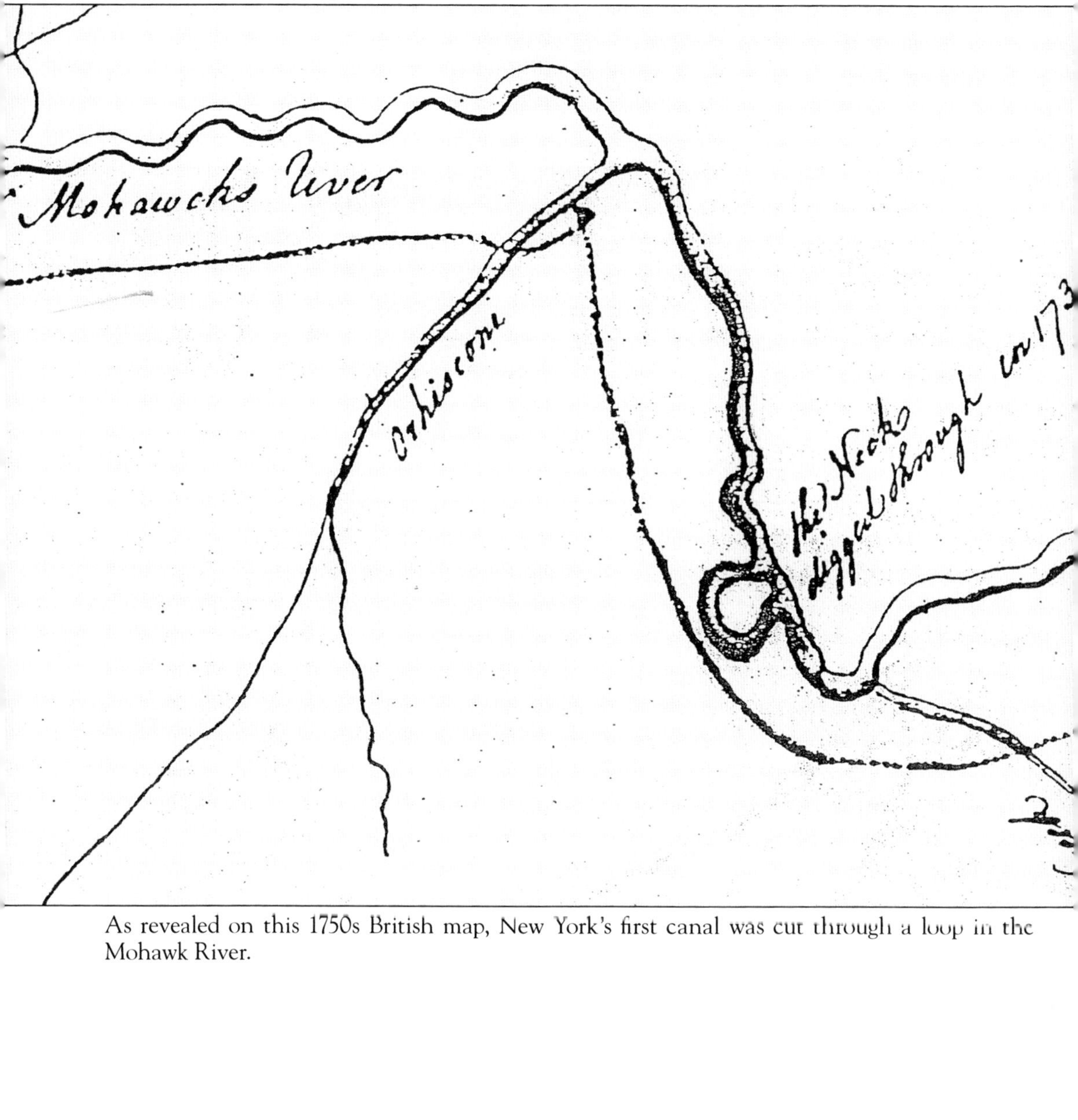

As revealed on this 1750s British map, New York's first canal was cut through a loop in the Mohawk River.

On the cover: Seen here are the Thomas family children in the year 1895 on the farm located on the River Road. They are, from left to right, William, Anna, Irving, and Roy. Not shown is Ray, Roy's twin. Roy is holding his pet fox. Farm boys would find a baby fox on the farm and raise it as a pet dog. This was before they knew there was a disease called rabies. (Author's collection.)

IMAGES
of America

MARCY

Raymond F. Ball

ARCADIA
PUBLISHING

ISBN 978-0-7385-5524-9

Published by Arcadia Publishing
Charleston SC, Chicago IL, Portsmouth NH, San Francisco CA

Printed in the United States of America

Library of Congress Catalog Card Number: 2007930419

For all general information contact Arcadia Publishing at:
Telephone 843-853-2070
Fax 843-853-0044
E-mail sales@arcadiapublishing.com
For customer service and orders:
Toll-Free 1-888-313-2665

Visit us on the Internet at www.arcadiapublishing.com

To my daughter-in-law Debra Ball.

Contents

ACKNOWLEDGMENTS

This page is not large enough to list all the historic societies, libraries, cemeteries, clerk's offices, archives, and Web sites that have helped me in the past almost 30 years of genealogy and local history research. God surely blessed me by bringing so many good and helpful people into my life. My sincere, humble thanks to all.

This book is dedicated to my daughter-in-law Debra Ball. She was a great help to me in research and typing and was always eager to be useful with never a complaint of using her time. One year, we traveled over a 1,000 miles searching for and photographing markers. She was my inspiration and tireless helper. Two years ago, Debbie was stricken with cancer of the stomach. Whenever we left to go home, we would give each other the thumbs up sign. The last time she could hardly lift her arm, but the thumb was up and the smile was faint. She fought a hard battle, but at age 41, the cancer won the fight. The memory of my helper is all through this book.

INTRODUCTION

Marcy history is rather unique, but at the same time not unlike that of several other towns that extend the length of the Mohawk Valley in central New York. Thousands of years ago, at the time of the great Ice Age, the ice covered most of what is presently New York State. This ice was nearly one mile in height and covered most of Lake Iroquois, which was one of the ancient Great Lakes, now known as Lake Ontario. From the Lower Hudson Valley north to Albany and beyond to the St. Lawrence existed Lake Albany, and it also was frozen over with thick ice.

About 12,000 years ago the ice began to recede or melt, and as it did, it left behind the Catskill and Adirondack mountain ranges. These must have appeared like islands in the large body of water. The St. Lawrence and Champlain Valleys drained out in a few hundred years, but Lake Iroquois showed no sign of changing. To the west, it had been slowly draining into what would become the five Great Lakes. At Little Falls, the main lake narrowed down to a break in the rock strata. Here the escaping water pressure was so great as to cut pot holes about three feet in diameter and four feet deep into the solid rock.

This escaping water only added to the water level below, which archaeologists have named Lake Amsterdam. The water found a small opening in the lower rim of this lake and began to escape through it, and the pressure of the water behind kept working away, making a larger opening. After several thousand years, this small opening was worn away and has become what is called the "noses"—the natural gateway to the Mohawk Valley and the entire west.

This break in the mountain range is the most important geological event that occurred since the Ice Age, for without it we would still have a giant lake, there would be no gateway for settlers, boats, trains, cars, and trucks, and the Township of Marcy would never have been.

Instead Marcy is located on what would have been the north shore of the lake, on a plateau of rich sandy loam composed of thousands of years of lake bottom silt and rich vegetation. The recovery and new growth took hundreds of years. Compared with the show that nature put on over the last 10,000 years, what could we as people do in only 400?

But try we would. Our early settlers came right after the Revolutionary War, not from Europe, but from the New England states.

Originally this entire area was called "Deerfield," and it will be remembered as the place where the Native Americans burned the settler's homes; the march by Gen. Nicholas Herkimer and his citizen army to the bloody battle of Oriskany and the siege of nearby Fort Stanwix. Most of this was portrayed in the movie *Drums along the Mohawk*.

After a few years, some settlers moved to the western part of Deerfield and began new settlements in the heavily wooded wilderness. The year was 1793, and this was the pioneer beginning of our future town. The first chore they faced was for two men to drive a wagon the 50 miles to Onondaga Lake and dig enough salt to last until the next season. Then they had to get the salt home safe and dry to share with each family. This was no small task when there were no roads, just woods and wilderness.

Most settlers tried to arrange their arrival for the late spring, if the weather cooperated. They would leave from the New England states in late March or early April and have their possessions in a wagon pulled by oxen or horses. This was a rough time of the year for both man and beast, as they would encounter late winter snows and the rainy season. Many a wagon broke down with a broken wheel, and lucky was the settler who had a spare wheel with him. Even luckier was the settler who was with a group of men that could help lift the wagon and install the new wheel. This meant cutting down a tree and using the trunk as a long pole to pry up the wagon out of the mud high enough to remove and replace the wheel.

Before leaving Deerfield, each settler would purchase or obtain rights to a plot of ground that appeared proper for their needs. The wagon served as shelter while some land was cleared and planted. The trees that were cut down were reduced to the trunks for building a cabin and the branches for firewood. It is hard to comprehend what these people endured and the mental anguish of knowing that they had from springtime until late fall to clear the land, get a crop, erect a shelter for themselves and the animals they had, and provide warmth before the onset of winter.

The settler's plots were just that—plots of land of so many acres and of various shapes and sizes. There were no roads, just random trails. To get to a certain plot, it was necessary to cross over your neighbor's and other plots. Early town government decided that a road system was necessary and voted to unite all the trails into a public road system. How to do this without money seemed impossible, so it was decided that each settler would be responsible for the road going by or through his property. This system carried on for many years until government grew and a taxation program brought in income to provide for roads and bridges.

Should the roads have a name or number? That was a big question early on in town. Many settlers had little education, so it was feared that they would not be able to read numbers. But they did seem to know where others lived, so it was decided to name roads by the name of the original settler on that road.

Life went on about the same as it would in any farm community with one exception—the hamlet of Stittville. With the railroad going through the village in the 1850s, things changed. Businessmen saw an opportunity in the available labor supply, water power, and good receiving and shipping.

Soon numerous factories were built and with the excellent schools, Stittville became a good place to live. But disaster struck several times in the form of large fires, which burned entire neighborhoods of homes and businesses right to the ground. The village had everything going for it, except no water and no fire department or fireman. It would be many years before the arrival of city water and hydrants.

But the future of the hamlet of Stittville and the town of Marcy was now at stake in a big way. Over the years, the mills in the village had all come under control of the Oneida Knitting Company, and that organization decided to liquidate. The Stittville plant and 15 village homes were auctioned off in a huge auction. Thus in the year 1917, at the stroke of the auctioneers gavel, came an end to early manufacturing in Stittville and the town of Marcy.

One

Mohawk Explorers

Native Americans used the Mohawk River as one of their main modes of travel. Early settlers followed their example. Starting about 1693, long before any settlements in this wilderness, navigators who were engaged in trade and exploration used the waterways that connected Albany with Lake Ontario. They traveled in canoes and lightweight boats called bateaux. These bateaux were propelled by using long, metal-tipped poles, used to push the boat through the water. The Mohawk River, because of its meandering effect, had many loops or "ox bows" as they were called. One traveler wrote in his diary that they camped that night at a bend in the river. Come morning, they proceeded to pole their bateaux up the ox bow, and at dusk, camped at the next bend in the river. From there, they could look over and see the previous night's campsite. They had labored all day and gained a distance of only several hundred feet. On one such trip, the boat crew, using only shovels, dug a channel from one loop to the opposite loop just wide enough for the boat. In time, the natural effect of the water would widen this channel. This became New York State's first canal, and it is identified on at least a half dozen British maps as the "neck digged through in 1730."

This site in Marcy is fully recognized by the New York State Museum and is now on both the New York State and National Registers of Historic Places.

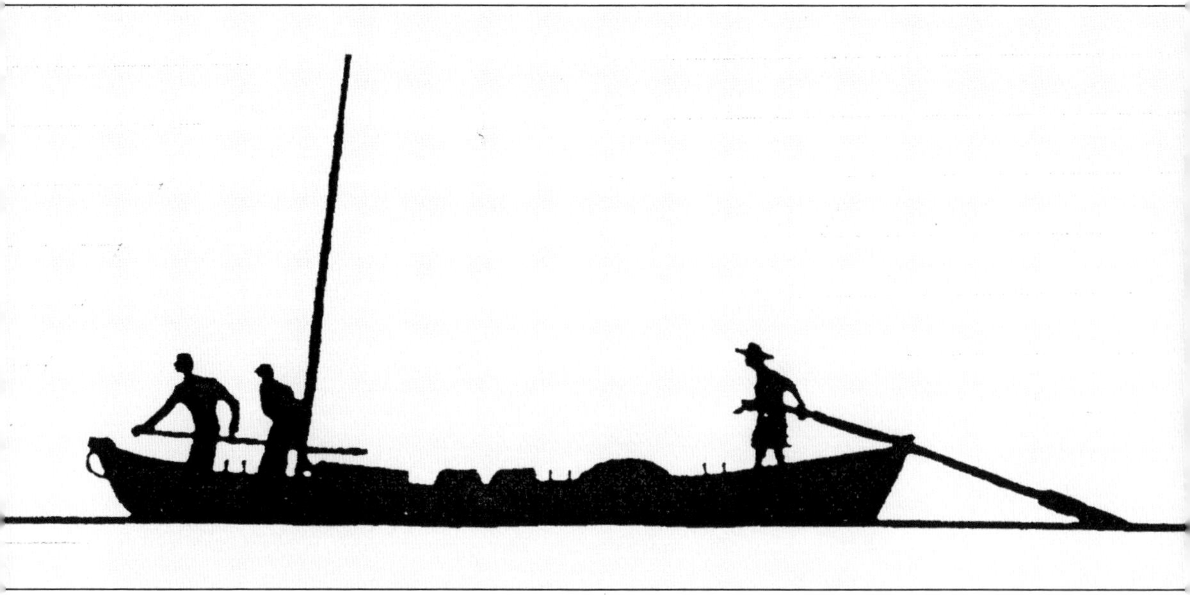

Light, flat-bottomed bateaux, like this three-handed version, were the most common carriers of people and cargo on the Mohawk route in the 1700s.

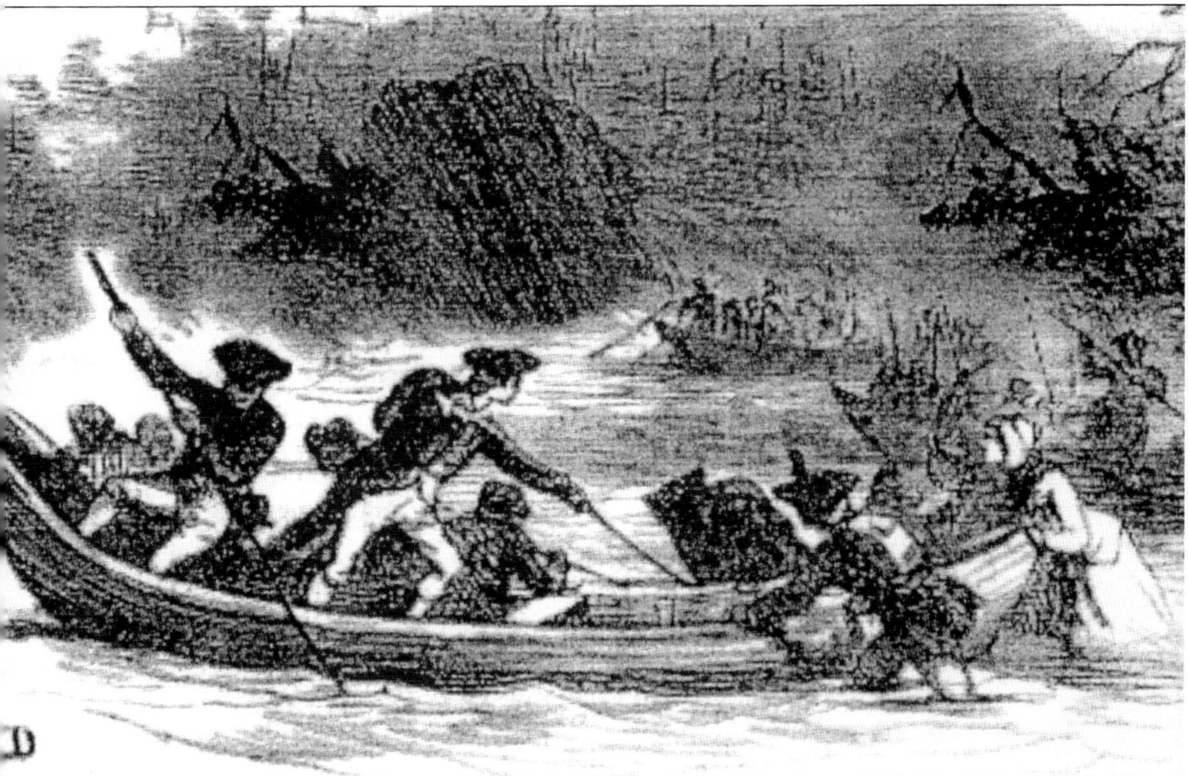

Seen here is a New York State Museum drawing of pioneers polling and pushing boats up the wild and rapid-filled Mohawk River in the early 1700s.

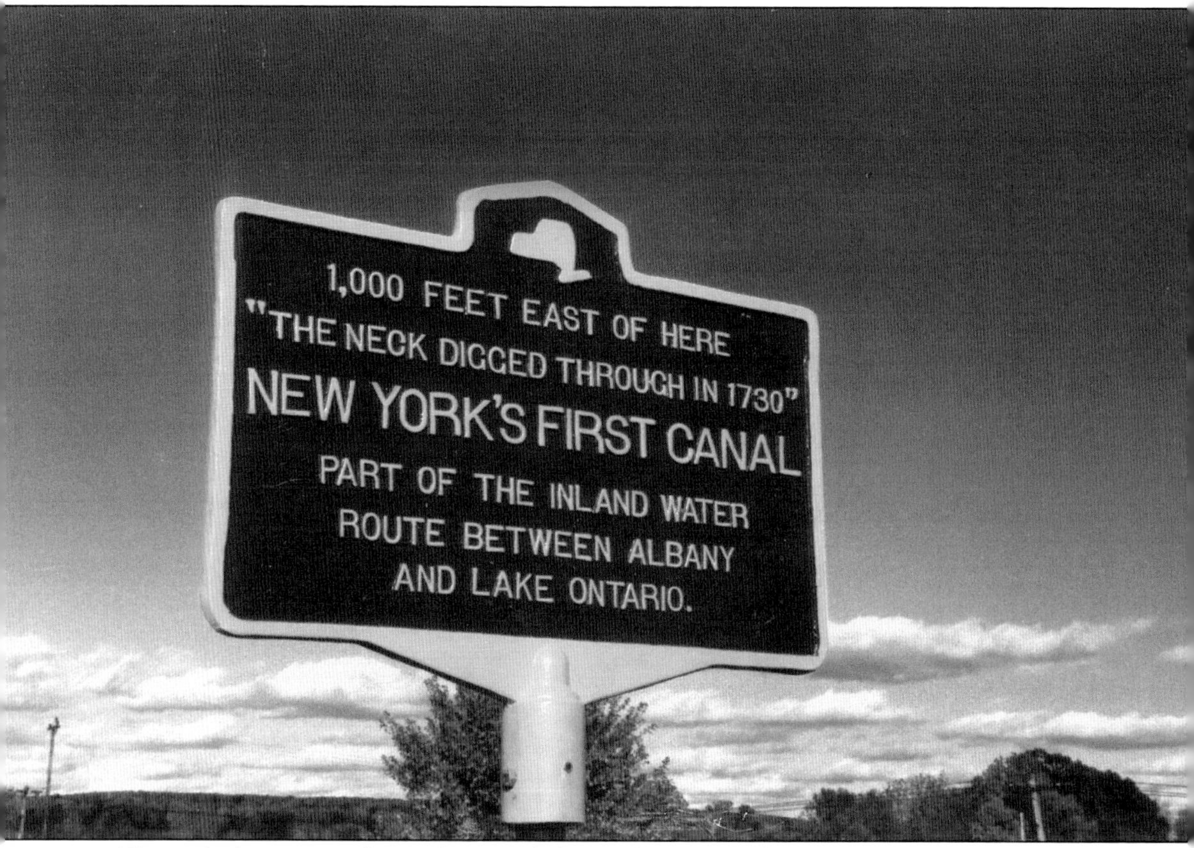

This is the historic marker at the site of "the Neck," New York's first canal. This was a major part of the waterway between Albany and Lake Ontario.

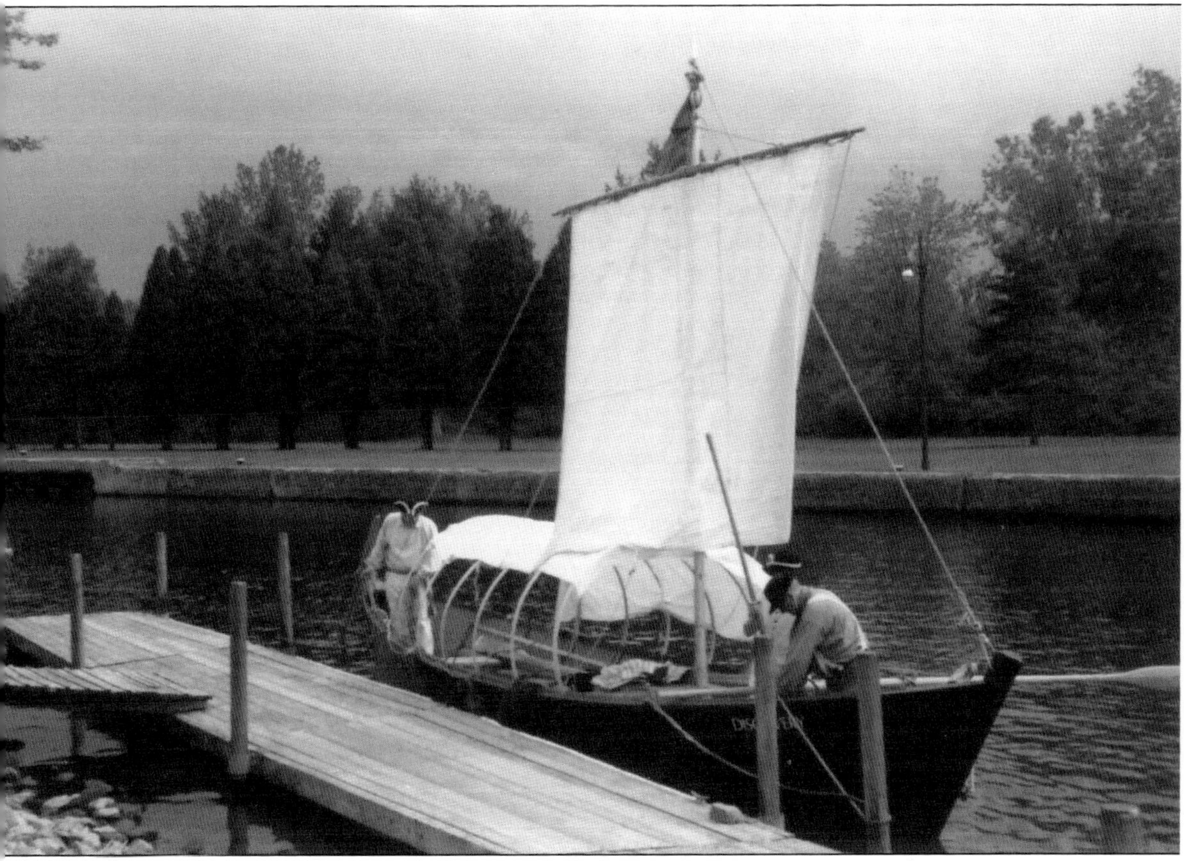

Philip Lord, from the New York State Museum, and his assistants are pictured with a bateaux on a special trip from Albany to Lake Ontario to prove how pioneers made the trip. No complete bateaux has ever been found, except the remains of one submerged in Lake George. Any attempt to remove it would cause it to break apart. However, a complete set of blueprints was found in an old boat-building shop near Schenectady. From these plans the above replica was built, and it is now in the New York State Museum at Albany.

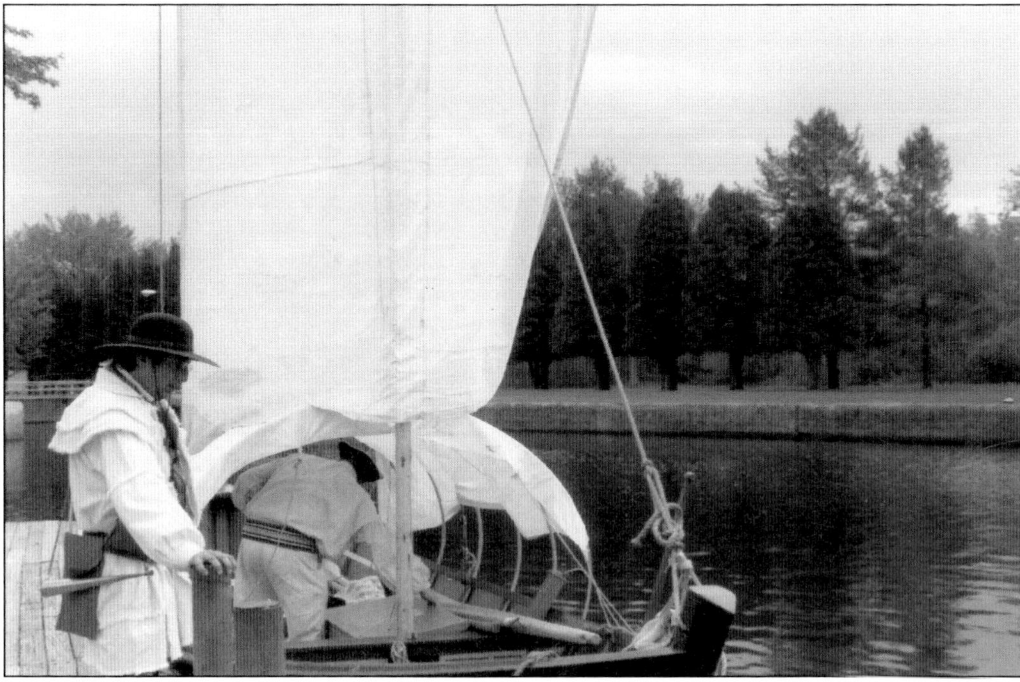

Philip Lord of the History Department at the New York State Museum shows how a bateaux could be fitted with a canvas cover to protect against adverse weather and even a sail to help with movement when there was a westerly wind.

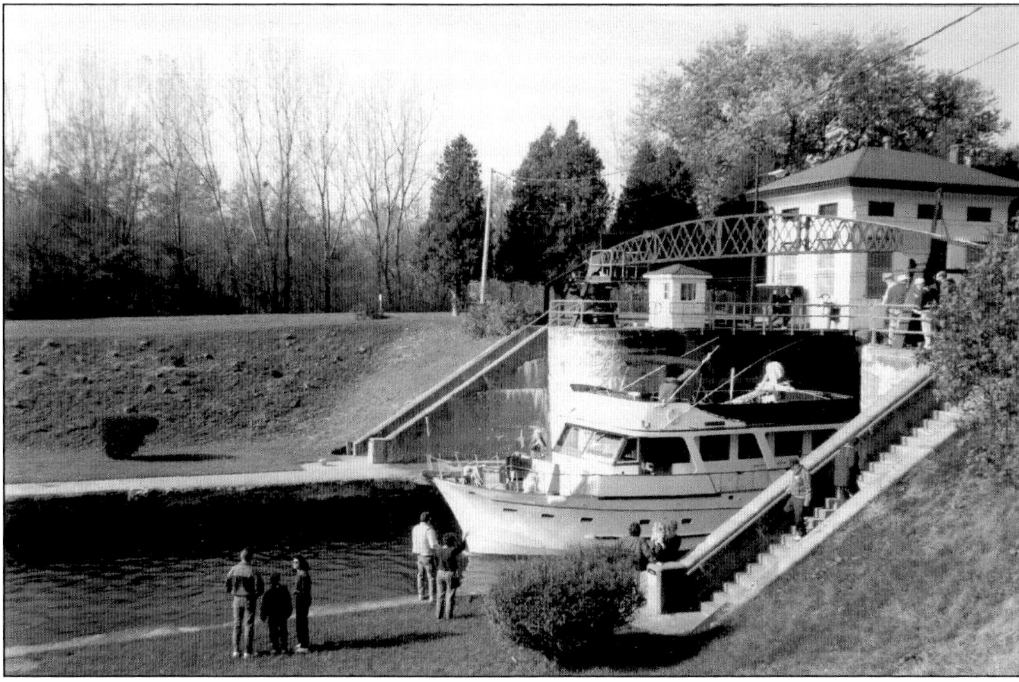

The present-day canal built in 1912 and a boat going through lock 20 on the way from Toronto to the Caribbean are depicted here. Cruise ships and private pleasure boats have largely replaced the cargo barges.

Two

Early Settlers

In 1773, the first settlers came to this area with their families, namely George Weaver, Mark Damuth, and Christian Reall. They built cabins, cleared land for farms, and lived peacefully for nearly three years until the colonies revolted and the Revolutionary War began. A friendly Oneida native named Blue Back warned the settlers of an impending attack by Tories and their Native American allies. The settlers fled for their lives back down the valley to "Little Stone Arabia," a small fort in Schuyler near Palatine.

In the summer of 1784, after the Revolutionary War, these three families moved back to Deerfield and rebuilt their farms. In 1788, a sawmill was erected on Nine Mile Creek and soon settlers came to the area, and in a few years, it became known as Red Mills.

Later in the early 1800s, the settlement was renamed Stittville after Robert Stitt who built the first store and small hotel.

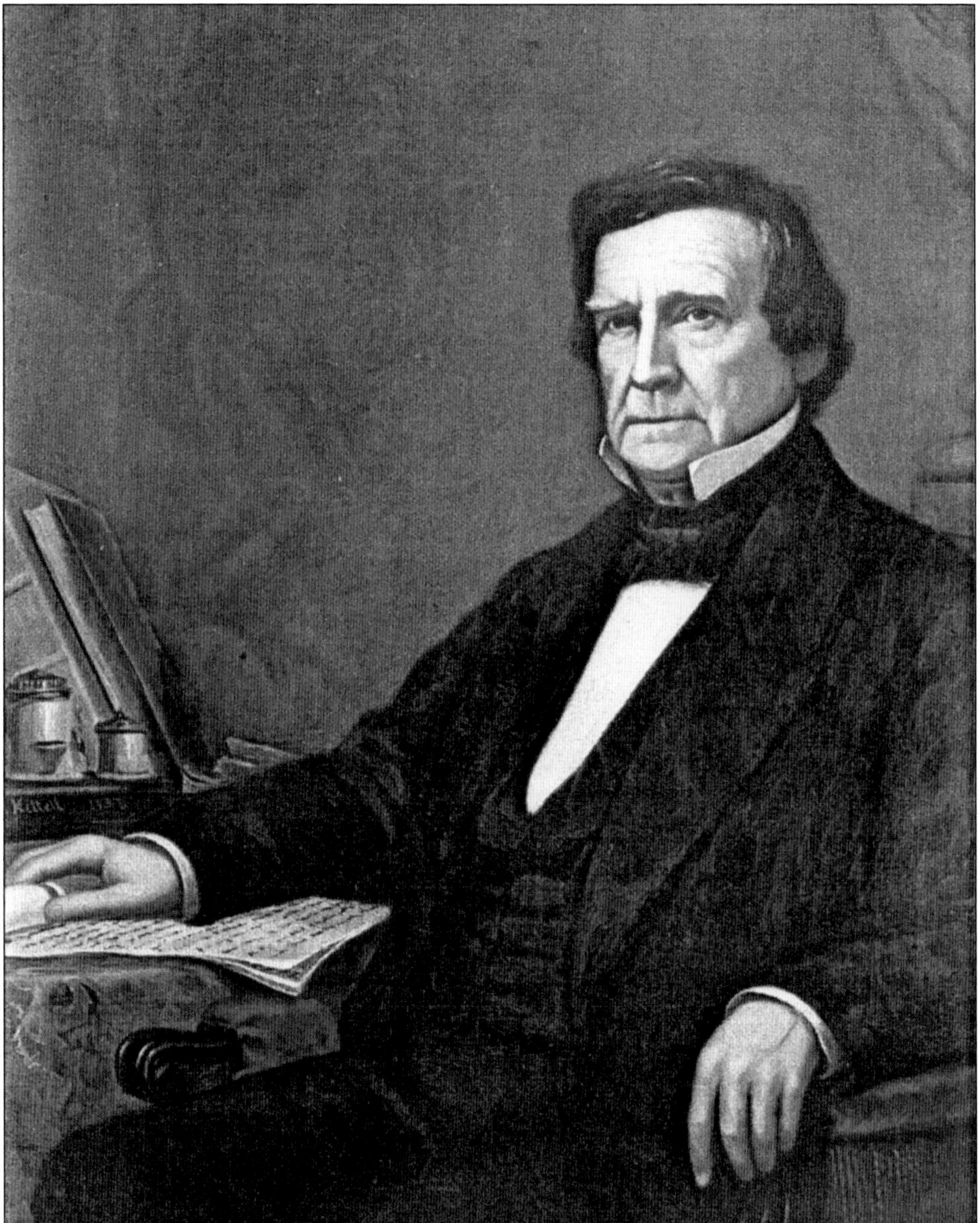

Shown is a portrait of Gov. William L. Marcy. The original painting is in the New York Historical Society.

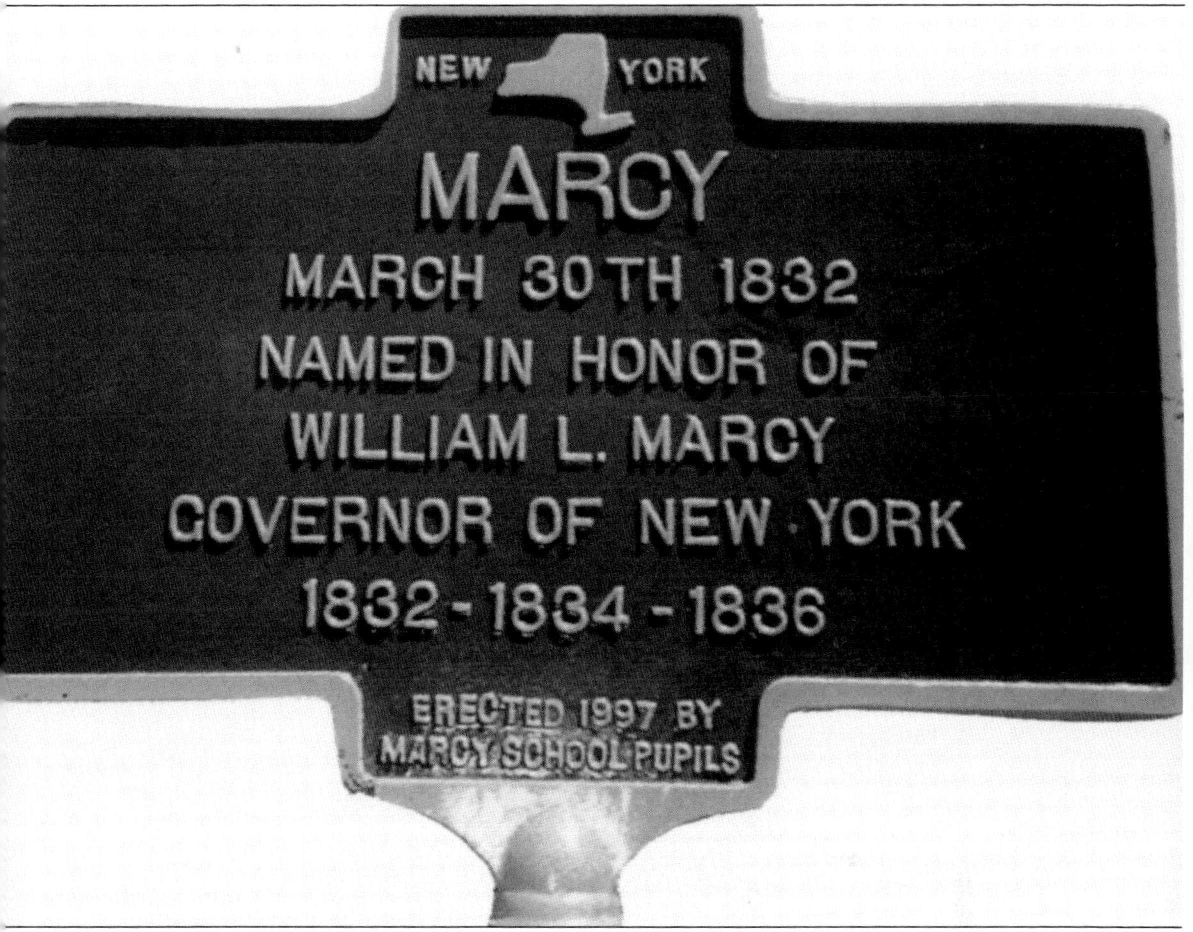

This historic marker honoring the birth of the Town of Marcy and Gov. William Marcy was erected in 1997 by Marcy schoolchildren.

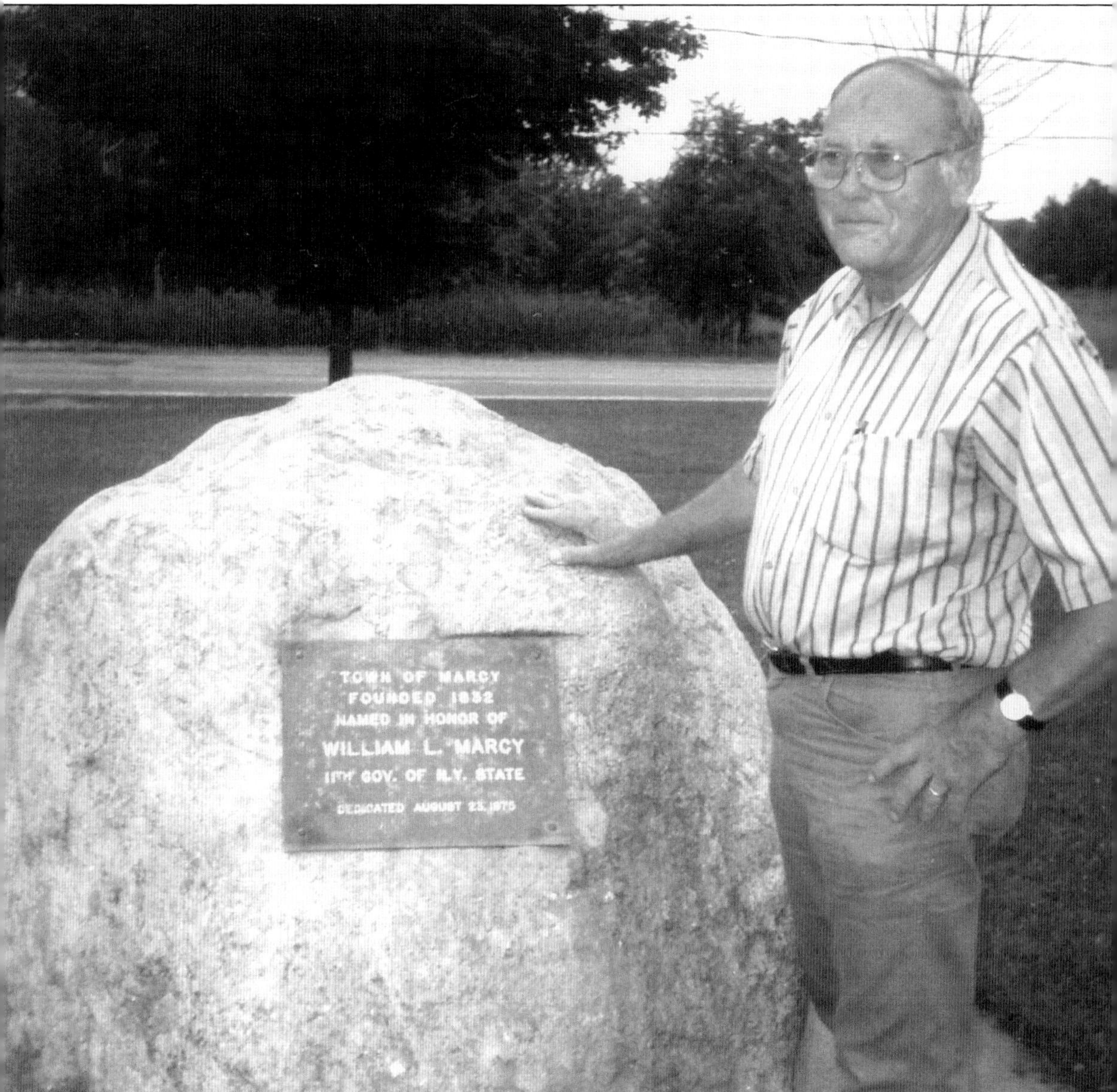

In 1994, Dale Marcy, the great-grandson of William L. Marcy, traveled here from Kansas to see the town named after his ancestor.

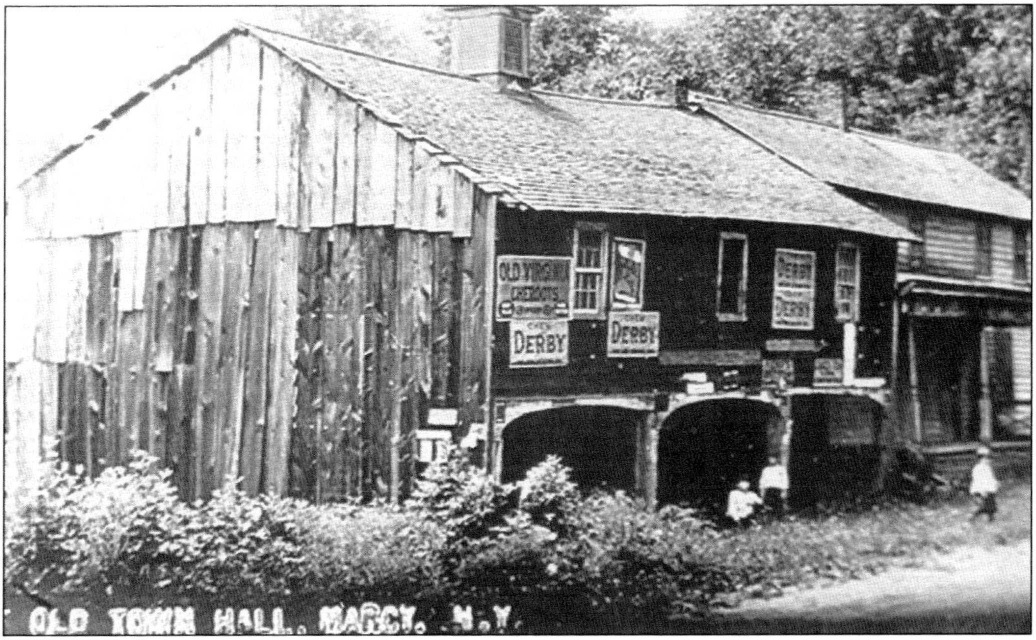

This is the only photograph of the old town hall. The town board members would meet in each other's homes during inclement weather and in this barn, if conditions allowed. It was considered a luxury since horses could be put underneath it during a storm.

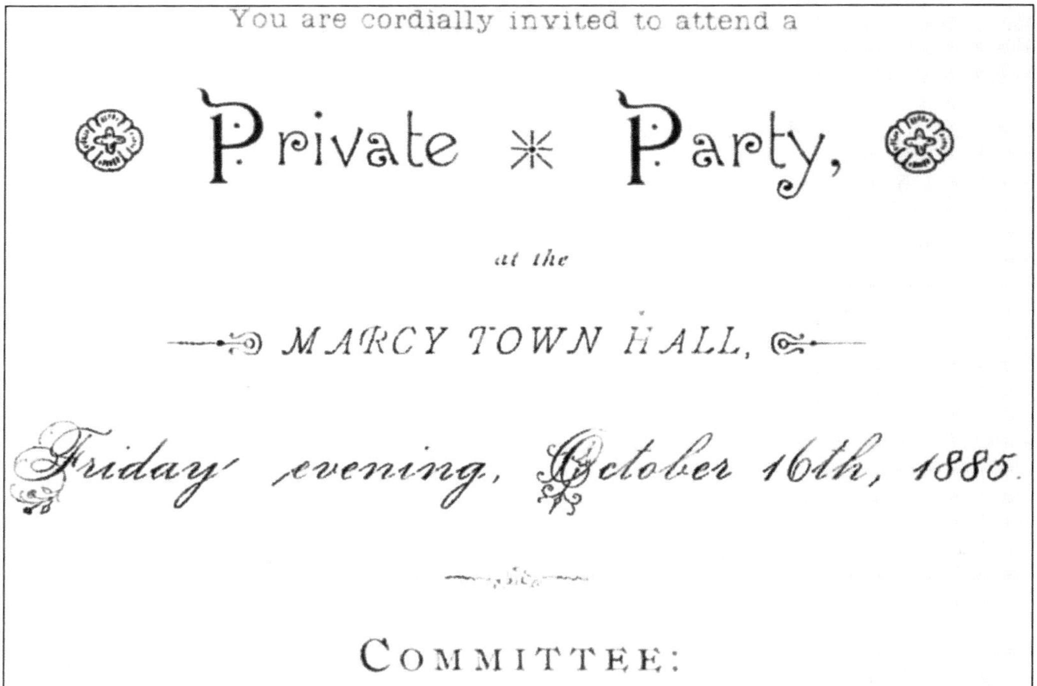

You are cordially invited to attend a

Private Party,

at the

MARCY TOWN HALL,

Friday evening, October 16th, 1885.

COMMITTEE:

John Pickett. D. J. Davis.

The town hall also served as a meeting room for private parties, and, as this invitation shows, it was being used for that purpose at least up until 1885.

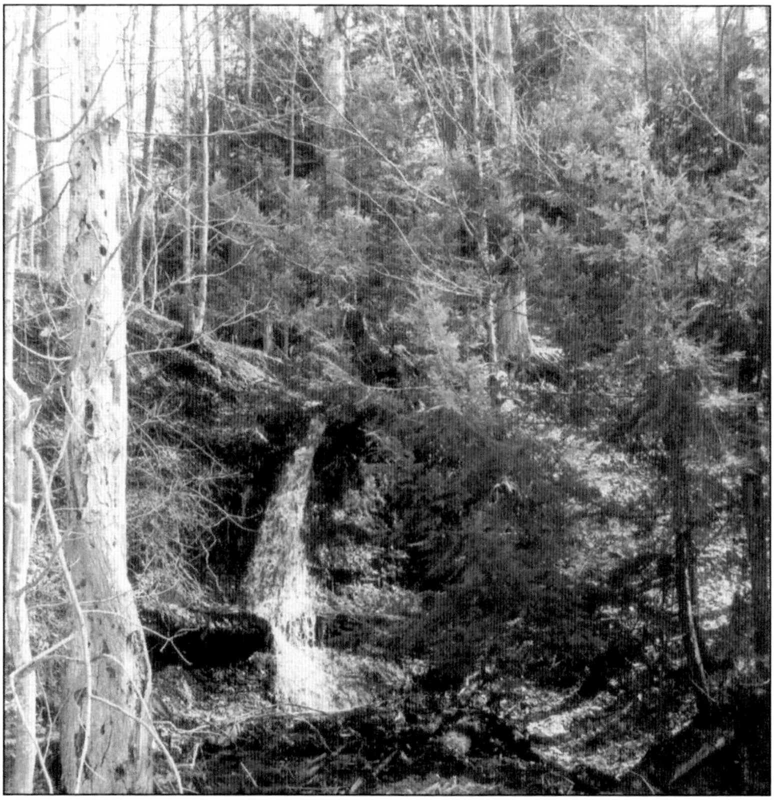

Ritchie Falls, off Ritchie Road, has been running like this since early settlers discovered it in 1788. The falls originate from an underground source and empty into the Nine Mile Creek.

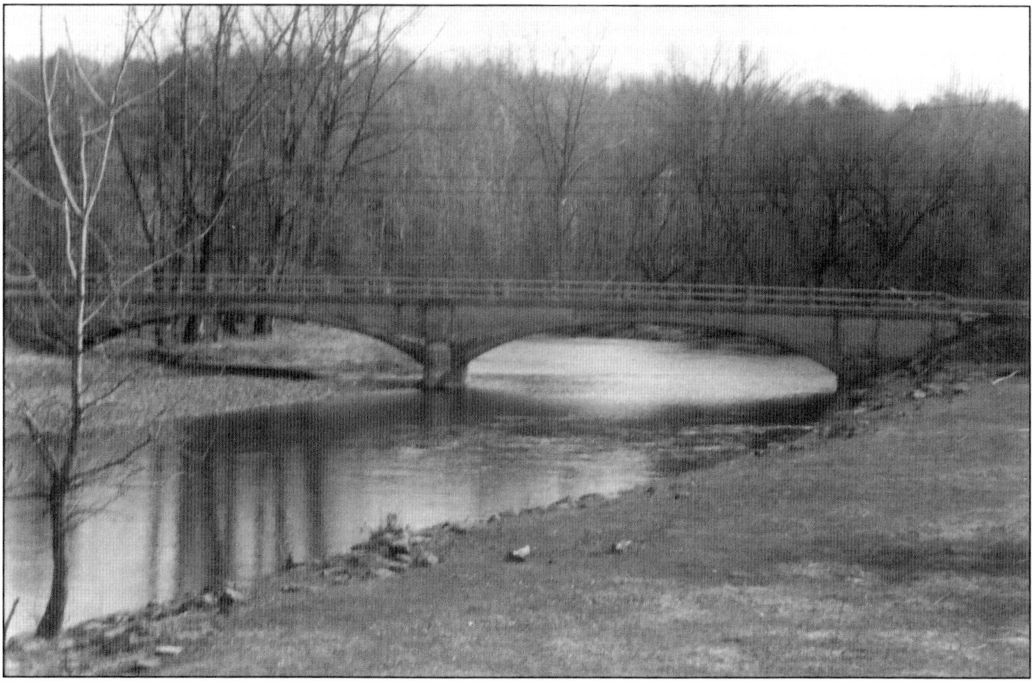

Nine Mile Bridge is shown in late fall, when the water is low. During the spring runoff, the water will be about three feet higher, as indicated by the high water mark.

Three

A Town Is Born

The town of Deerfield was very large and shaped like a backwards letter J, with the lower part extending west about seven miles. The main settlement was primarily in the lower west end near the Mohawk River. From here to the main corners in Deerfield was about eight miles. If a man had a good horse and buggy, he could make the trip along the old Native American trails through the wilderness, conduct his business, and be back home by dark. That is if the weather was good and dry. In winter or rainy weather, the trails through the woods were almost impossible to navigate. In the early 1820s, frustration and the feeling of isolation from Deerfield led the settlers to petition the legislature for action. It took two years of lobbying, but finally, on March 30, 1832, a new township was created. At the time, the governor of New York State was William L. Marcy, a very popular man who had served in many different capacities. In his honor the settlers named the new town Marcy.

The hamlet of Stittville, since its beginning, was a part of the town of Trenton. The boundary line between Marcy and Trenton ran through the center of Stittville and this caused a lot of problems. On December 23, 1891, the boundary line was moved to the north, which put the entire hamlet of Stittville in the town of Marcy.

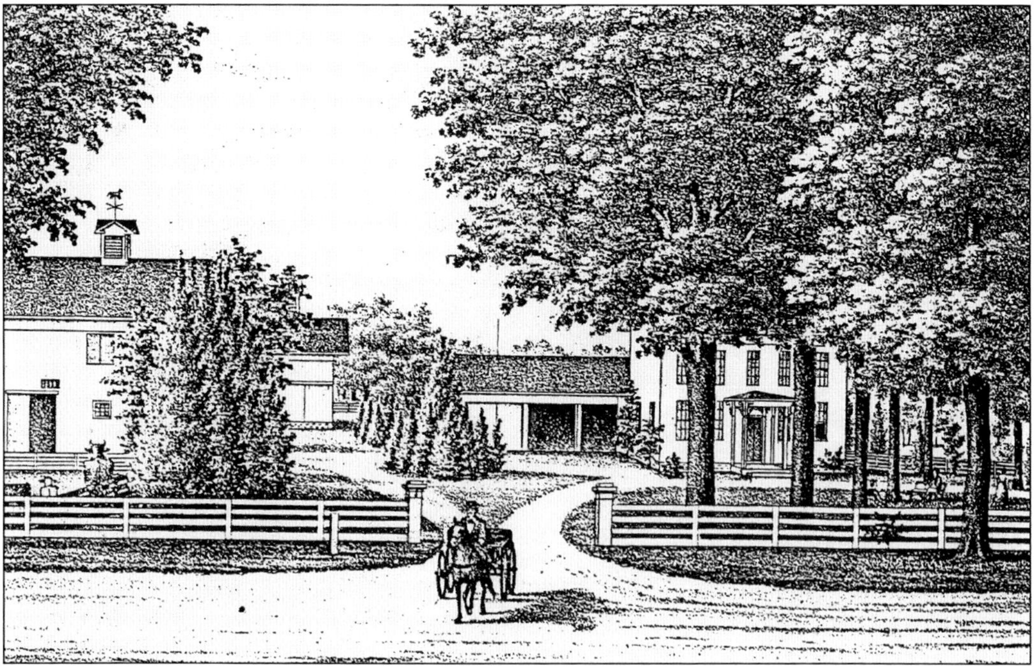

Martin Cavana was born in a log house in Utica about 1800. This is an 1860 lithograph of the Cavana homestead where, in 1823, his son James was born.

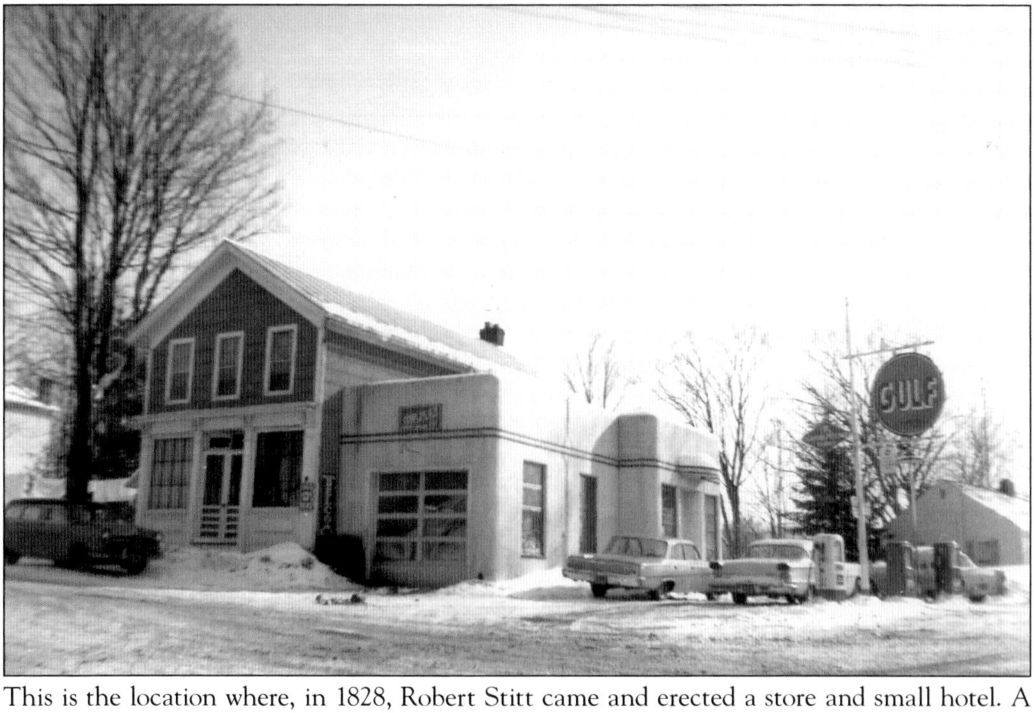

This is the location where, in 1828, Robert Stitt came and erected a store and small hotel. A small village developed in the area, and the residents named it Stittville in his honor. In the 1930s, a new owner added a gas station onto the side of the present house.

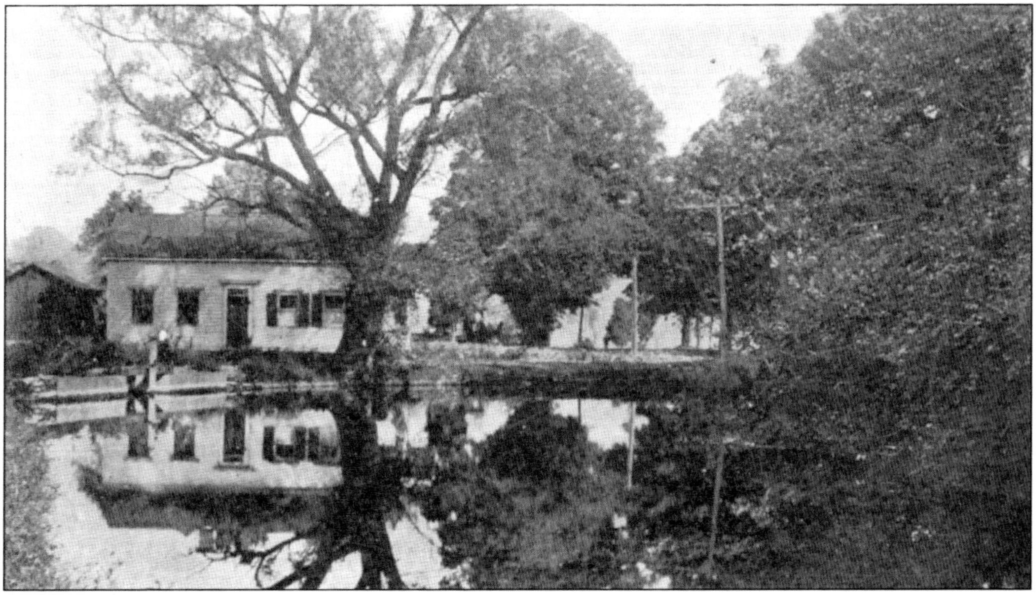

Water diverted from Nine Mile Creek by a dam flowed through a dike to form this pond near the Stittville knitting mill and furnished power to run the mill. This was a familiar sight in Stittville for about 75 years until the dam went out. After that, the mill operated on steam power.

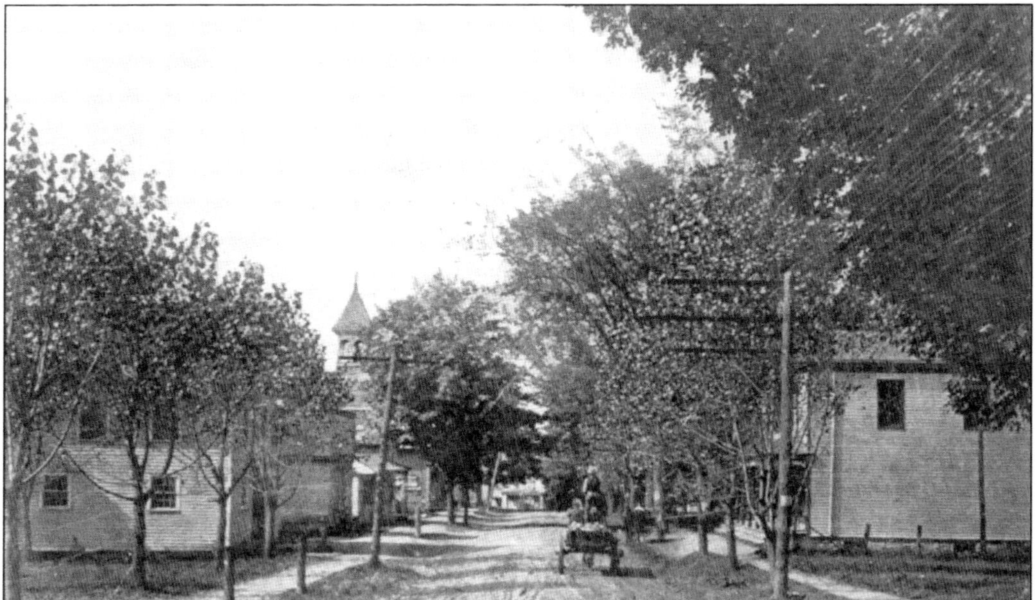

This view down Main Street faces the four corners. This shows the buildings as they looked prior to the fire the night of March 31 through April 1, 1910. All these buildings burned, including the Methodist church whose steeple can be seen in the background.

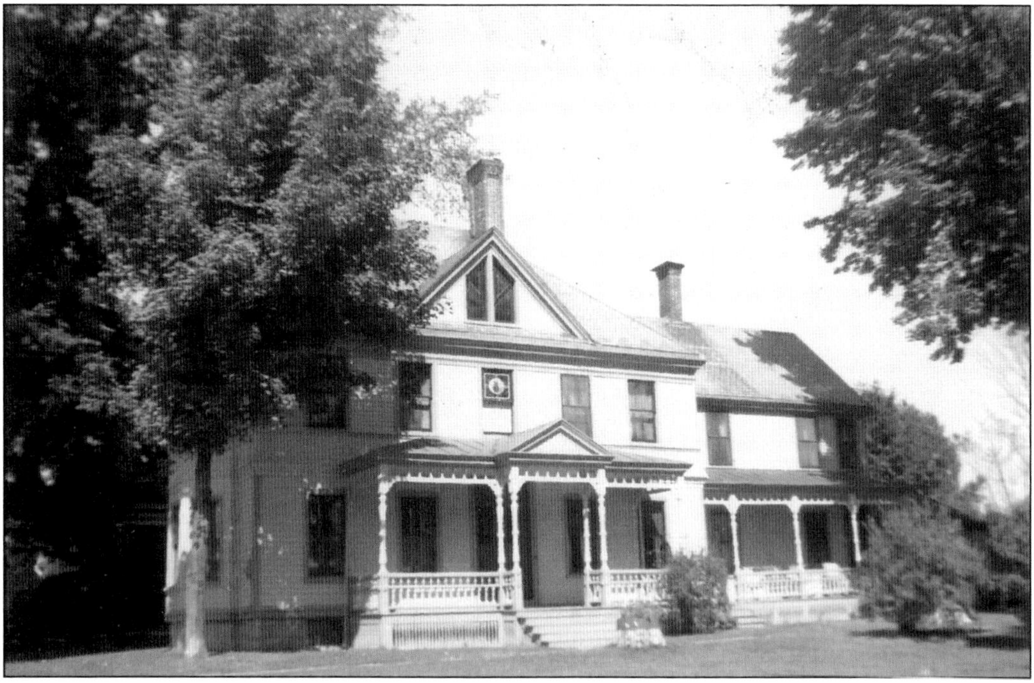

This was the home of Willard and Addie Raymer Atwood, believed to have been erected in 1890. It was on Maple Avenue near the four corners and faced the mill, which was run for many years by Willard in partnership with Charles Hackett.

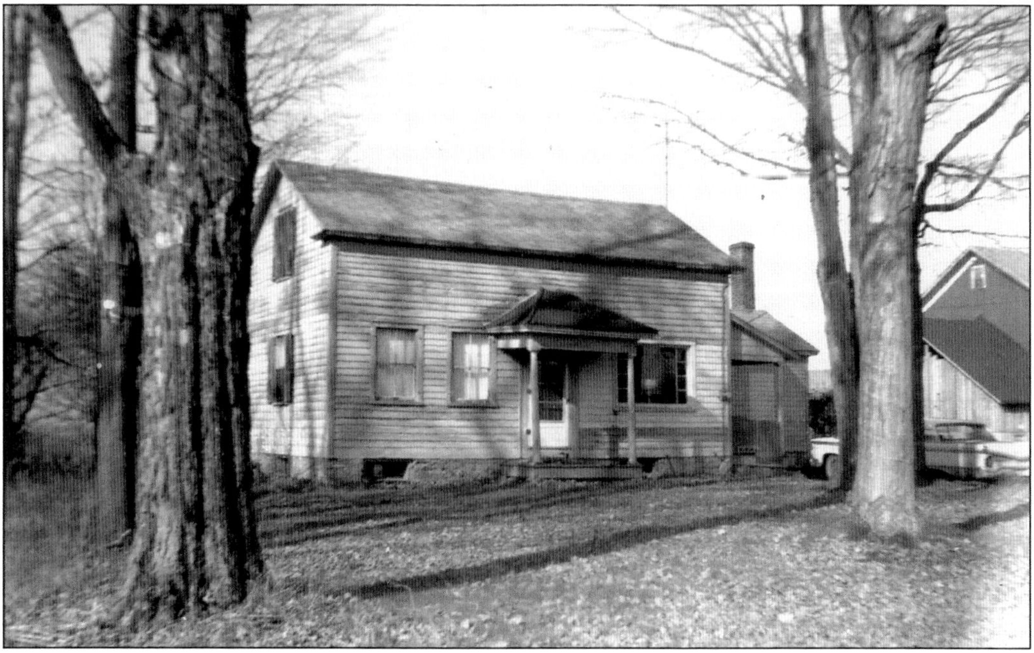

This house is on the farm that was once owned by Erastus and Hannah Raymer. It is on the Stittville-Marcy Road, the first farm on the west side of the road south of Benton Road.

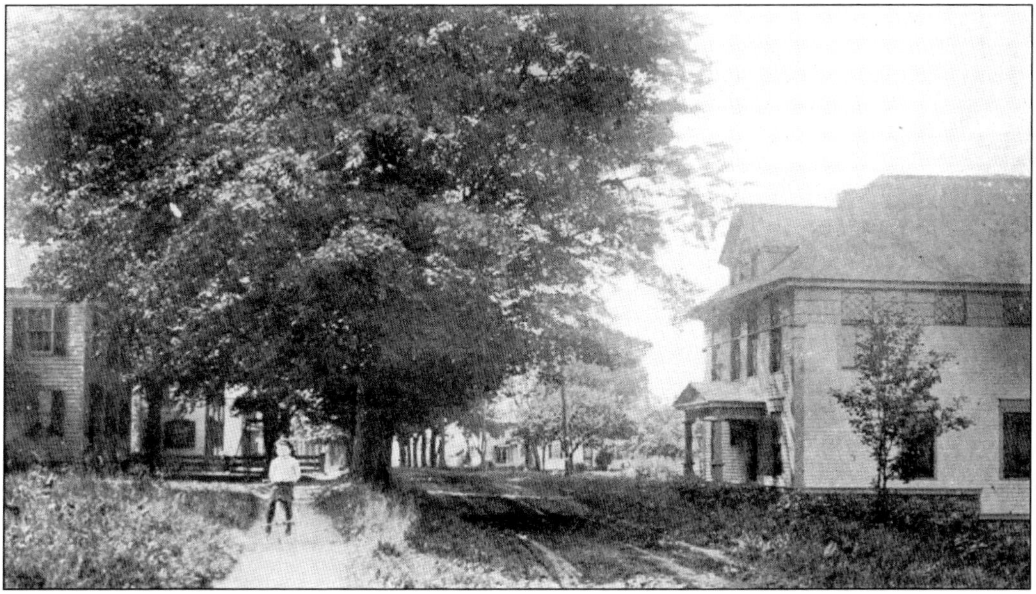

Seen here, East Maple Avenue in the hamlet of Stittville was a muddy dirt road, but it had nice sidewalks.

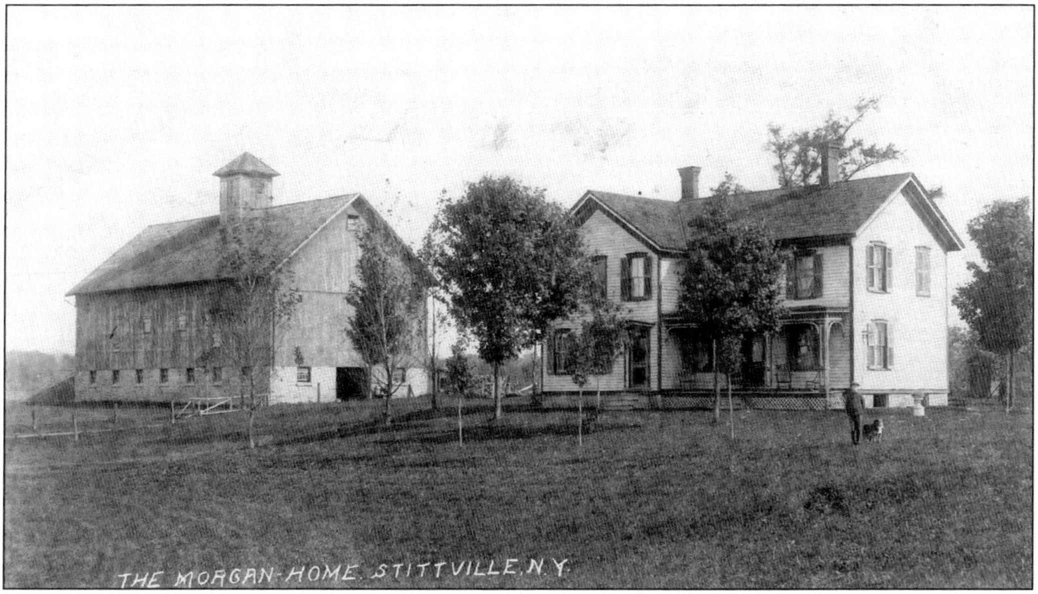

Asa and Elsie Morgan came to Stittville in 1800, and this was the Morgan home. Jennie Morgan, a former teacher, at one time served as town historian.

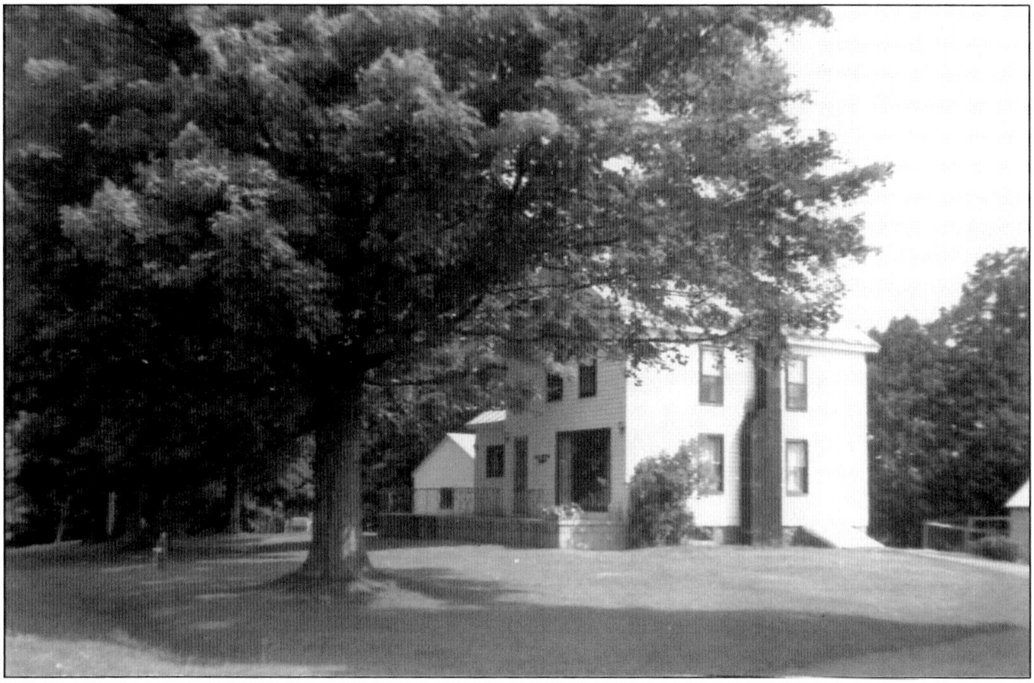

This house on Powell Road was owned by members of the Powell family for many years. It has been modified by the installation of picture windows on the front.

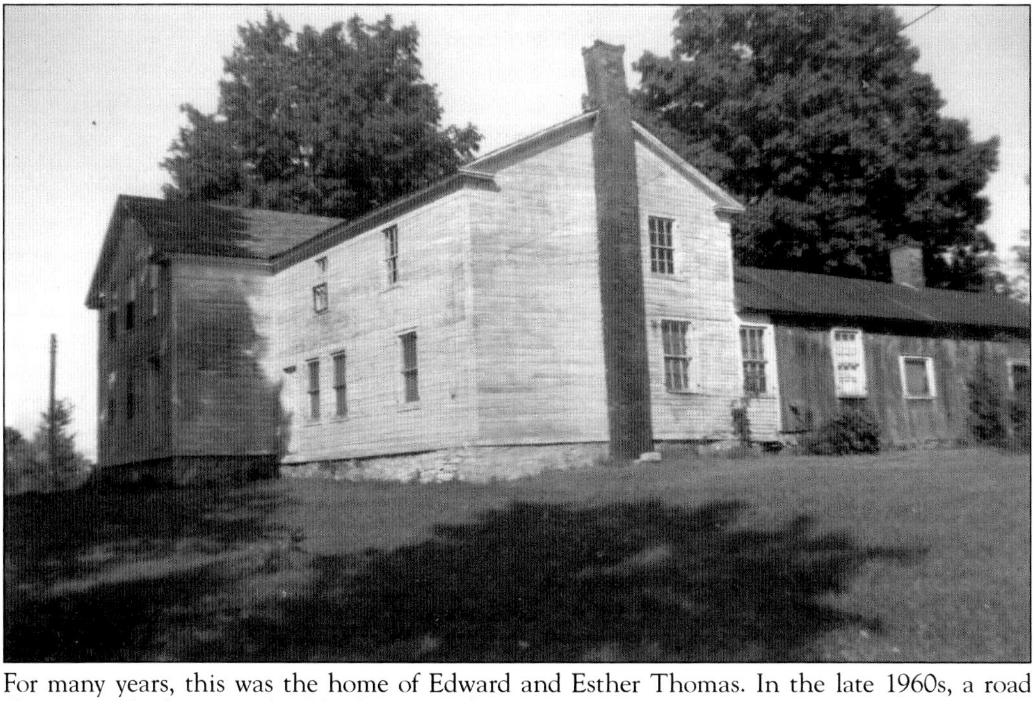

For many years, this was the home of Edward and Esther Thomas. In the late 1960s, a road change resulted in considerable change to this property.

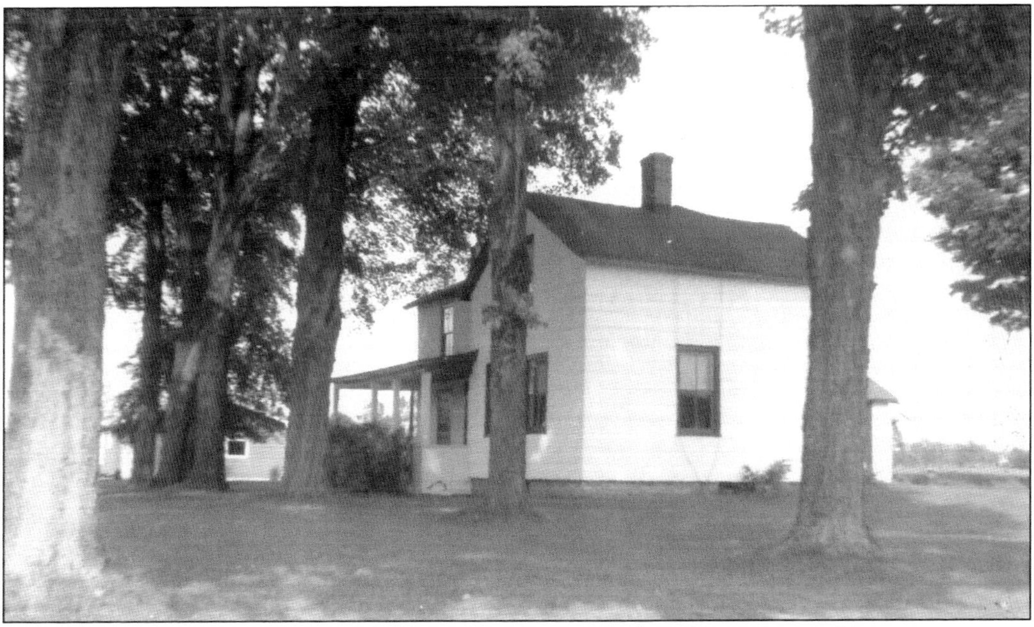

About a half mile south of the four corners is this simple box-design house. For many years, it was the home of Olin and Clara Powell Lawton.

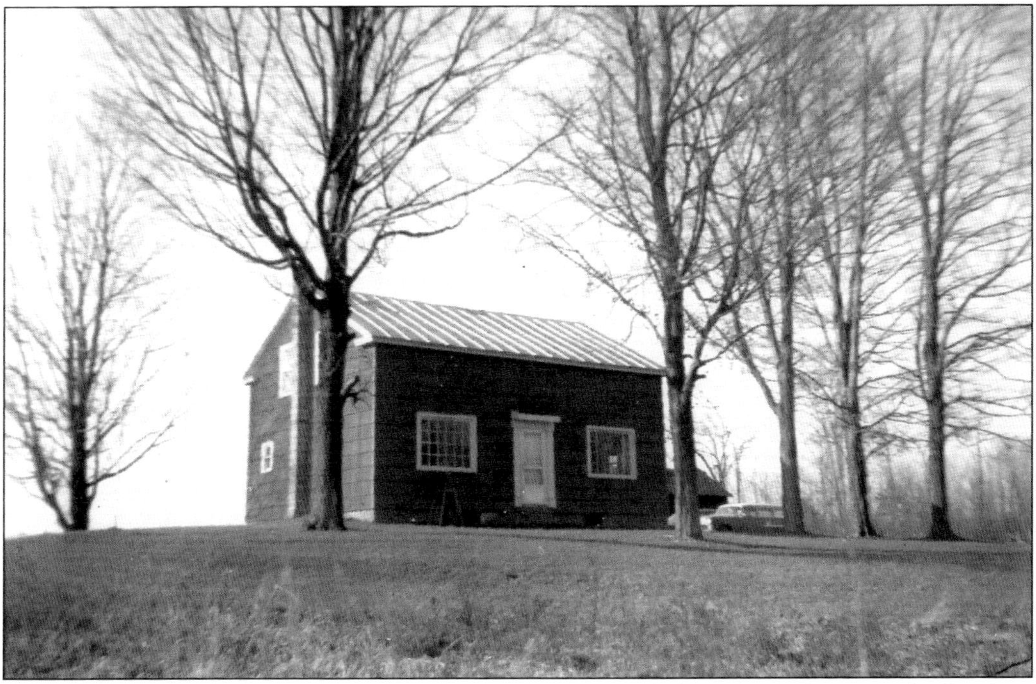

This is the former home of Isaac Raymer Powell, who used the power of Nine Mile Creek to run his sawmills and gristmills. The house was on Powell Road, which was named after the Powell family.

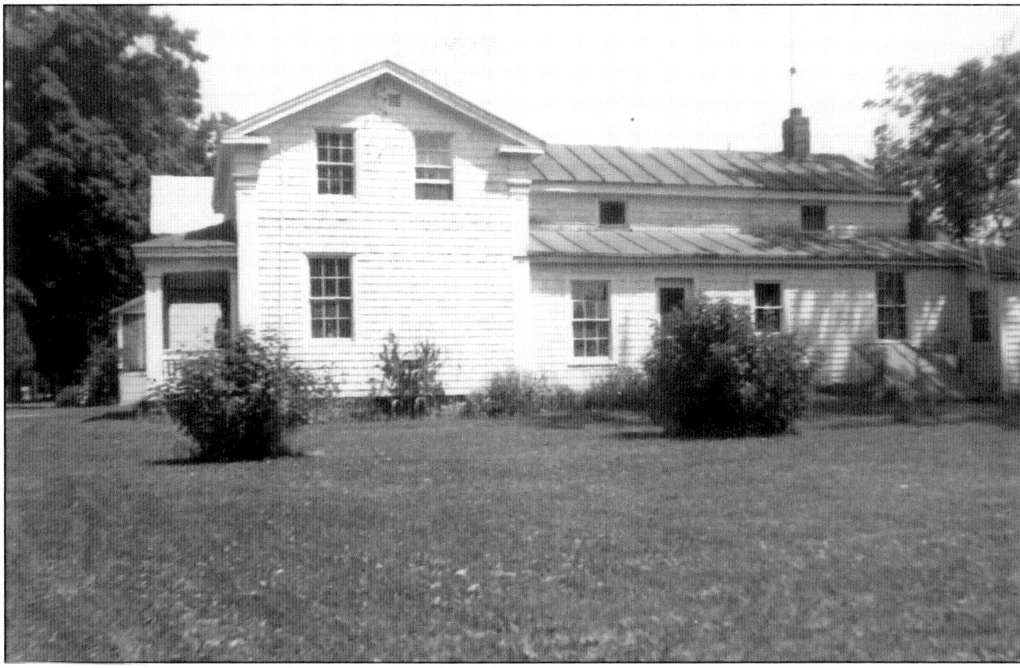

In 1810, this farm was purchased by Enoch and Abel Haskins from Amaziah Palmer of Deerfield. In 1813, it was purchased by Conrad Raymer and remained in the Raymer family for almost 100 years. The original builder may have been Azariah Raymer.

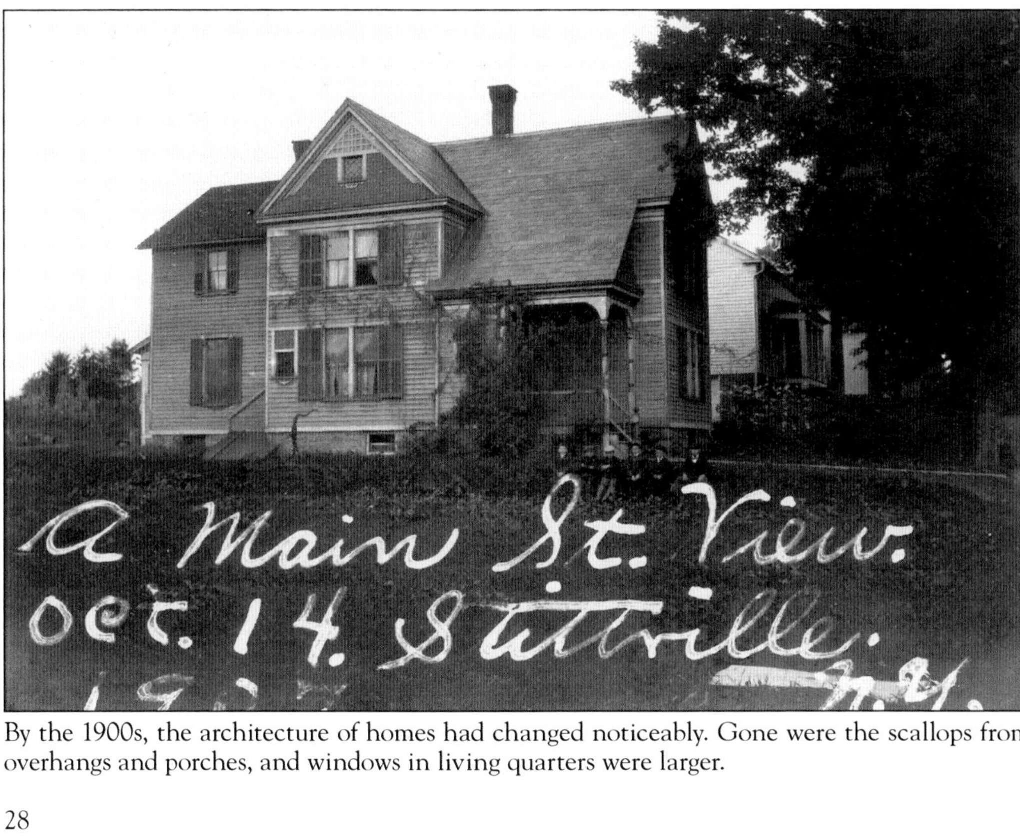

By the 1900s, the architecture of homes had changed noticeably. Gone were the scallops from overhangs and porches, and windows in living quarters were larger.

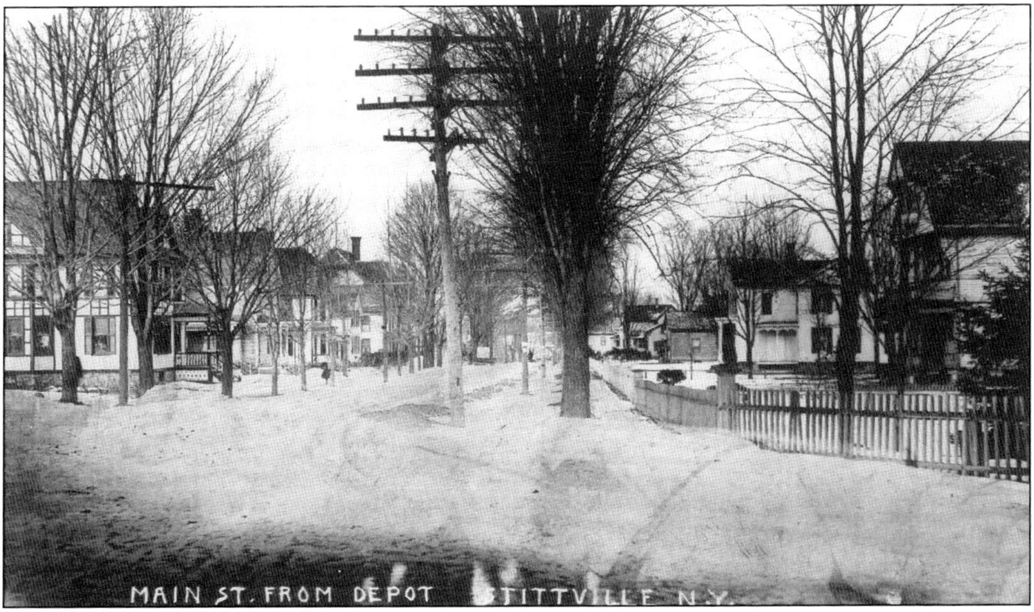

Main Street, Stittville, in wintertime is seen here about a year before the great fire. Notice the road is not plowed nor the sidewalks shoveled.

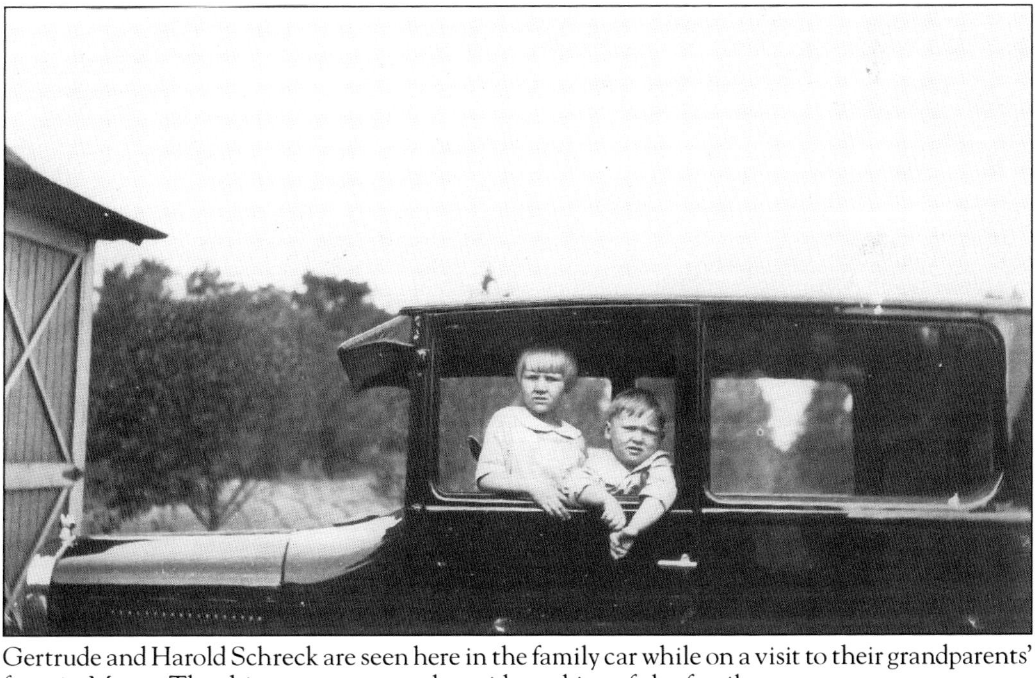

Gertrude and Harold Schreck are seen here in the family car while on a visit to their grandparents' farm in Marcy. The shiny new car was the pride and joy of the family.

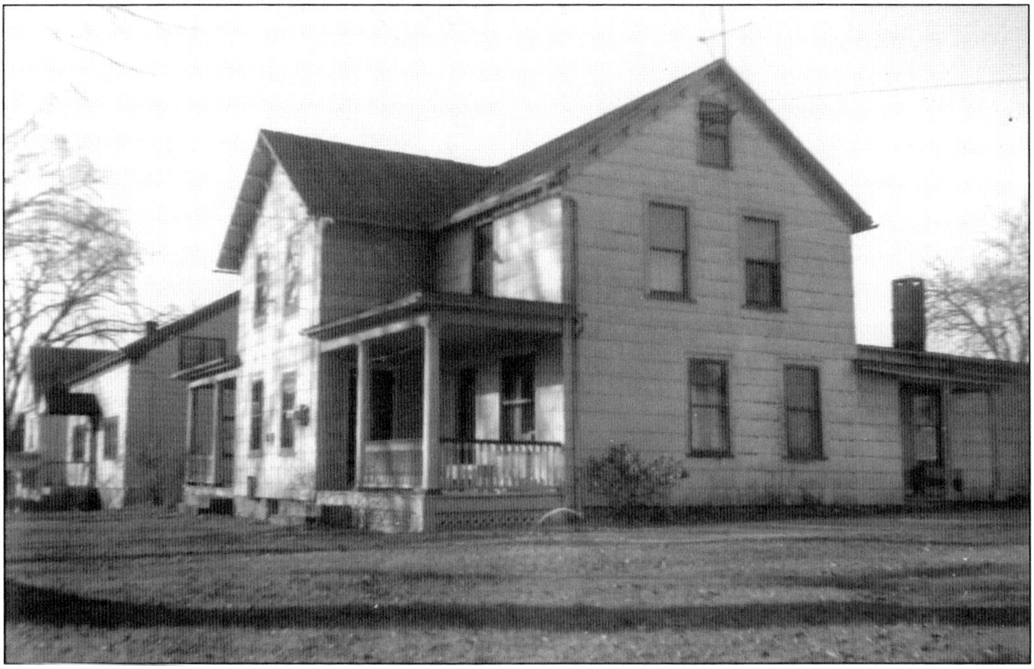

On the north side of Main Street, nearer to the four corners then Railroad Street at the other end, is this house, which was home to Maria Raymer Wescott up to the early 1900s. More recent owners have modified the house to suit their needs.

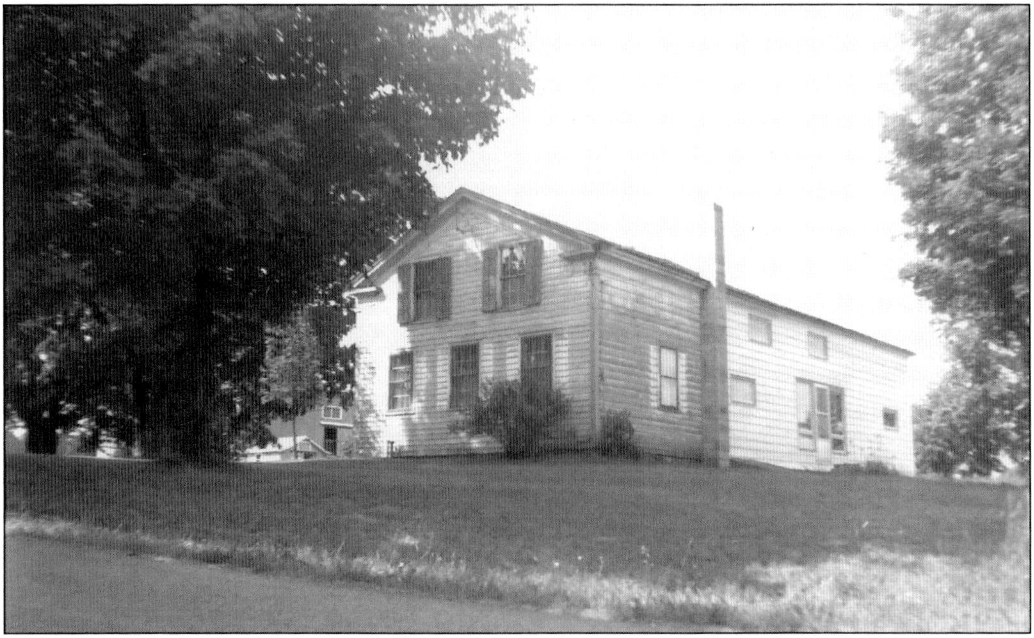

On December 10, 1841, this property was sold by Ingham and Caroline Townsend to George and Nancy Raymer Powell. At that time, it was known as Lot No. 18 of Sumners patent and consisted of 100 acres of land for $1,700. This farm on the Powell road, about two miles south of Stittville on the bank of the Nine Mile Creek, has been known as the Powell homestead for many years, although it is presently owned and occupied by others.

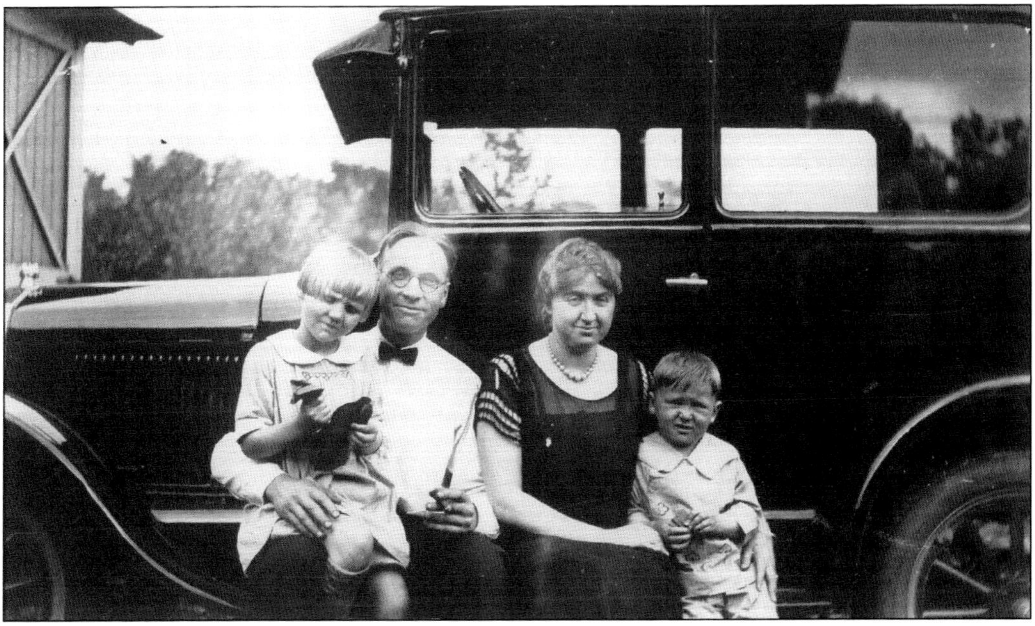

Seen here from left to right are Gertrude with her daddy, Jerome Schreck, and Mary Schreck with Harold. They are on a regular visit to the farm on Glass Factory Road.

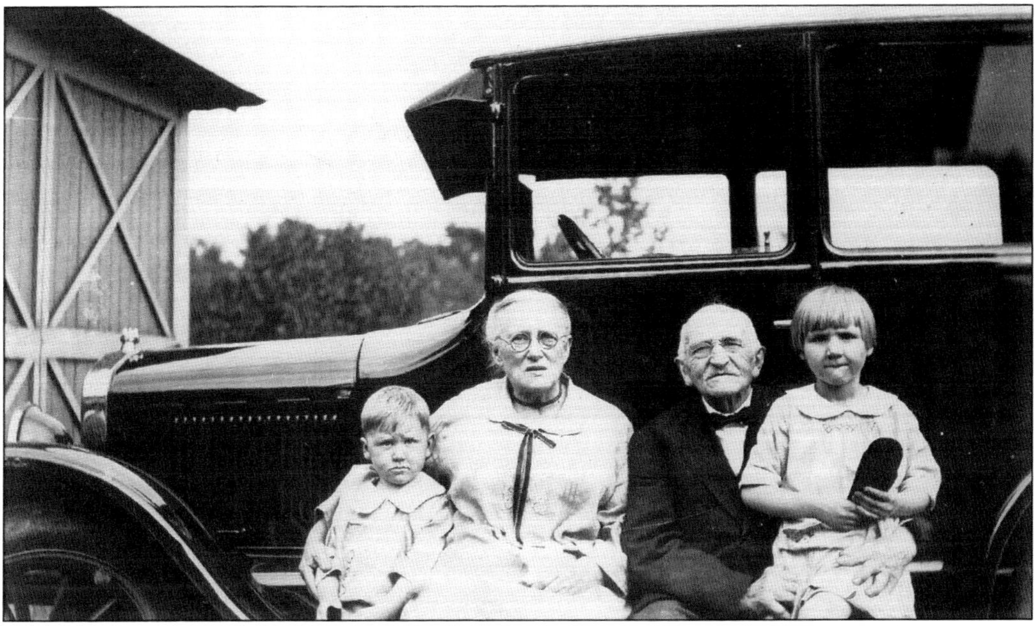

Seen here are, from left to right, Harold, grandparents Mame and Bill Roesing, and Gertrude.

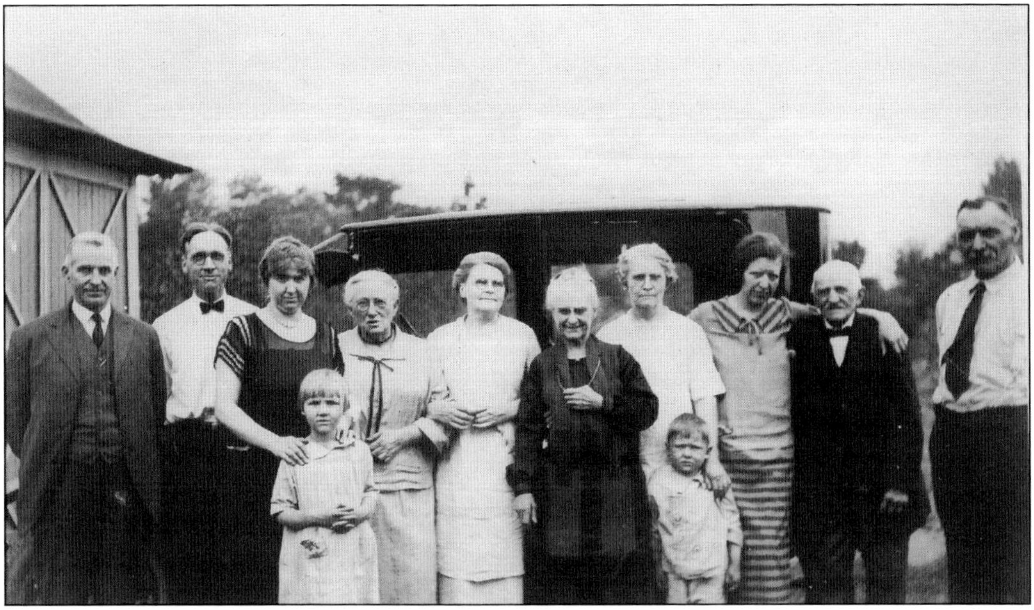

This family gathers together, before telephones, to get all the news. The children, in front, are Gertrude and Harold Schreck. In the back are, standing from left to right, Tom Lynch, Jerome Schreck, Mary Schreck, Mame Roesing, Mary Schreck, Sara Roesing, Mary Schreck, unidentified, Bill Roesing, and Adam Schreck. There are five generations here in all. Young Harold would go on to become a B-17 pilot, flying bombing missions over Germany from England.

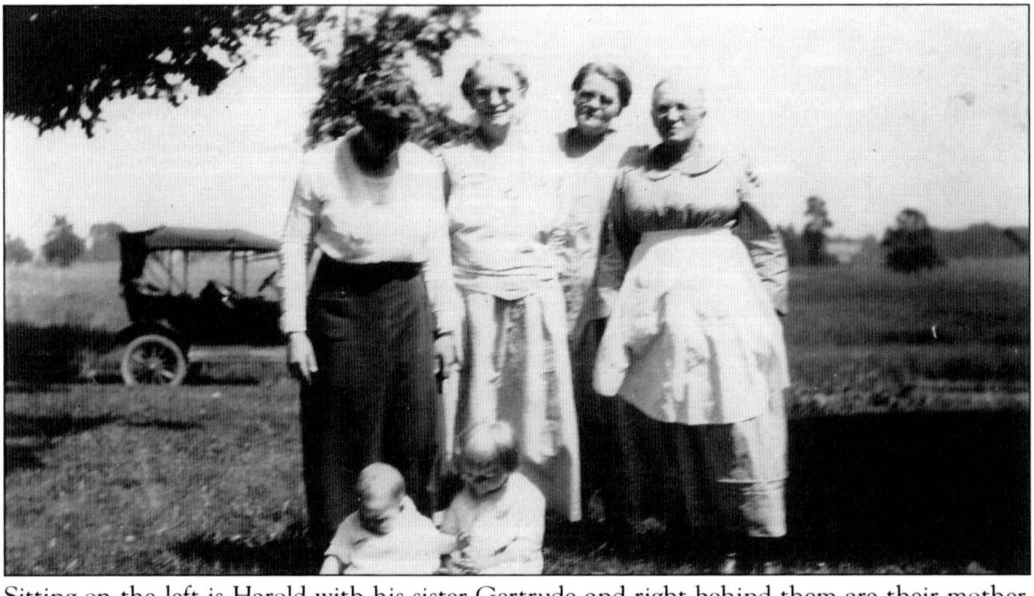

Sitting on the left is Harold with his sister Gertrude and right behind them are their mother, Mary Schreck, grandmother Mary Schreck, Dona Lynch, and grandmother Mame Roesing.

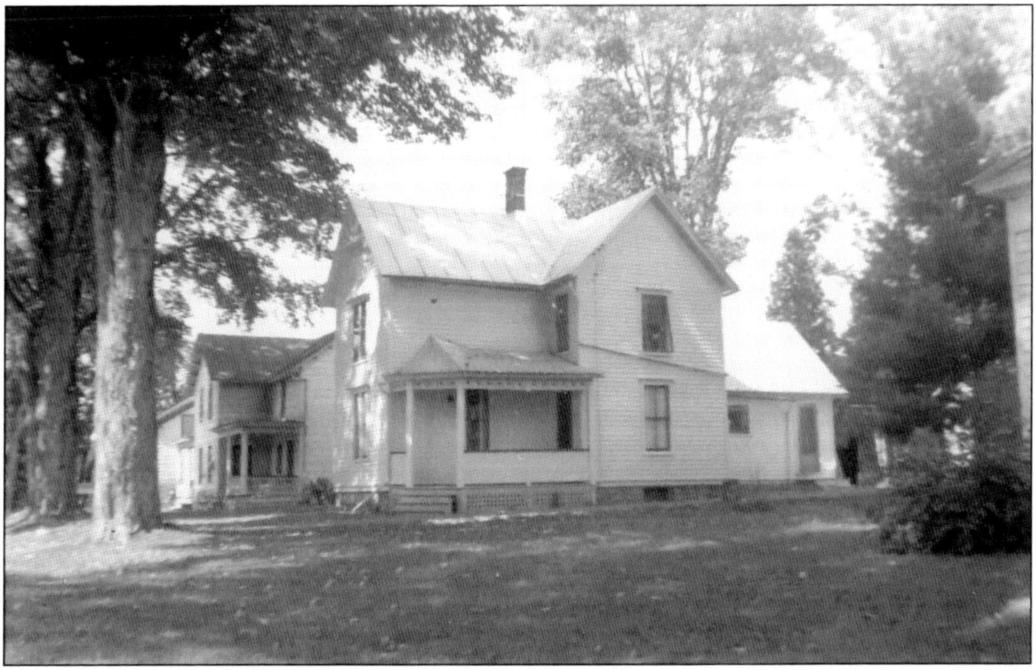

This house on the north side of Main Street, about in the middle of the block, was the home of Ralph and Elizabeth Sherwood Raymer. Families tended to stay in Stittville, and over time, there was much intermarriage. The houses would get sold to the next generations, and the family names would thus continue on the same property.

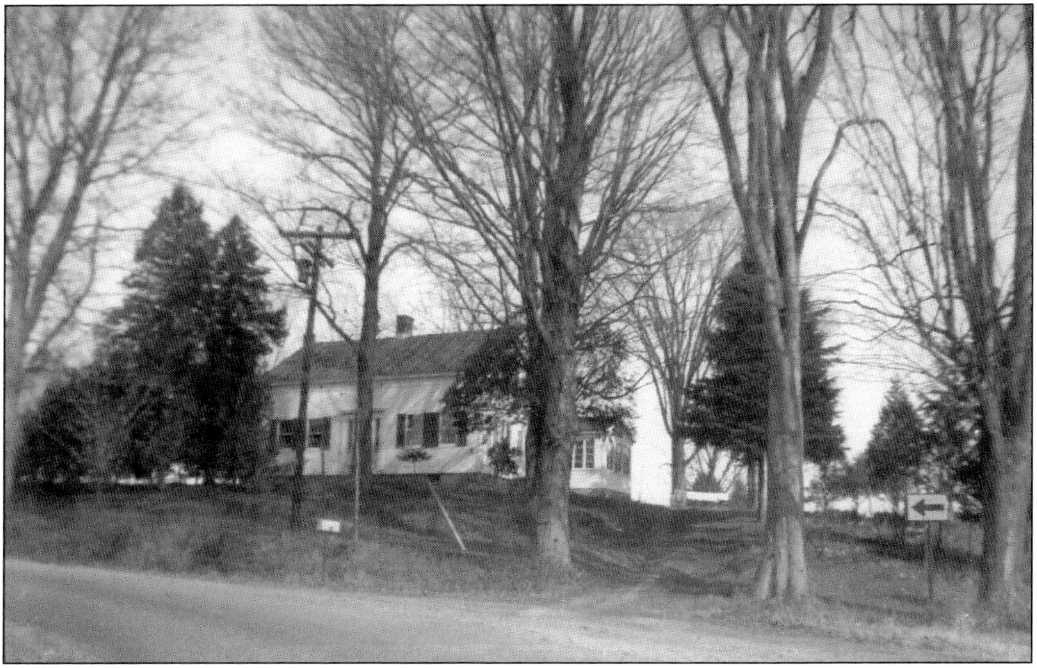

Half hidden by trees, this home on the Powell Road is about two miles south of Stittville. It is the first place on the right, just past the Nine Mile Creek Bridge. The Melaneton Raymer family lived here many years, and later, the Alma Steinbacher family called it home.

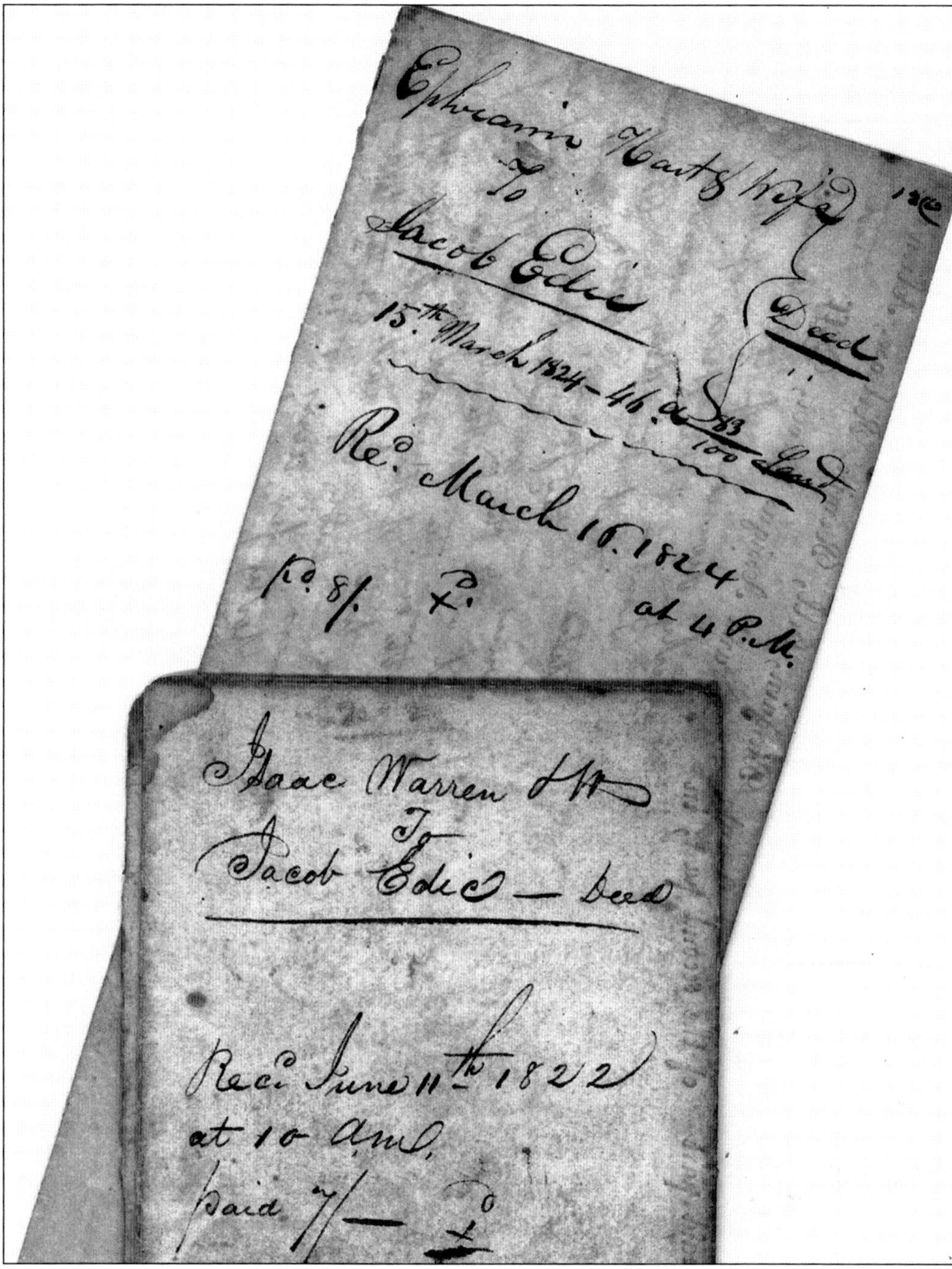

Over the years, Hollywood and cable television have shown images of pioneers and early settlers as being gung-ho characters, with an axe in one hand and a rifle in the other hand. Actually the settlers had much the same procedure to go through as is done today. First they picked out the plot of ground that appealed to them from a map or actual visit, and then the purchase procedure followed by a deed and/or mortgage. Finally they would visit the town office, or more likely the county office, where the paperwork was recorded. Sample deeds from 1812 to 1827 are shown here.

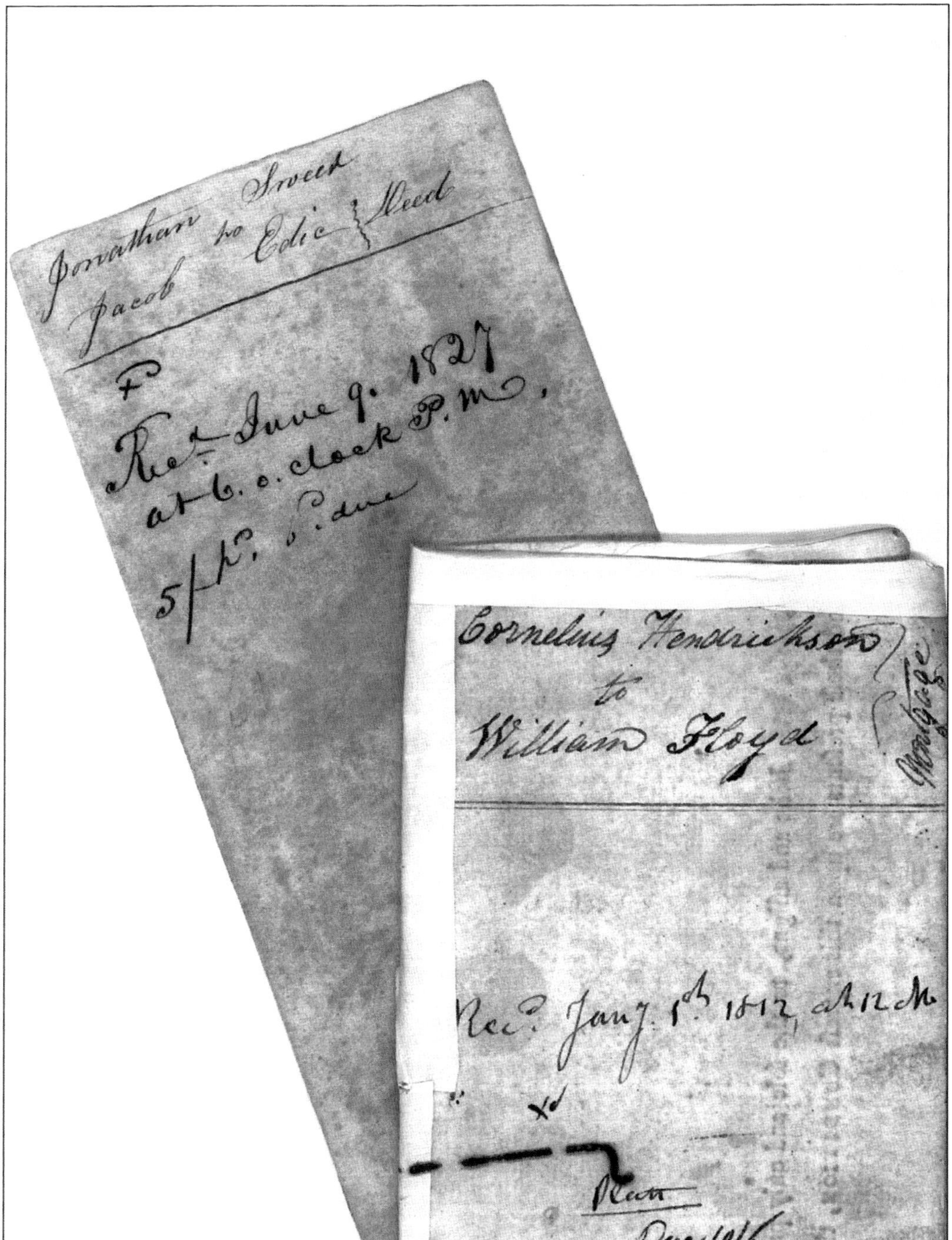

Throughout history, there have always been those who have and those who have not (or very little). Not all settlers had the finances to purchase a home or a farm. Enter the moneyman, who would lend the funds to the hopeful young settler. If the crops came as planned, or the diary worked, the loan was paid off, and the homestead survived. It is interesting to note in reviewing hundreds of these mortgages that the same names appear over and over again as lenders, and even some of the most prominent names appear as borrowers, along with regular people.

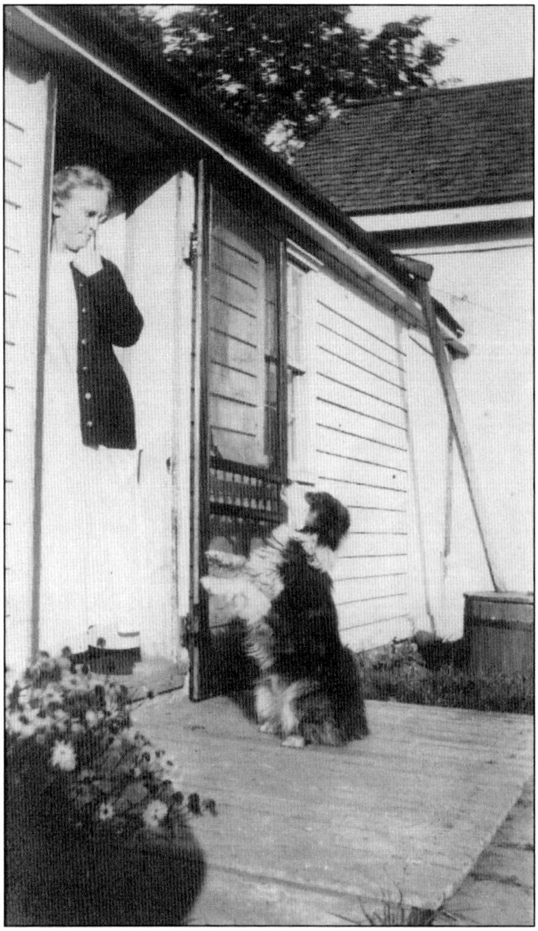

Pictured is a family dog, a friend and guardian. Every family had at least one dog, guardian of the property, watchdog, protector, fire warden, entertainer, and trustworthy friend.

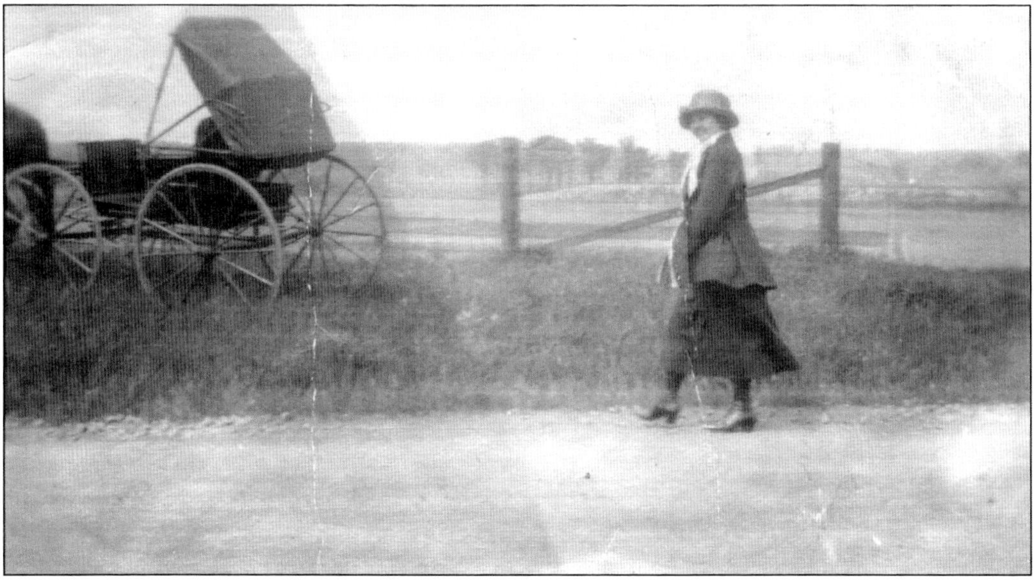

Mary Glasarowski visits Grace farm in Marcy in 1919. Later that year, she married Albert Kula.

Four

The Agricultural Life

Farm life in Marcy meant only one thing—work. In the early 1900s, there were over 500 farms in Marcy, some big and some small. One either owned and worked the farm or worked on someone else's farm as a tenant or farmhand. On a dairy farm, the livestock required attention and milking seven days a week. But farm life had one good feature in that generally there was enough to eat, since every family had a garden plot for potatoes and vegetables, dairy cows, chickens, hogs, and a small orchard. In fact, during the Great Depression, the average Marcy farm family did better than their city counterparts. Then World War II came along and provided a market for everything the farm could produce. The profits enabled the farmer to purchase new modern equipment, which eventually allowed a reduced workweek. The new modern automobile allowed quick access to nearby cities and job opportunities that even attracted new generations from the farm families.

By 2000, the number of farms had decreased to only six and only a couple of these could still be considered large. Today it is not uncommon to see a car stop by a farm so that a parent can allow the children to see cows or to watch a tractor pulling a hay baler. What used to be a common way of life in Marcy has now become a curiosity.

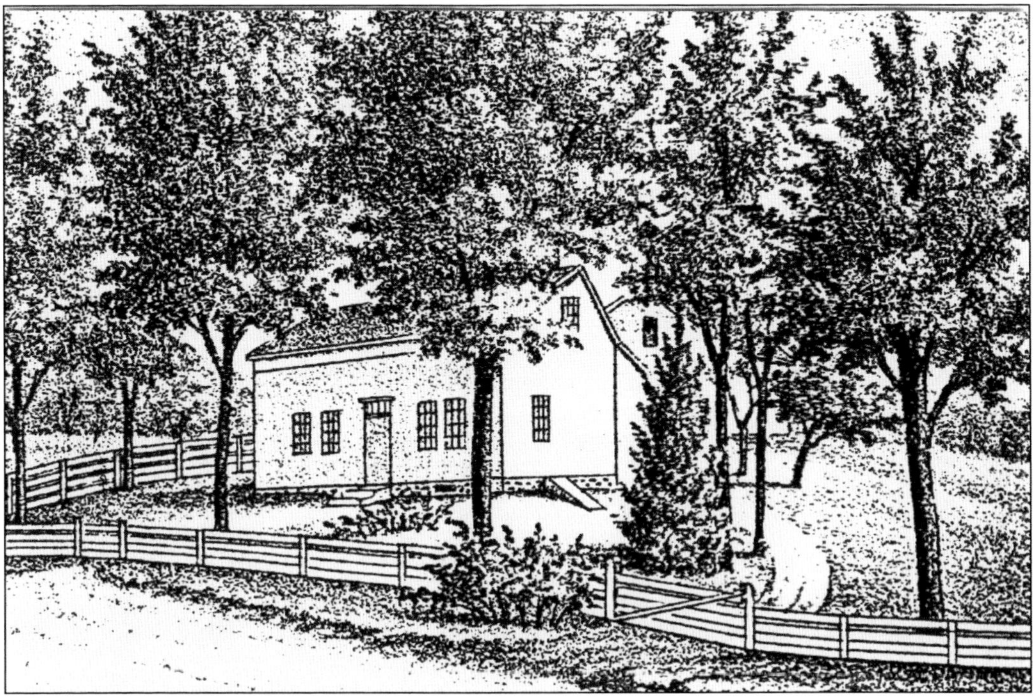

An 1860 lithograph shows the Martin Cavana homestead on Cavanaugh Road on the east side about two miles heading north.

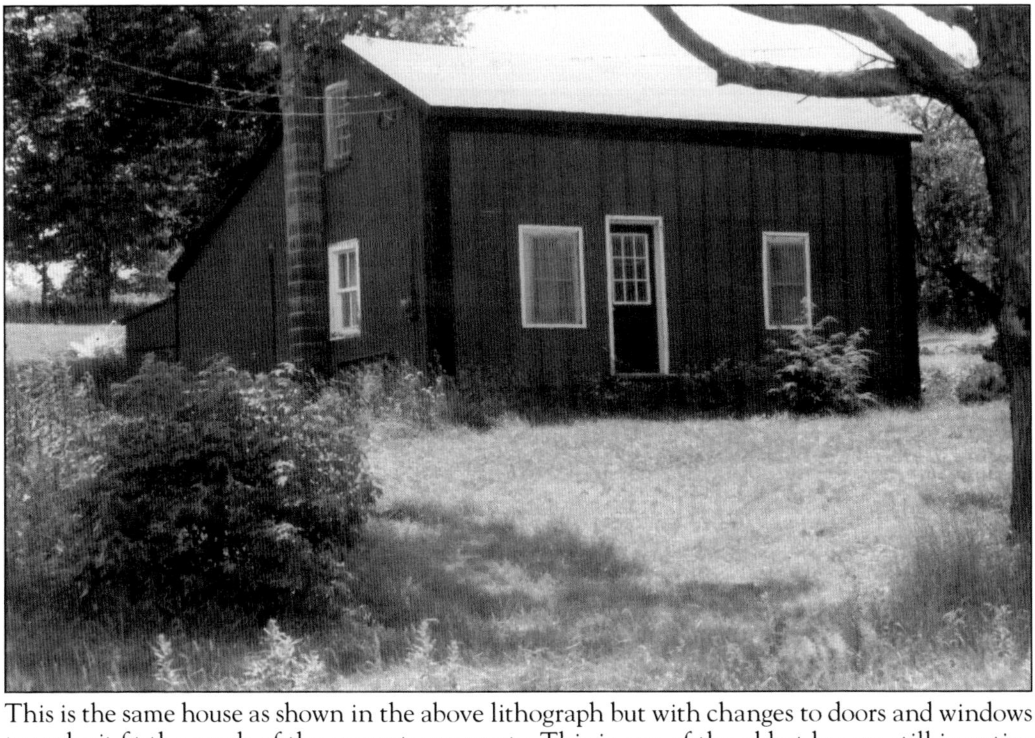

This is the same house as shown in the above lithograph but with changes to doors and windows to make it fit the needs of the present occupants. This is one of the oldest houses still in active use in Marcy.

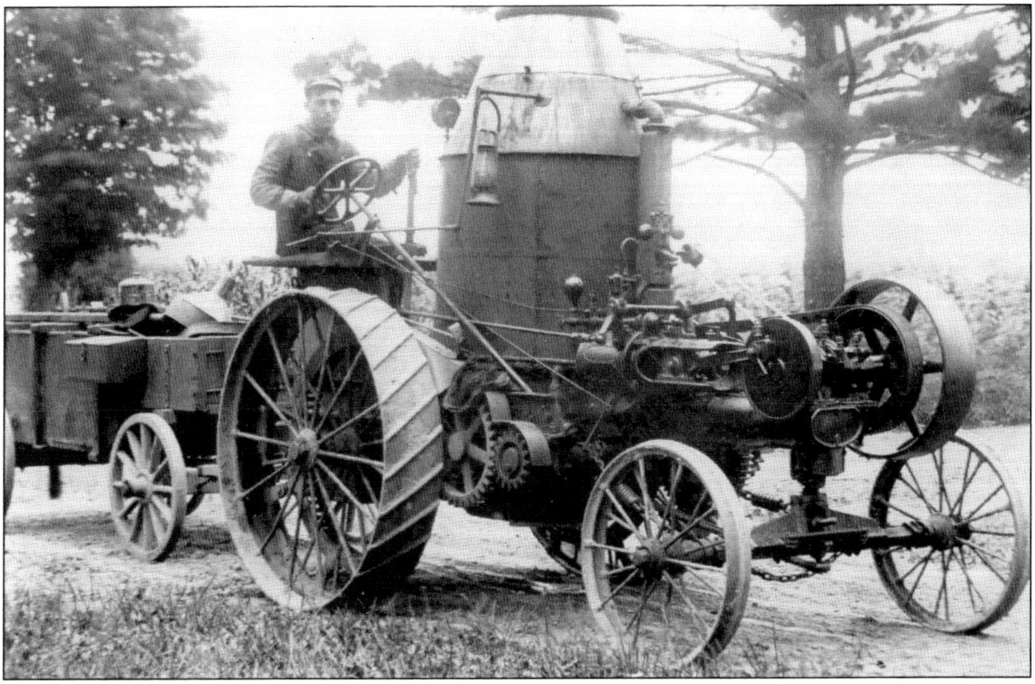

Roy Thomas and his twin brother, Ray, went into the business of custom harvesting for other farmers in Marcy and Deerfield. Their machines were more like steam engines on wheels rather than the tractor design known today.

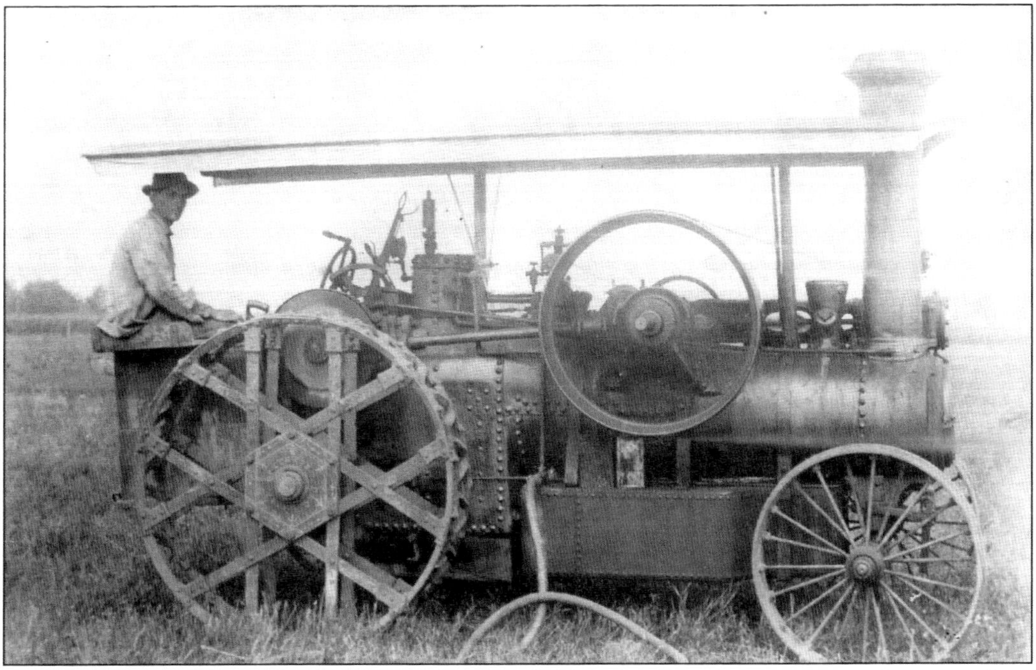

Ray is pictured with another steam tractor. He and his twin brother, Roy, went from one farm to the next during harvest and would be gone for weeks at a time, as the machines were to slow to drive home.

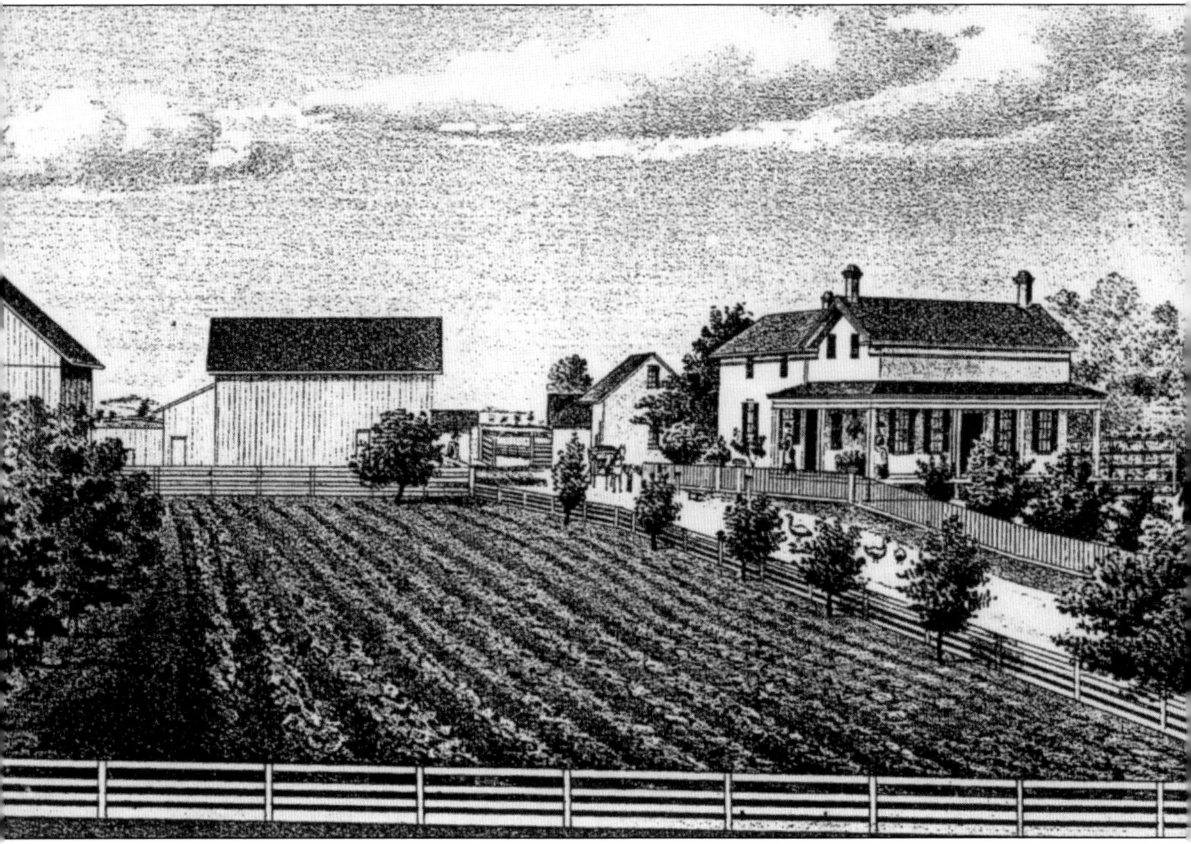

An 1878 lithograph shows the farm of Edward T. Marson on River Road, now the corner of Mohawk Street and Route 49. Mohawk Street now goes through where the barn stood. The farm was ruined by the building of the canal and thruway.

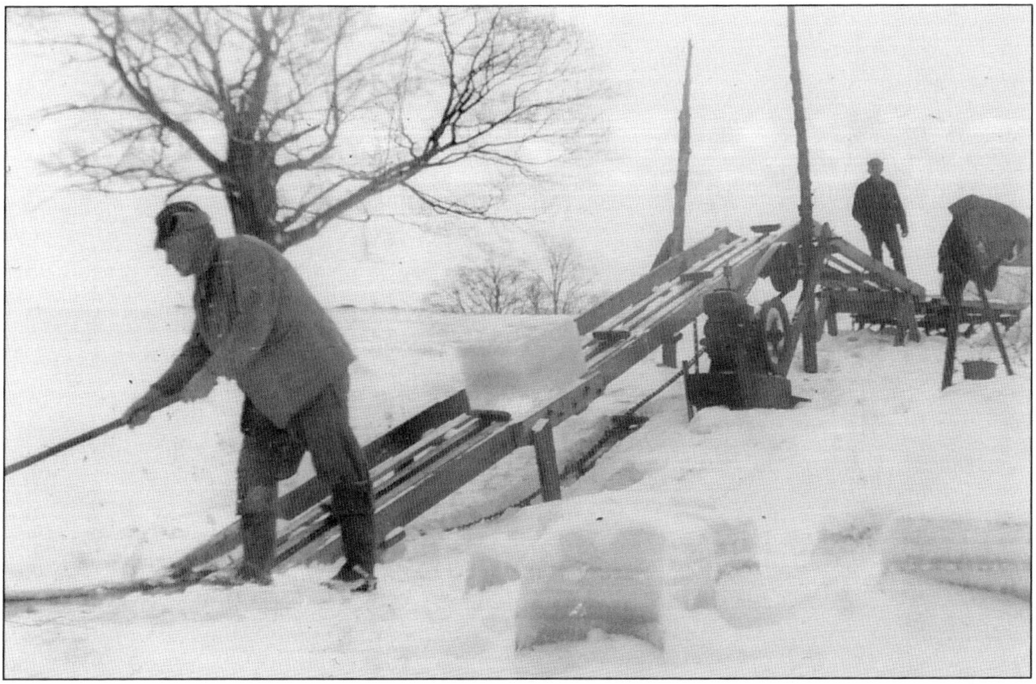

In 1942, Marcy farmers were shipping milk in milk cans on the milk train. This required a lot of ice to cool the milk, so most farmers cut their ice from their farm pond and stored it in an icehouse for as long as possible.

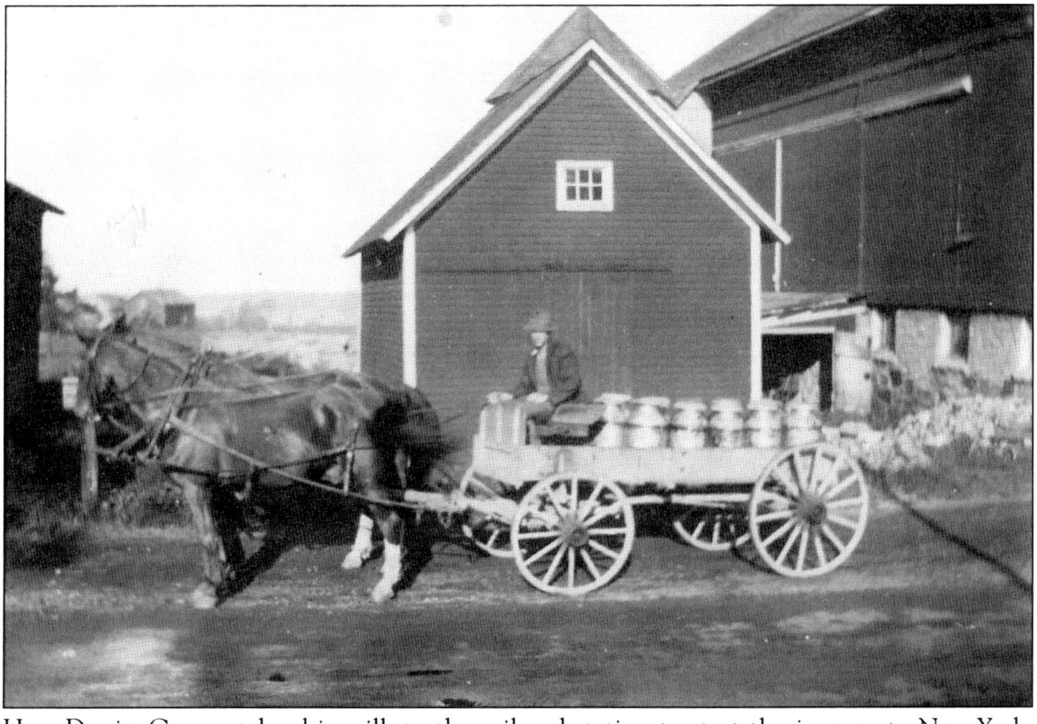

Here Dewitt George takes his milk to the railroad station to start the journey to New York. These barns have since been torn down to make way for a road project.

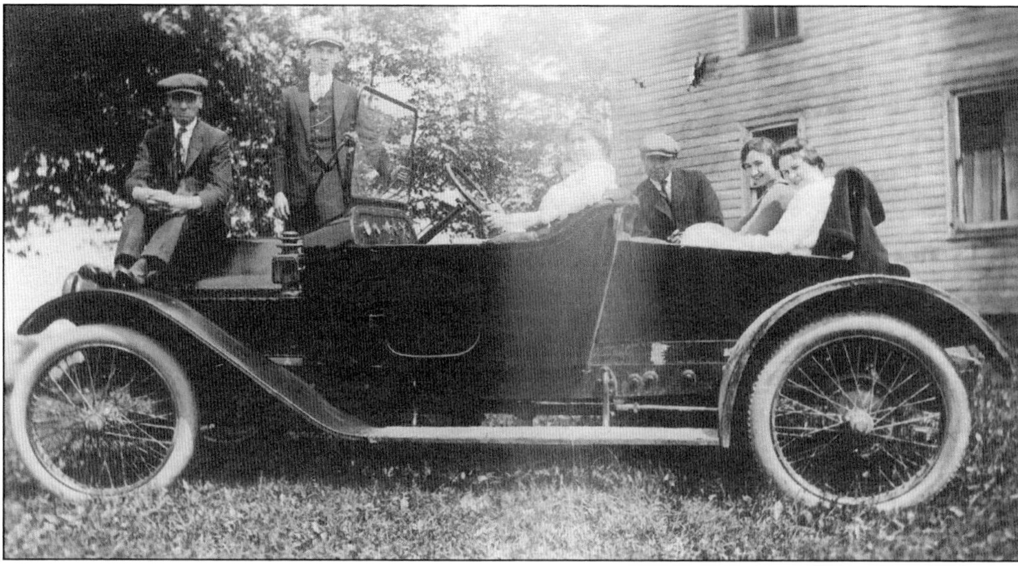

One's work was successful when one of those new-fangled automobiles could be afforded. Here the Schreck family enjoys the new automobile, and it has a rumble seat.

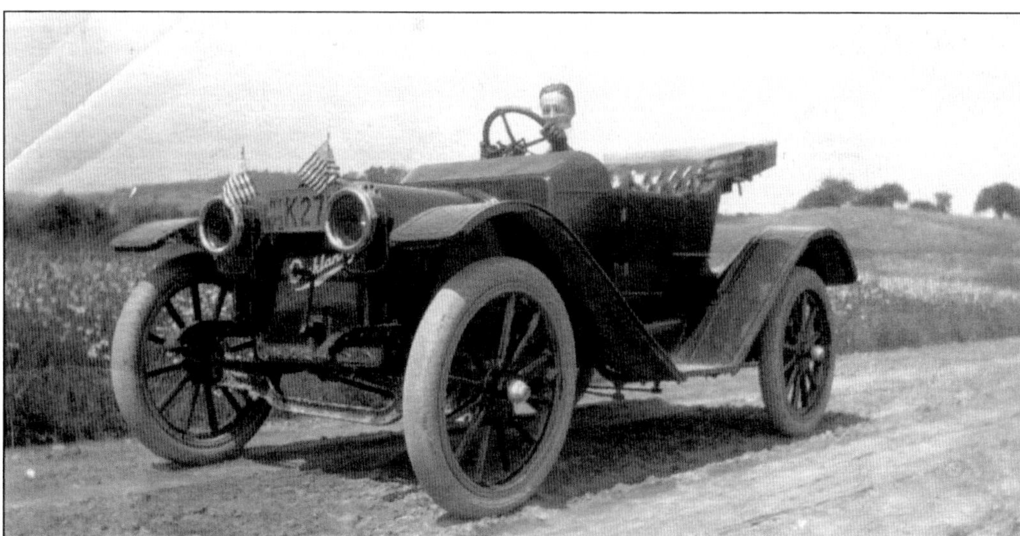

A convertible was the height of success, and this new model was even equipped with a hand crank to start the engine.

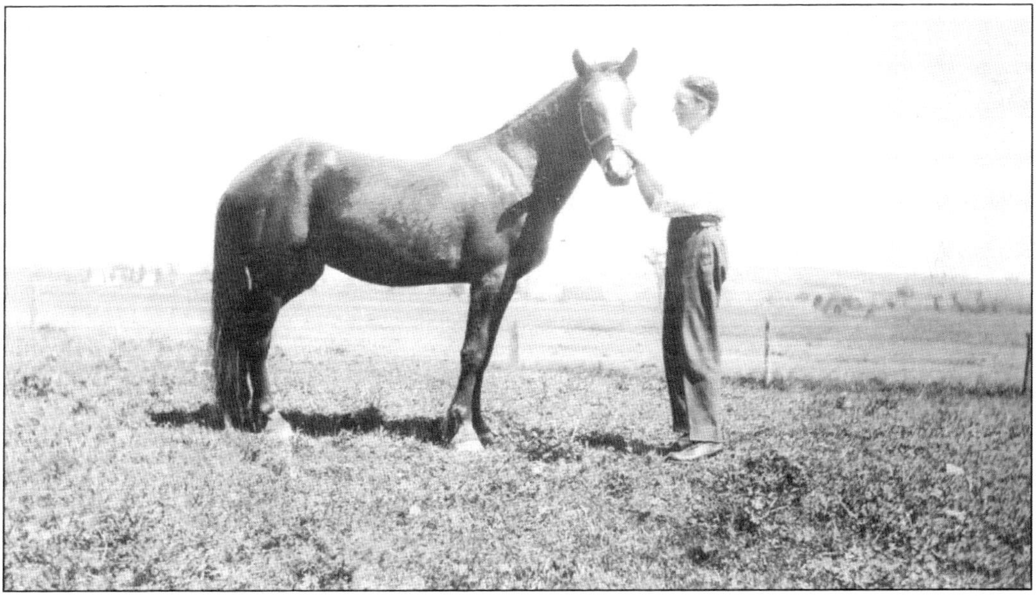

Some farmers used their horses for both work and pleasure, such as pulling a plow and pulling a buggy. If they could afford it, a farmer might have horses for each task.

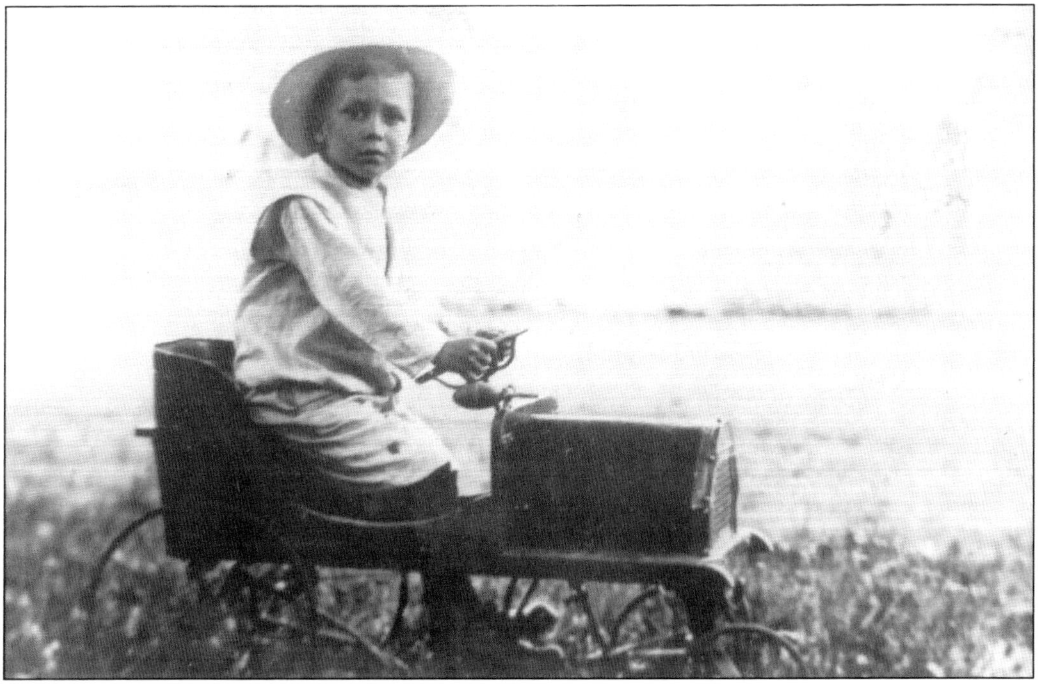

Kids are always the same. When dad got himself a new toy, the son had to have an automobile of his own. This model even had a horn.

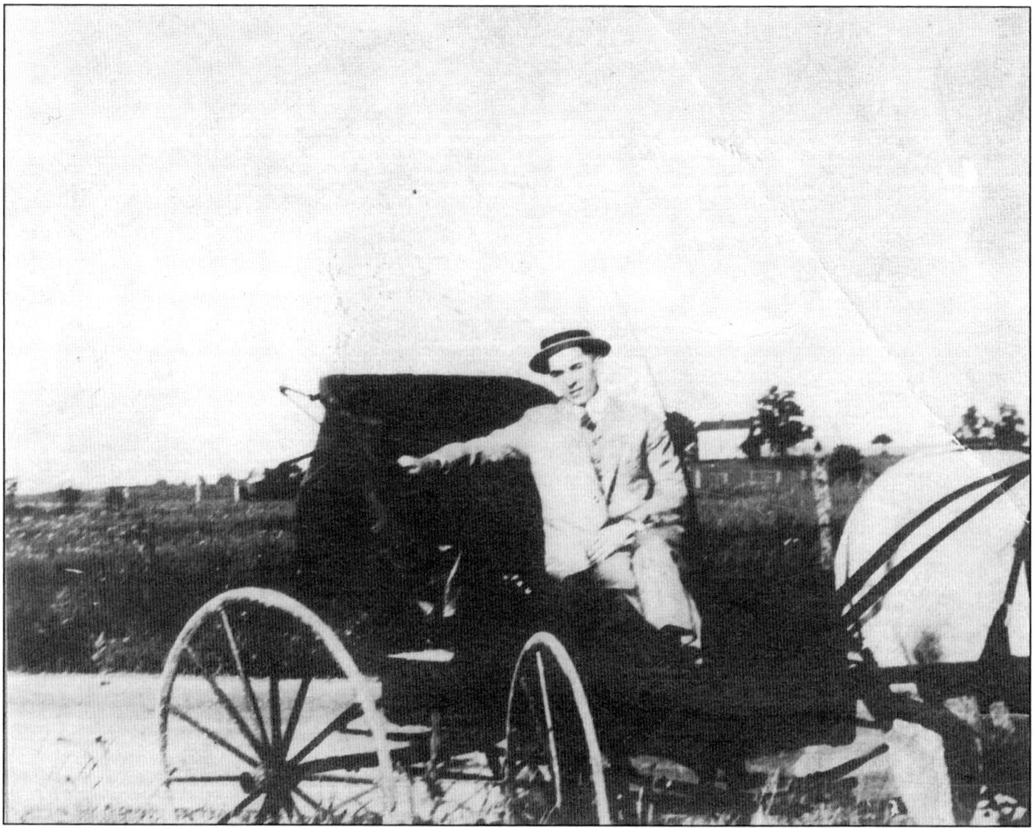

Having a date at Grace farm in 1919, Albert Kula poses in the buggy while Mary Glasarowski takes his picture.

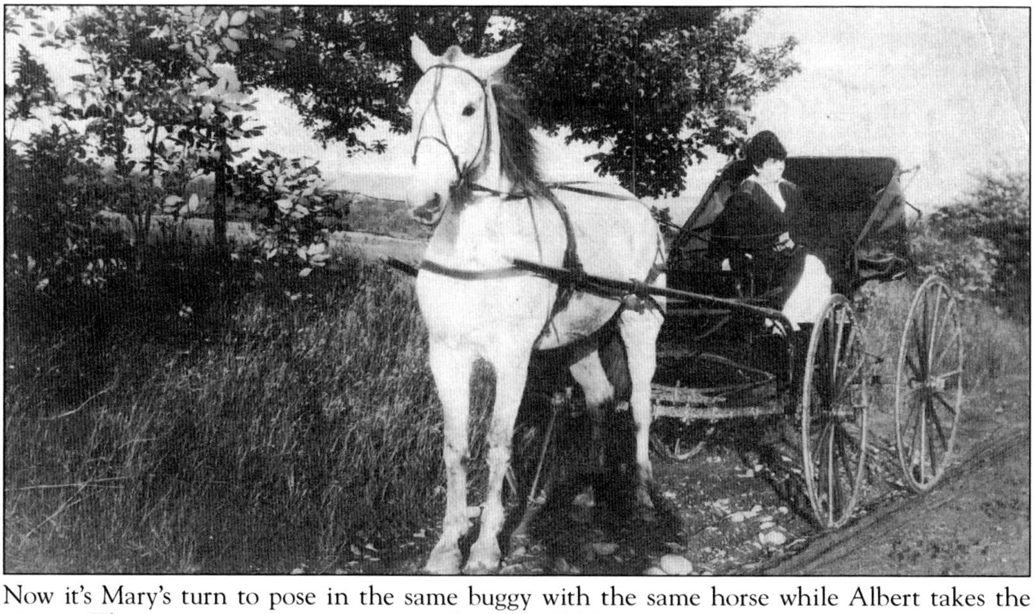

Now it's Mary's turn to pose in the same buggy with the same horse while Albert takes the picture. This was great entertainment in the early 1900s.

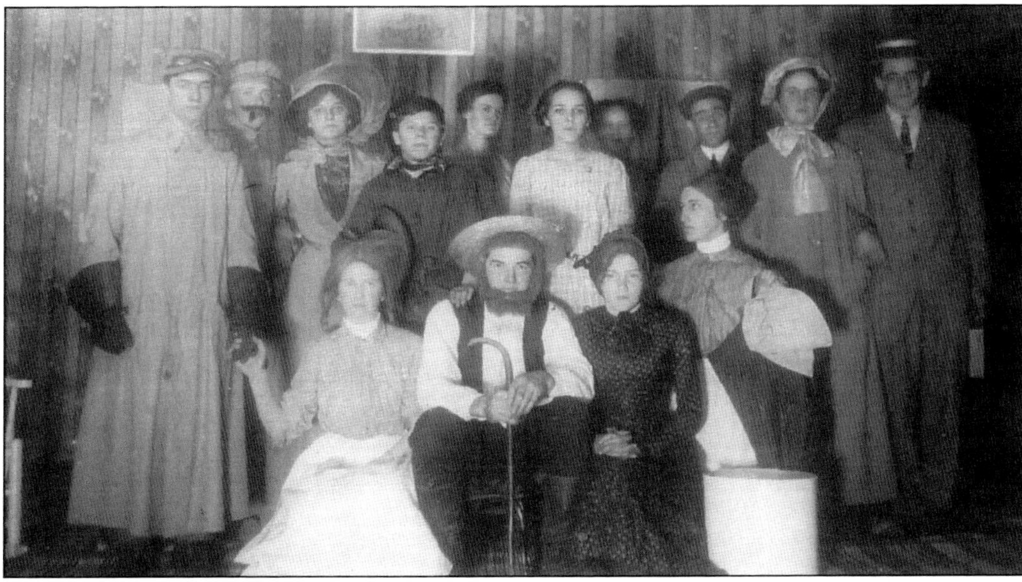

Farm life could be very boring without movies, radio, television, or theaters, so how did rural families make do? They made their own entertainment with fairs, horse races, spelling bees, quilt contests, barn raisings, and the like. Local plays were one popular event, which meant weeks of practice, stage building, and making costumes; there was perhaps six weeks of activity for one night of show time. This event was a bargain at 25¢ admission or 35¢ reserved seat.

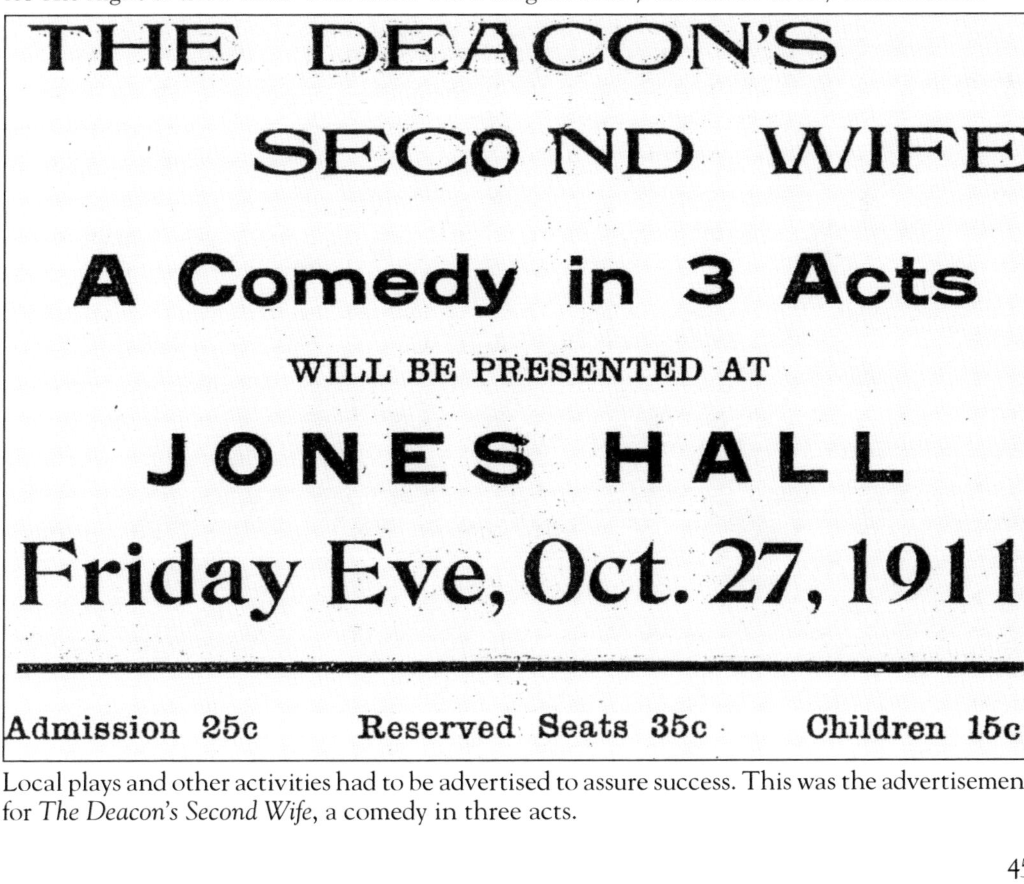

Local plays and other activities had to be advertised to assure success. This was the advertisement for *The Deacon's Second Wife*, a comedy in three acts.

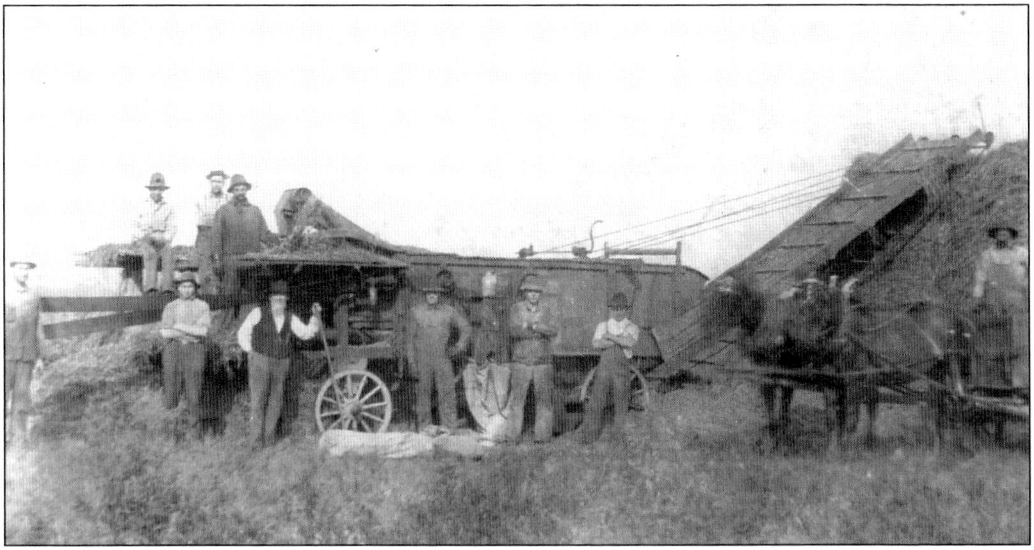

Harvest time on Marcy farms was a time of everyone pitching in and helping at all the neighboring farms until the crops were in the barn or silo, as shown in this 1910 photograph.

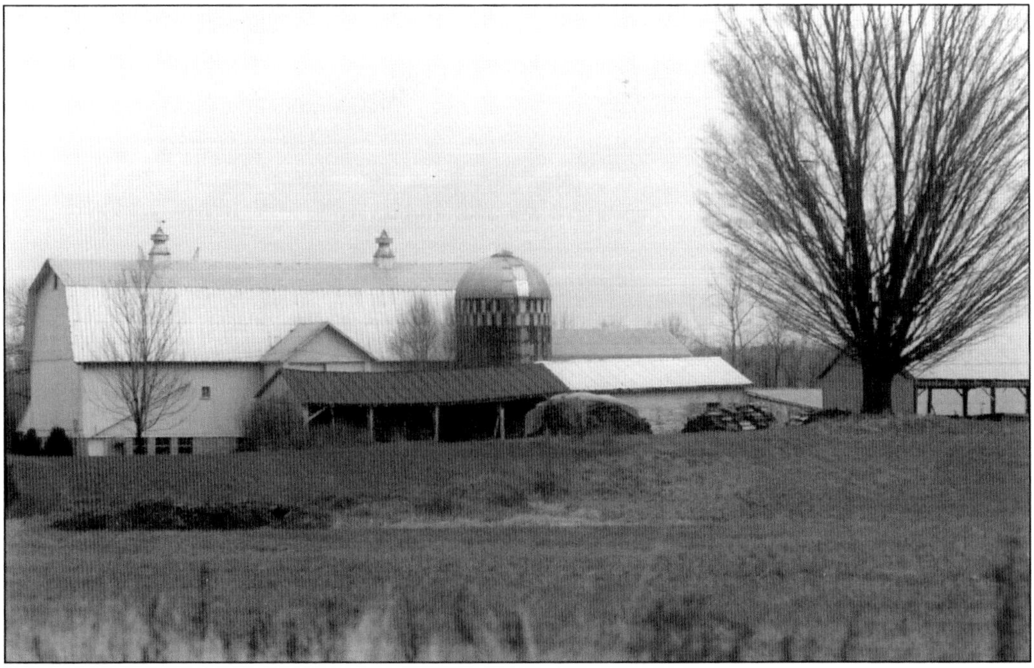

The family-type farm of 100 years ago has now grown into a larger family farm of today. But even these new farms with modern tractors, machinery, direct milk pick up, and electric power are having a hard time surviving.

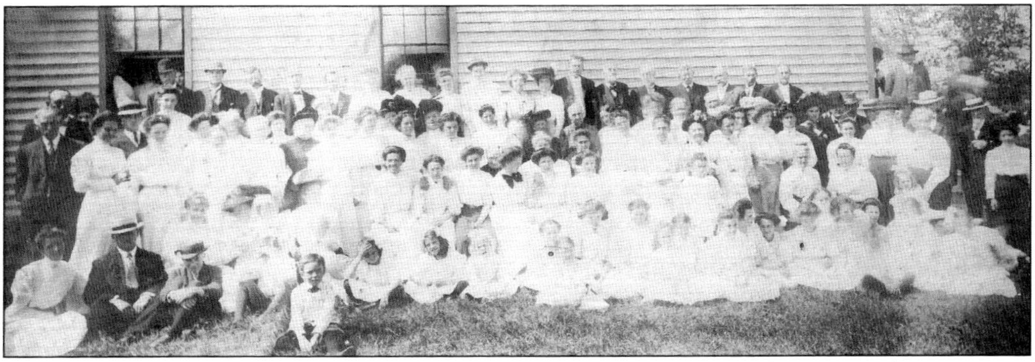

In this 1901 photograph of a Grange meeting, the sociable aspect can be seen in that everyone is dressed in their Sunday best to make it a joyful, happy experience.

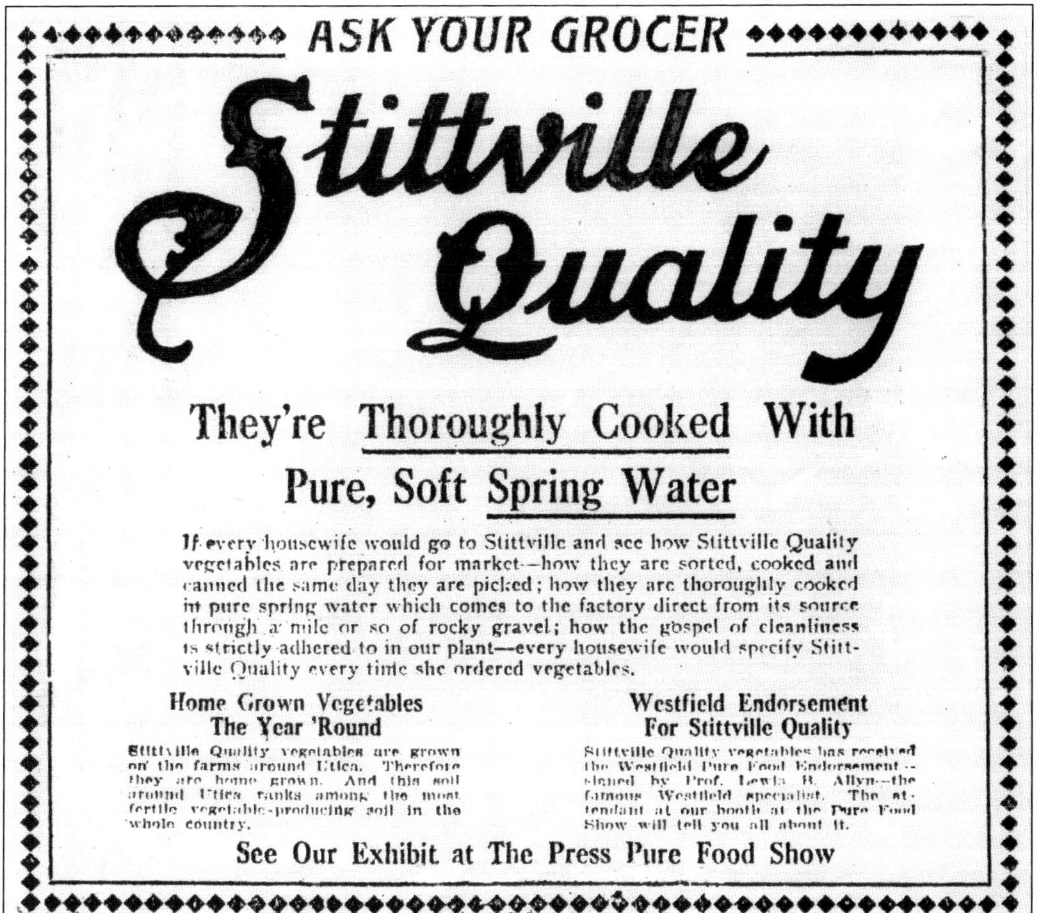

Many towns had a canning factory to process locally grown produce.

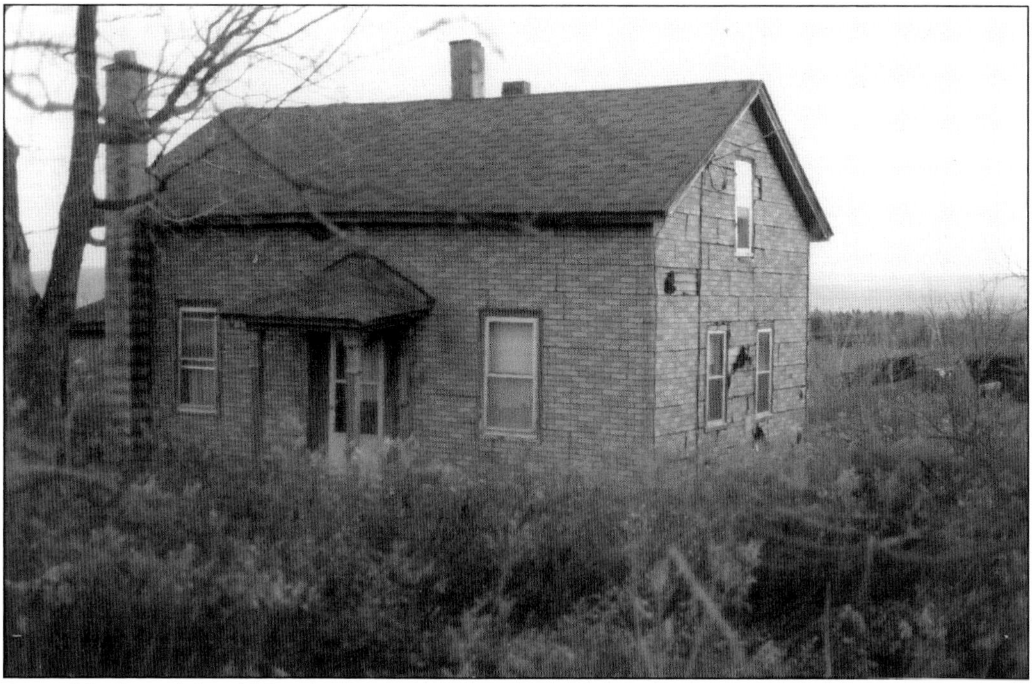

One of the last of the old farmhouses in Marcy is shown here. Notice the simple box design, usually with a kitchen and a general-purpose room and two bedrooms. Some homes had a second-floor loft area or maybe even two sleeping rooms. An outhouse was right outside the back door. Stoves provided the heat. Some had dirt floors. This house was torn down a few years ago.

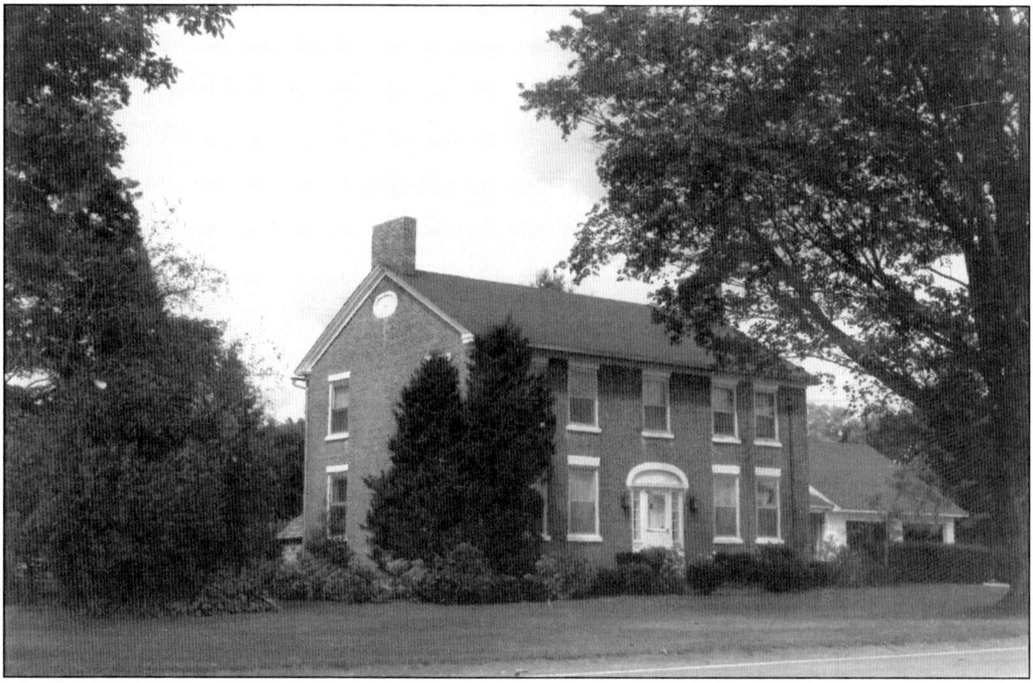

Maple Lawn Farm is one of the most beautiful old homes in Marcy. People driving by on Route 291 actually slow down to appreciate the beauty of this farm home.

Five

Railroads Change Everything

In 1853, a group of investors from Boonville obtained a state charter and proceeded to build the Boonville-Utica Railroad. Early studies convinced the investors that it was impossible for any locomotive to pull a train up over the Deerfield hills, so a route was selected to go through Marcy, following the least slope, through the Crane Creek lowlands and on into Stittville. The route was well chosen, and in just three years, the line was open to Remsen, and shortly thereafter into Boonville. A station was opened near Berean Baptist Church (now Marcy Community Church), and another at Stittville. Farmers could then ship their milk and produce to the outside world. Formerly one was born, married, and died all within the rural environment. But now one could get chores done early on Saturday and catch the train into Utica where young people could promenade up and down the city streets, see all kinds of people, and feast their eyes on store merchandise. They discovered that factory jobs in the city were paying $6 to $8 a week, and one only had to work 60 hours a week. This was even better than the dollar and a half per day that one could earn during the haying season. The world was a big, inviting place beyond the farm fences. Rural life would never be the same. And so, as the railroad changed the outlook for young rural people, it also changed what was to become the town of Marcy into another of the many hamlets of the township of Marcy.

The action shifted to the railroad stations at Marcy station and Stittville station. Soon both of these areas grew. They developed as passenger depots and shipping points for farm produce and manufactured goods from Stittville factories and receiving depots for goods coming into the area.

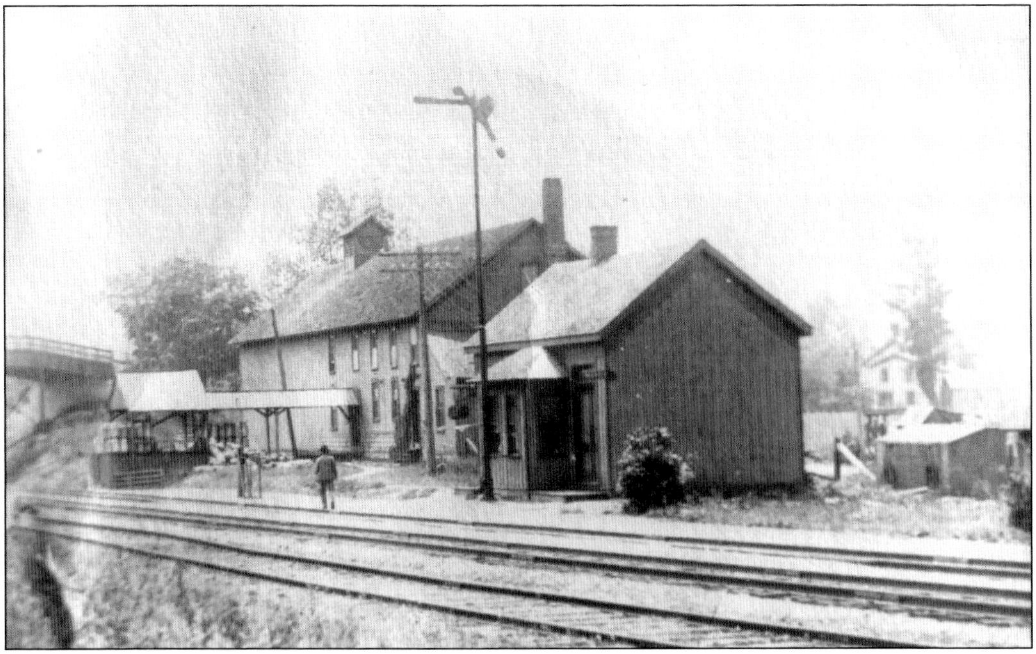

In this photograph, the Marcy railroad station is on the right and the Marcy milk station is on the left. When the train picked up its milk load at Holland Patent, they would telegraph ahead to Marcy that they were on the way. Men would then bring out the Marcy milk cans and ice and be ready to load the train when it arrived. The high-speed train then had the right-of-way to New York City with fresh milk.

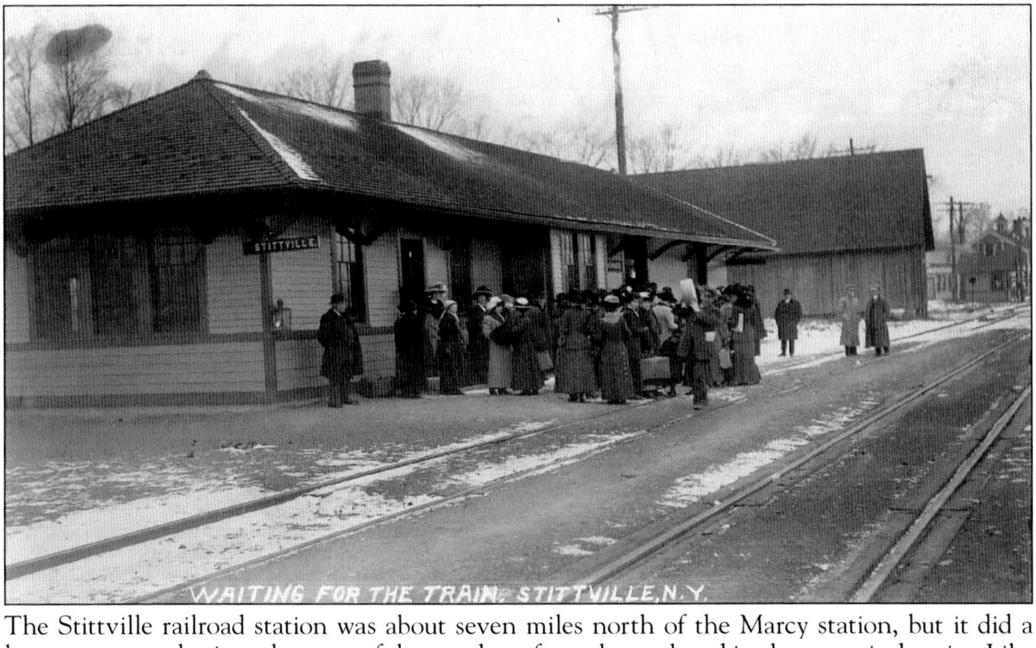

The Stittville railroad station was about seven miles north of the Marcy station, but it did a larger passenger business because of the number of people employed in the many industries. Like Marcy, they also had a milk station.

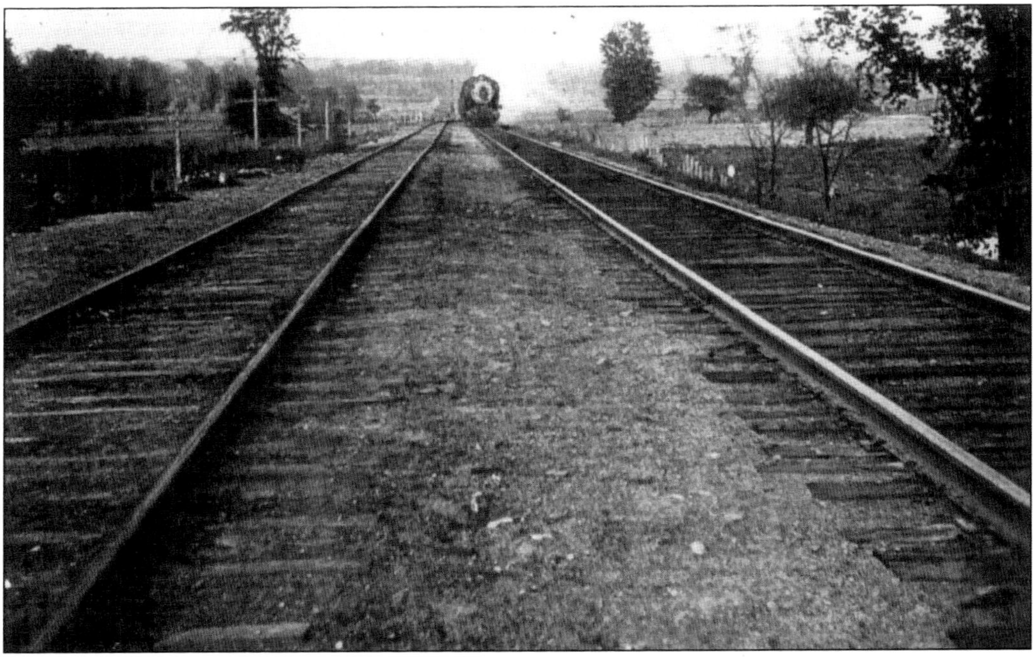

A 1911 photograph by the railroad company shows that two tracks were required to handle the number of trains. The engines were all high wheelers fueled by wood and in a few years by coal.

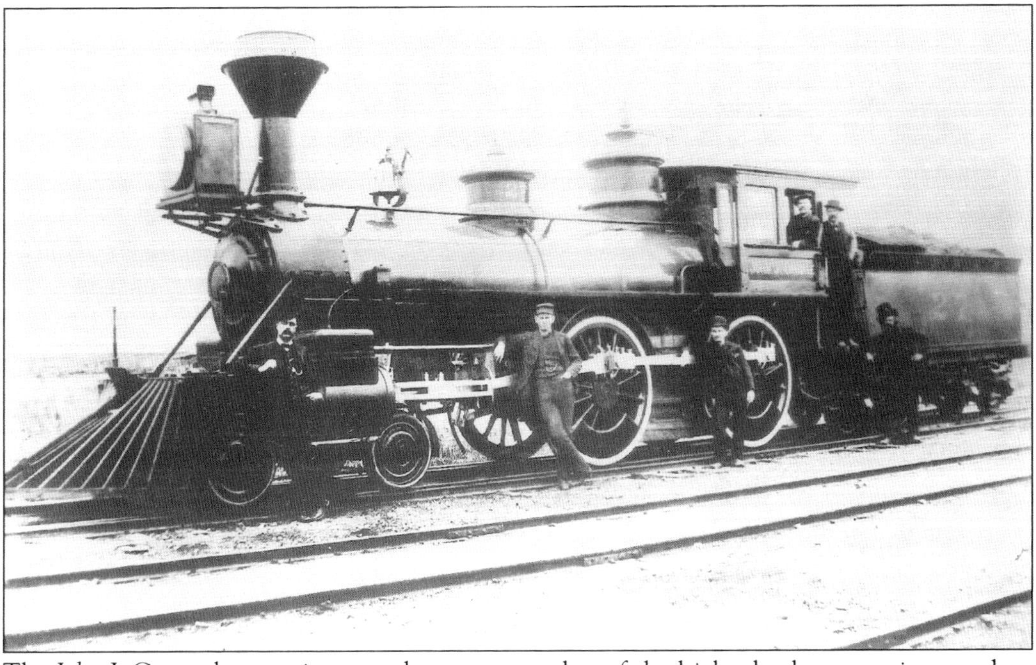

The *John J. Crause* locomotive, seen here, was another of the high-wheel-type engines used on the Utica and Black River Railroad stopping at Marcy and Stittville stations. (Courtesy of the New York Central Railroad Museum.)

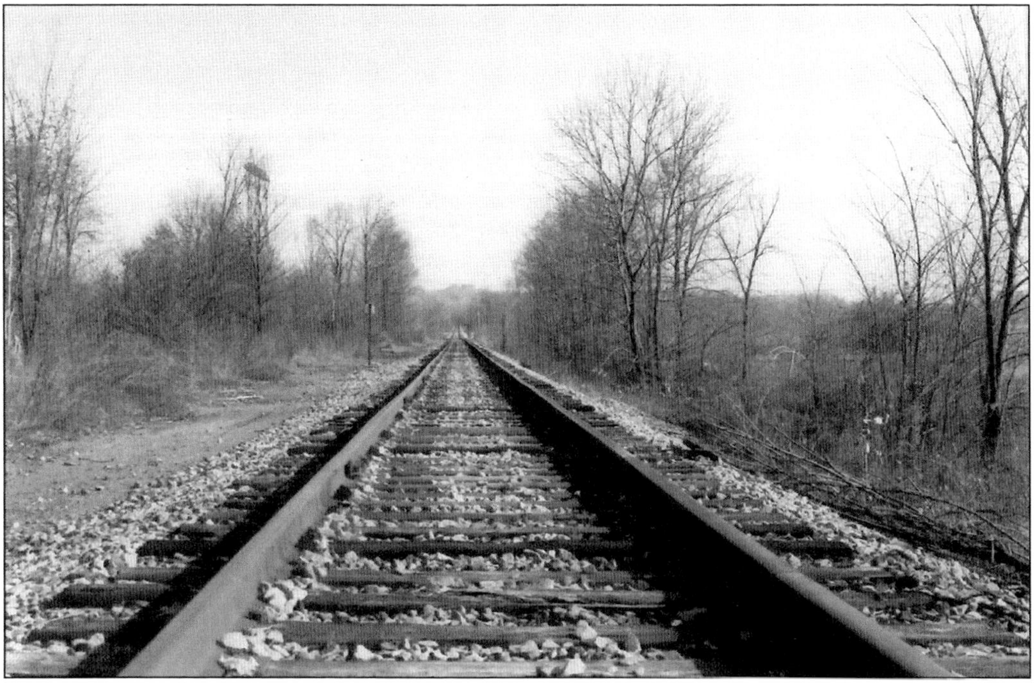

By 1999, the tracks had been reduced to only one. The big cause of this was invention of the stainless steel refrigerated milk tank truck and the new electronic controls, which allowed the railroad to make one track due the work of two tracks.

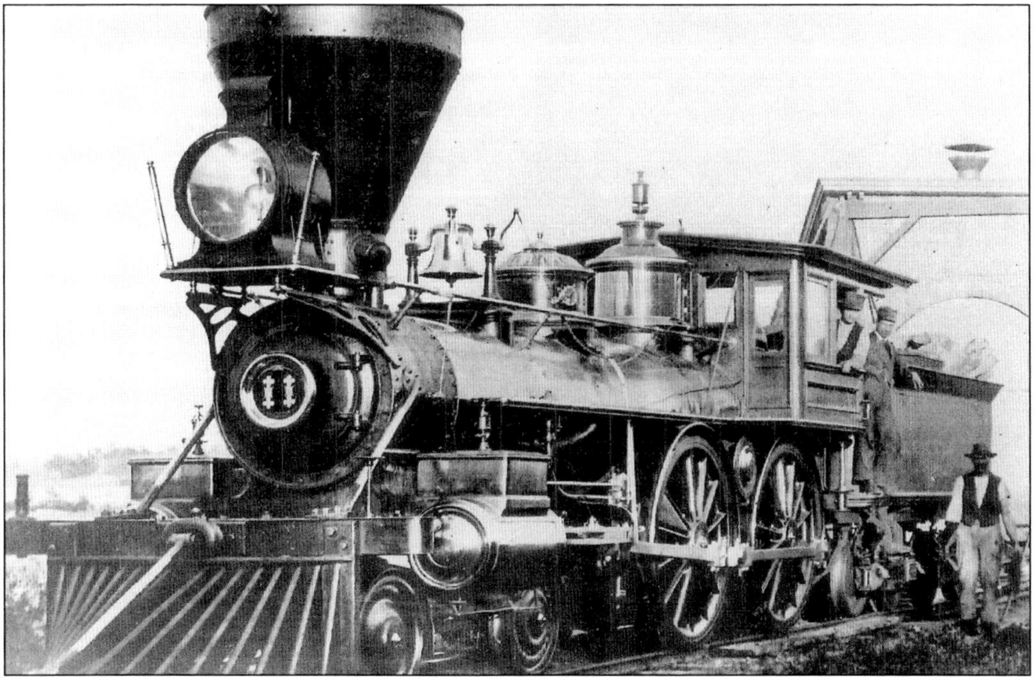

Technology was advancing rapidly after the Civil War as can be seen in this photograph of the *W. T. Hopkins* as compared to the *T. J. Faxton* locomotive first used in Marcy. (Courtesy of the New York Central Railroad Museum.)

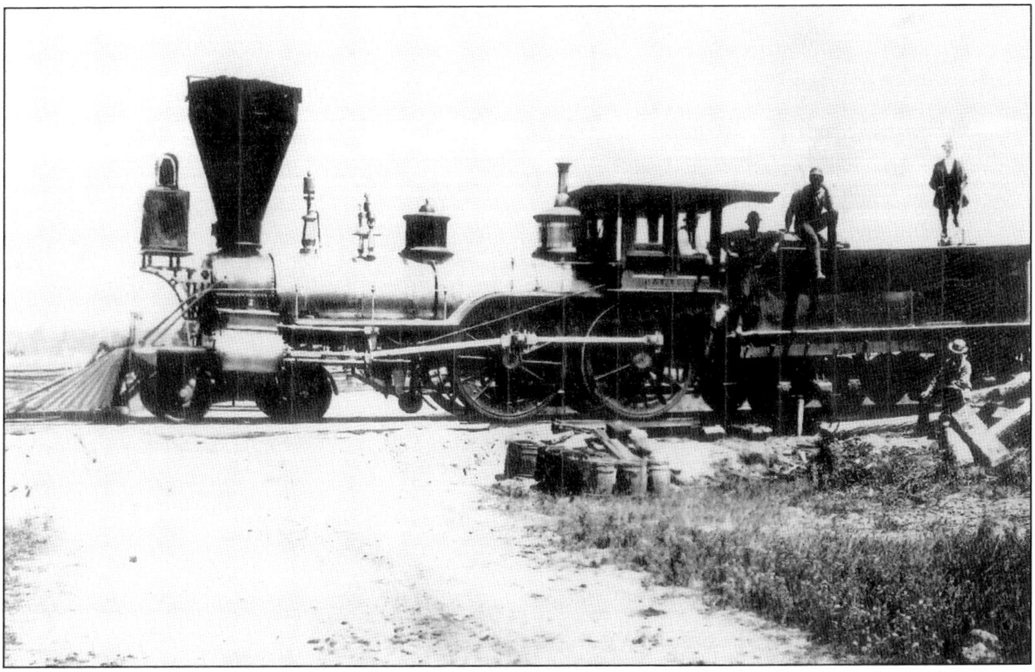

In 1855, the track was ready and the *T. J. Faxton* locomotive made the first trip through Marcy. (Courtesy of the New York Central Railroad Museum.)

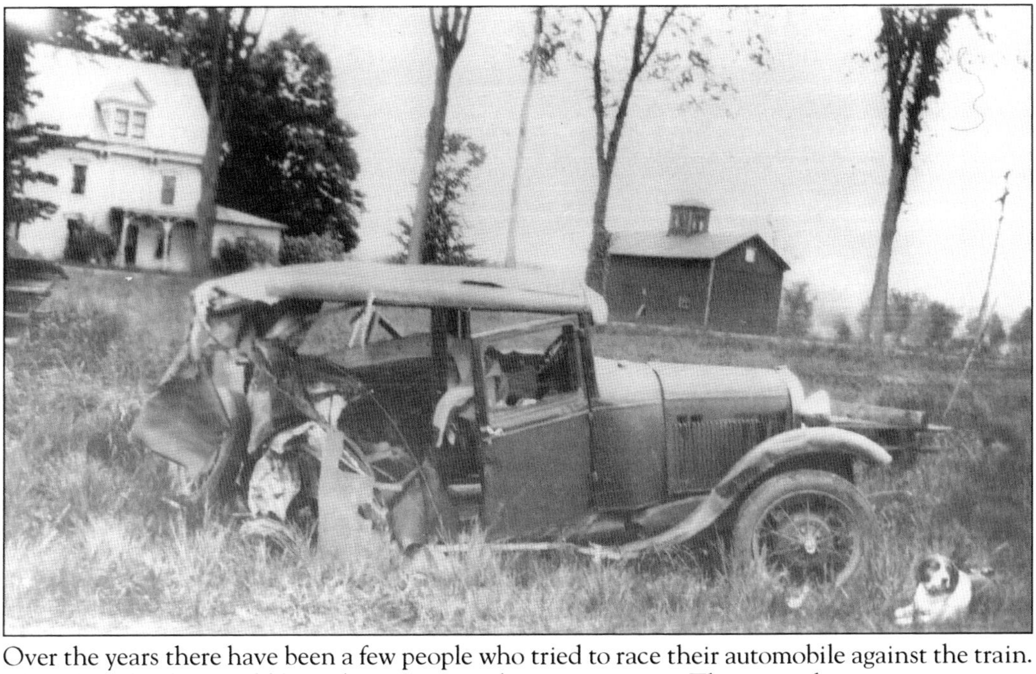

Over the years there have been a few people who tried to race their automobile against the train. They thought they could beat the train over the next crossing. The train always won.

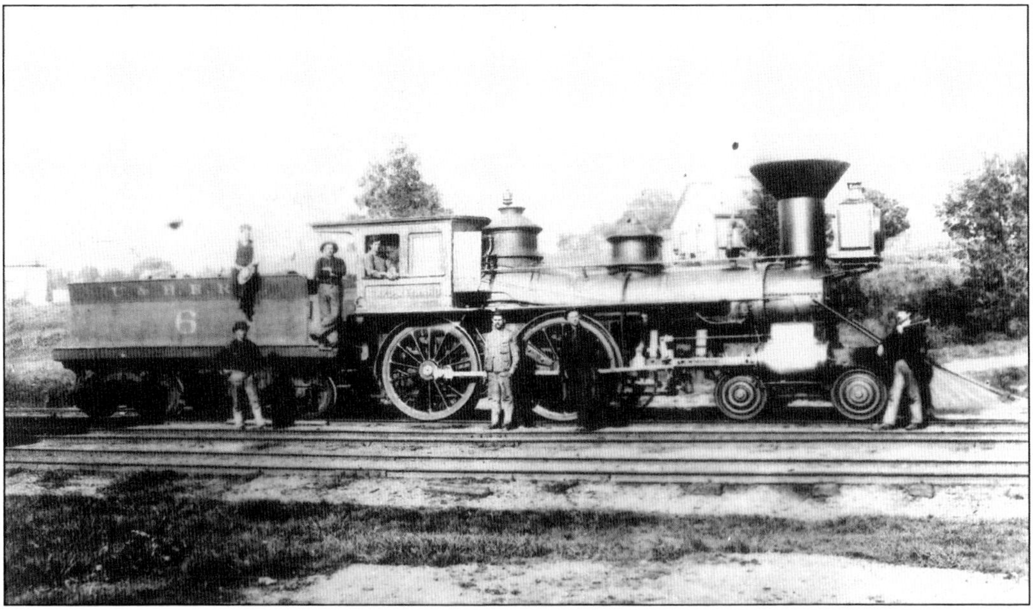

Many different engines made the Utica to Boonville run, but one of the favorite engines was called the *Isaac Maynard*. This was named after the conductor who became very popular with people living near a mail pickup and drop off station near Edic Road. The people decided to name their hamlet Maynard in his honor. (Courtesy of the New York Central Railroad Museum.)

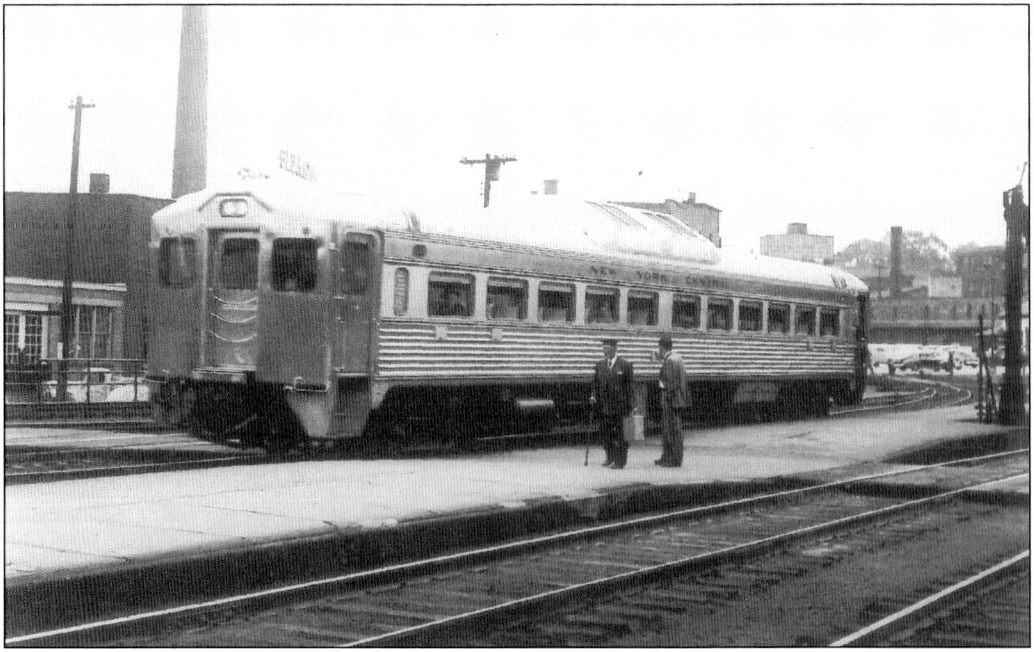

The last passenger train through Marcy was this Beeliner in 1953. It was a self-powered diesel, and it made its first trip with much fanfare between Utica and Watertown. After a few weeks, it ceased operation due to a lack of passengers, who preferred the automobile. (Courtesy of the New York Central Railroad Museum.)

Six

Roads, Canals, and Aviation

A big problem in Marcy, or in any rural community, was always the building and maintaining of roads and bridges. In 1836, $14 out of every $15 raised in taxes was spent on roads. By 1838, things were so bad that the town board voted not to accept any more trails to be made into roads. After the spring thaw, or following a heavy rainstorm, one or more of the wooden bridges would get washed out, causing a severe financial problem to rebuild the bridge.

The canal age came to New York State in the early 1800s and had an adverse effect on Marcy. The Erie Canal was built through Utica and Whitesboro, about eight miles south of Marcy. This meant that mills and factories tended to locate along the canal and businesses located in small rural towns tended to close or relocate. This situation continued for nearly 30 years until the building of the railroads. The fast trains meant a business could be competitive from a small rural town and so they came back to the area.

Once Marcy had the second largest airport in New York State—second only to LaGuardia field. The City of Utica built the airport, and it quickly became known as Marcy airport. All the important people in aviation were here several times in their career. The airport became famous for developing radio communications, beacon guidance, weather communications, and as a training center for mechanics and pilots during World War II.

Then after 50 years of aviation glory, the Marcy airport came to an end. A tragic fire destroyed the main hanger, and a new development sealed its fate. That development was the jet engine and jet plane. Marcy airport's runway was not long enough and could not support the new heavier planes. Marcy's place in aviation came to an end as the airport moved to a new location.

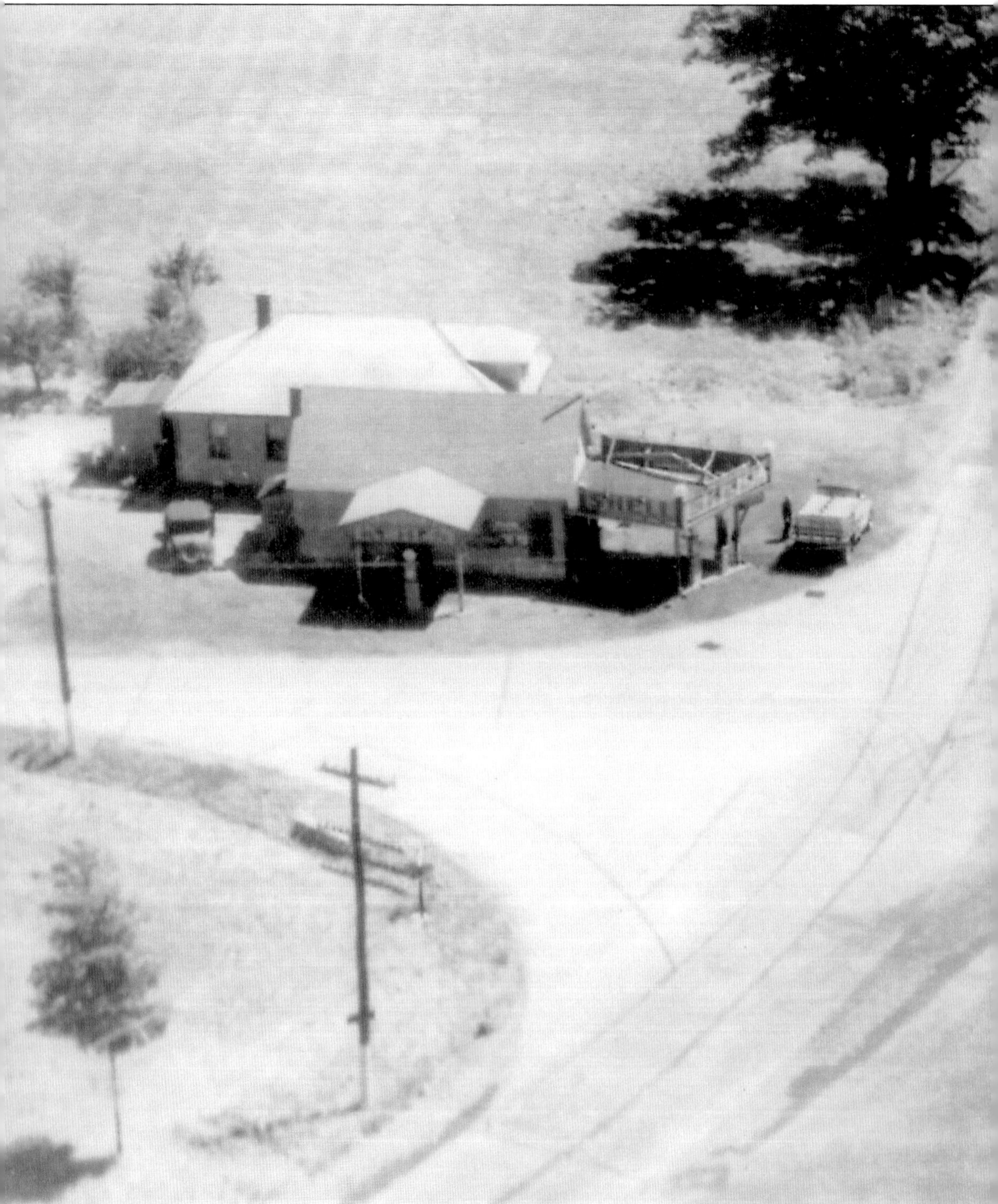

Cary's Corners, in Marcy, was the main business corner in 1920. The road to the right went to Whitesboro, the road to the left went to Stittville, and the road at the bottom went up over the

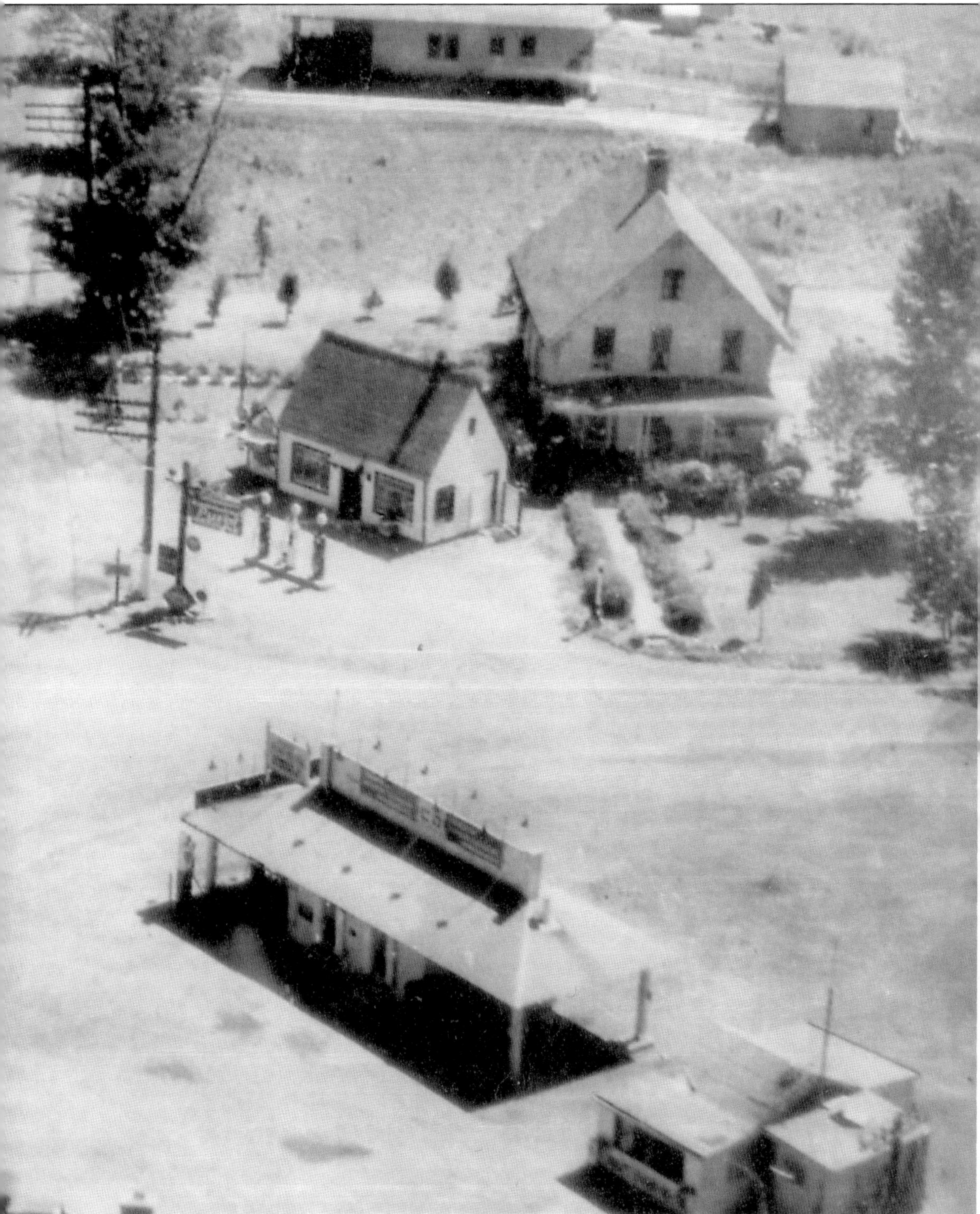

hill to the Marcy State Hospital. Gasoline was 11¢ per gallon, and a hotdog was 15¢.

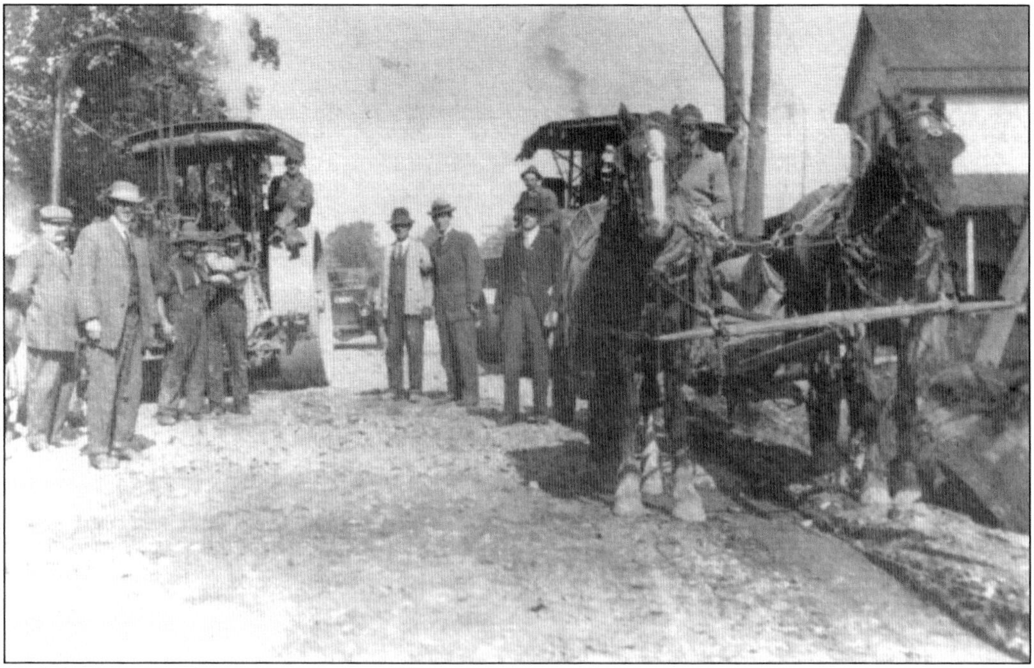

Early highway road repair projects used horses extensively, along with the new steamroller machine.

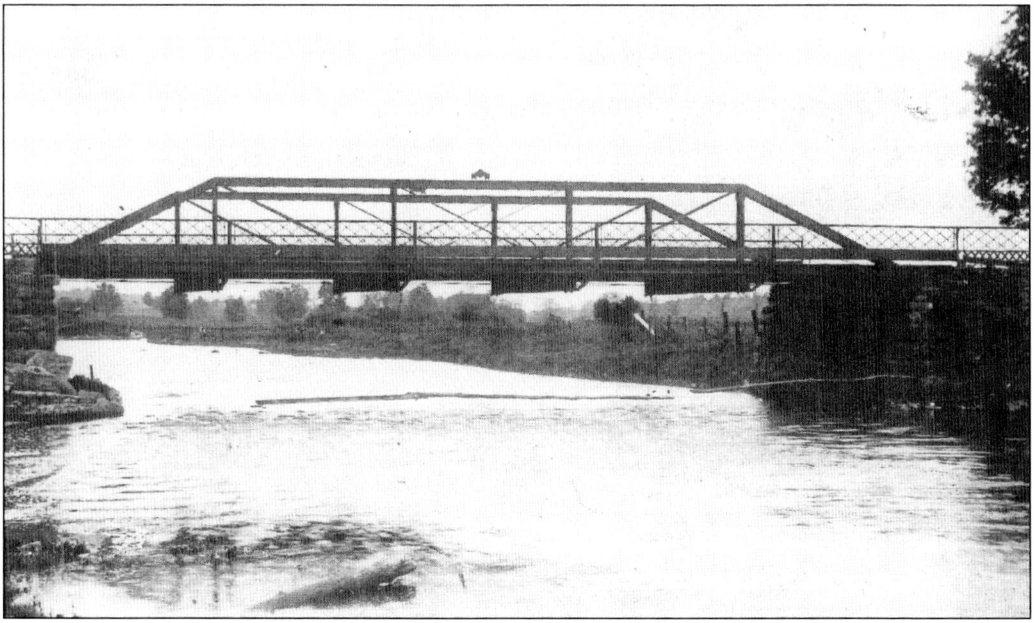

The bridge over Nine Mile Creek near the hamlet of Stittville and Route 291 is pictured here.

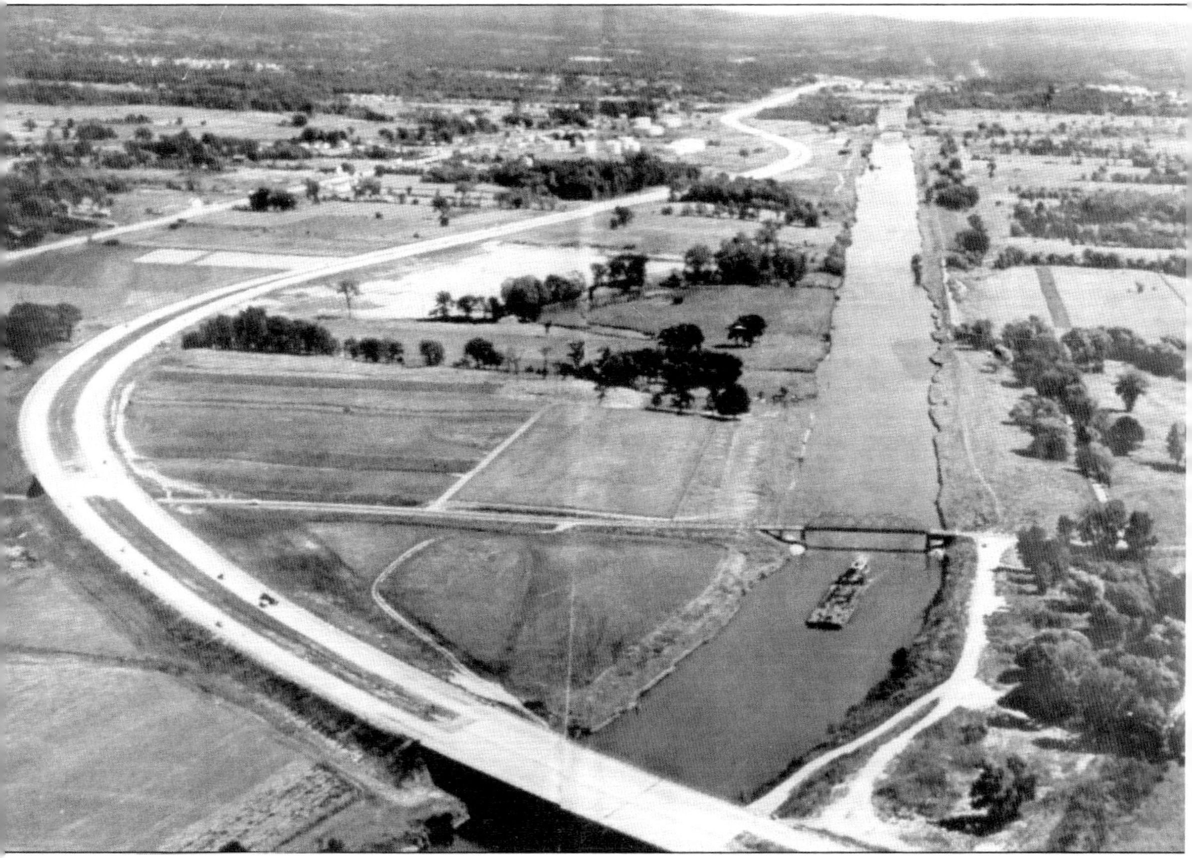

In 1952, the New York State Thruway was built, and it went through Marcy, taking a lot of choice farmland. This view, taken from a National Geographic plane, was used in the center fold of the magazine 55 years ago. Mohawk Street is in the forefront. The old one-lane iron truss bridge crosses the canal. Cars alternately took turns crossing the bridge. Choice farmland was cut in two. The Candella farm is a the extreme left where Mohawk Street crosses under the thruway. Route 49 is an oil-and-stone highway with nothing but farmland on either side. The only business is the fuel storage tanks in the center of the picture. Interestingly, the thruway made a curve in the road to go around the tanks.

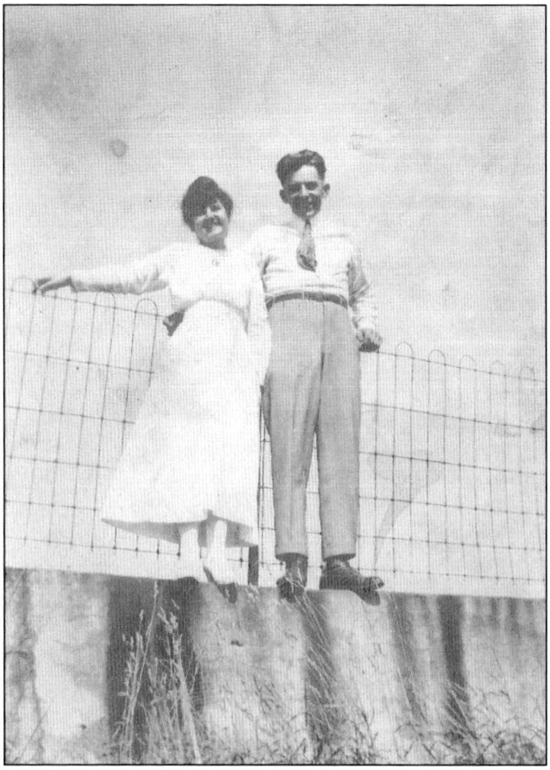

In 1919, Lock 20 was a favorite place to visit for many people, including Mary and Albert Kula.

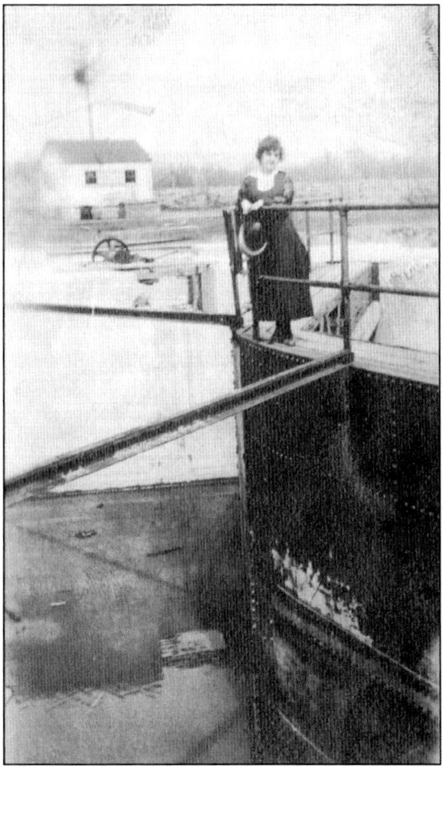

Here Mary is standing at the top of the canal gate. This was in the early days of construction; people are no longer allowed to walk out here and are held back by a safety fence.

Dick Botsford was one of the pioneer aviators at the Marcy (Utica) airport. He was qualified to fly almost any plane from a single engine to a giant trimotor plane. He had his own flying service; he was involved in all kinds of flying activities. As a flying instructor and Federal Aviation Administration inspector, he handled hundreds of aviators. One of his most prominent was Col. Charles A. Lindbergh, whom he checked out to fly the larger trimotor planes during World War II.

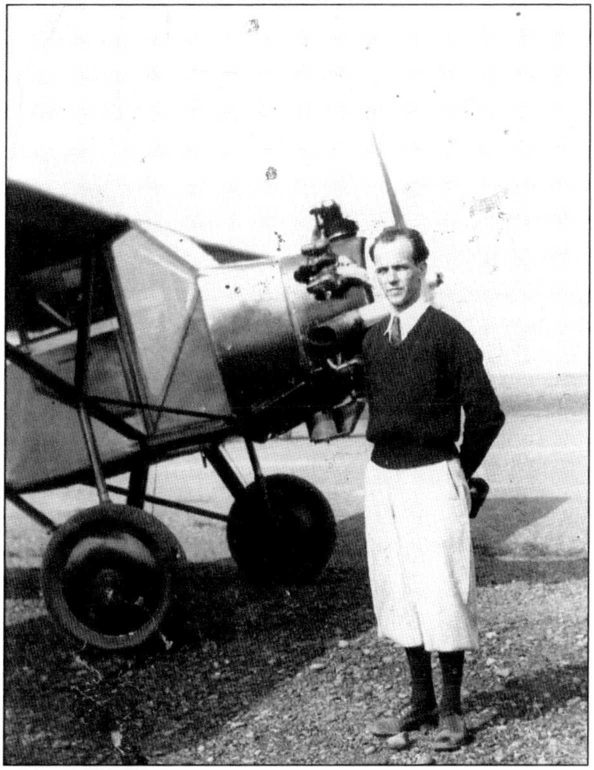

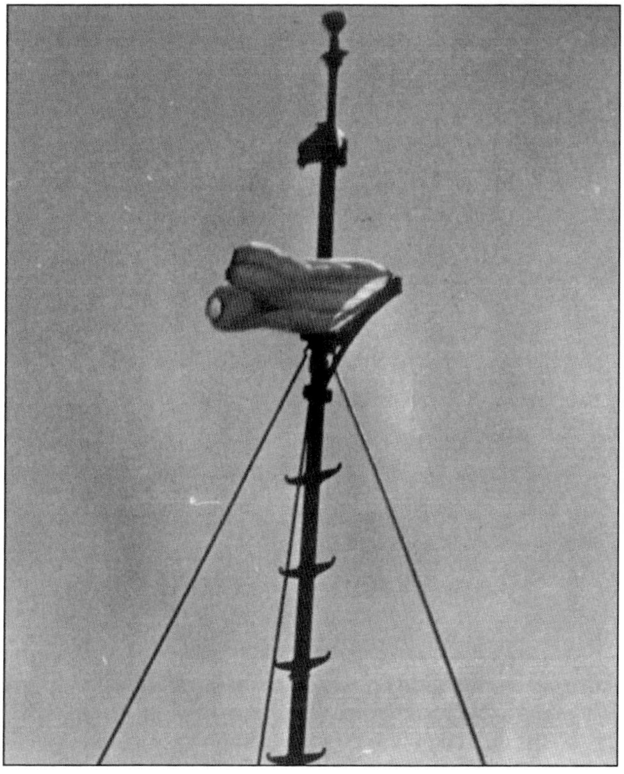

Every airport had a windsock, and by the direction the wind was blowing it told the pilot the direction of the wind to assist him in landing and takeoffs. One time at Marcy airport, an incident occurred where the windsock was gone and a replacement was not at hand. The naturally quick-thinking pilots knew just what to do—they went to a Utica department store and purchased the largest size woman's bloomers the store had and attached that to the mast. That pair of bloomers guided the pilots in and out for several days.

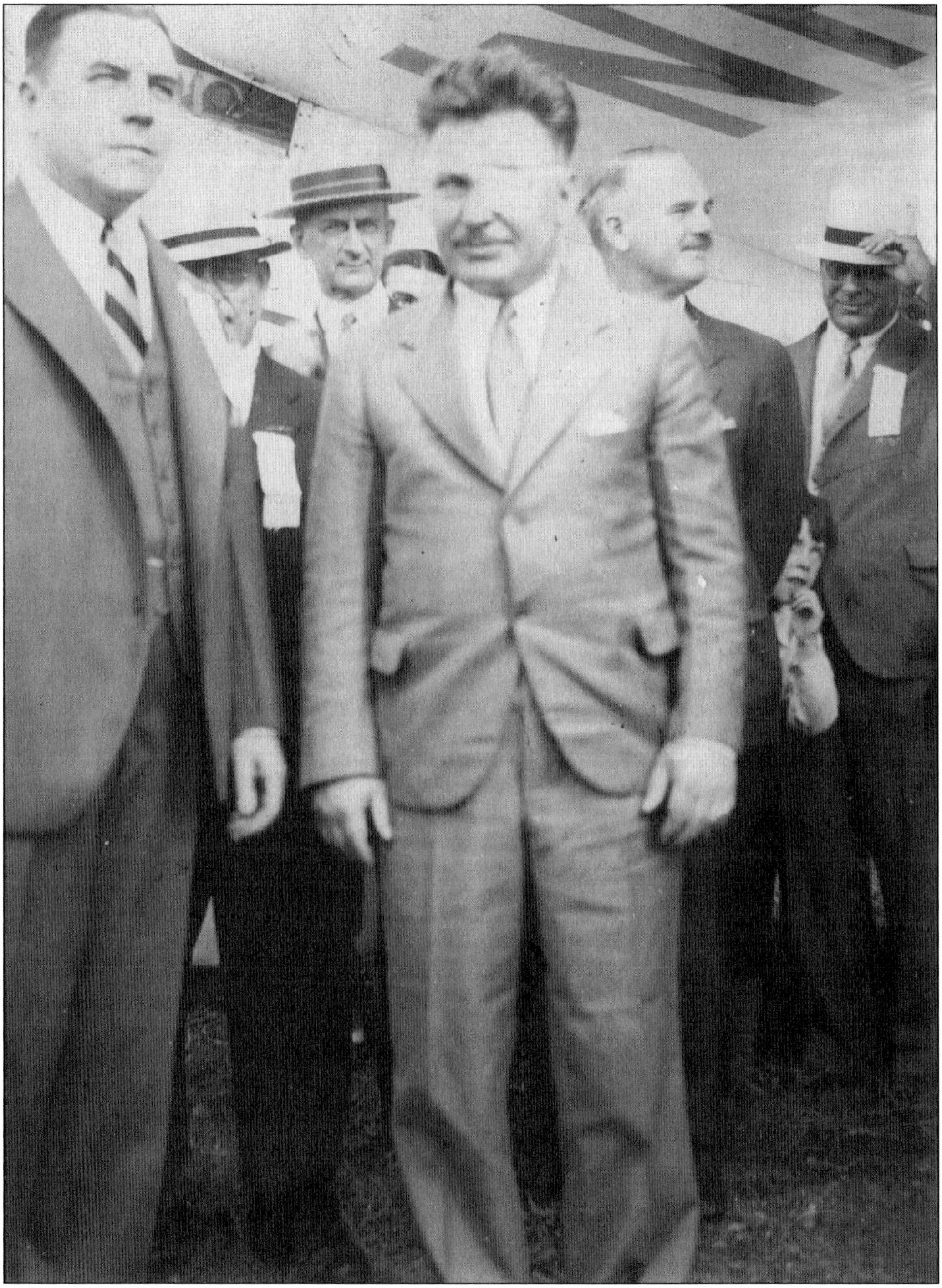

Wiley Post was a man of dreams. As a pilot, he dreamed of flying around the world. This would be an onerous task for any pilot, but Post only had one eye. In 1931, he did make the trip, but with a navigator. In 1933, he fulfilled his dream of flying around the world alone. It was a hero's welcome when he visited Marcy airport.

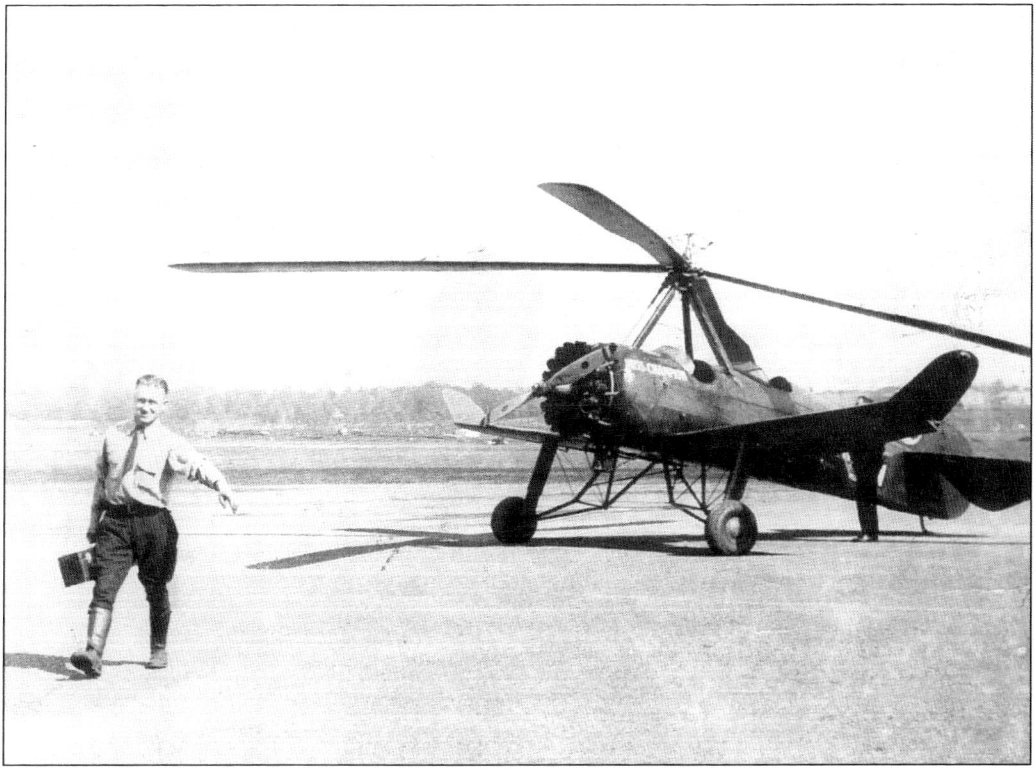

A frequent visitor at Marcy airport was this autogiro, the forerunner of the helicopter. The name of the pilot is unknown.

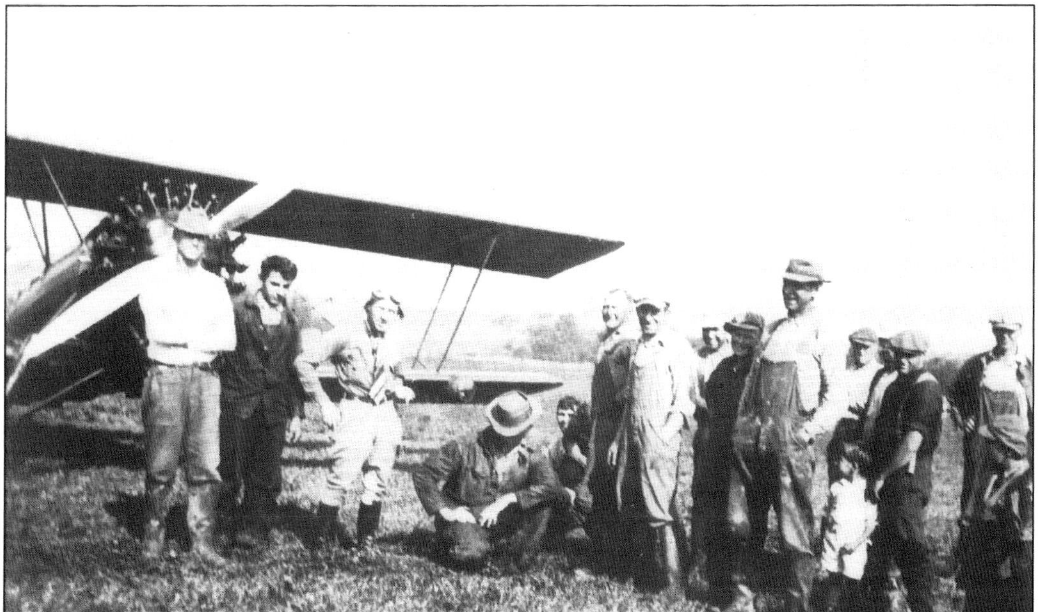

The airmail service was a busy activity at Marcy airport. But there were a few times it had problems. Here Cy Bittner, an airmail pilot, made a forced landing south of Utica due to engine trouble.

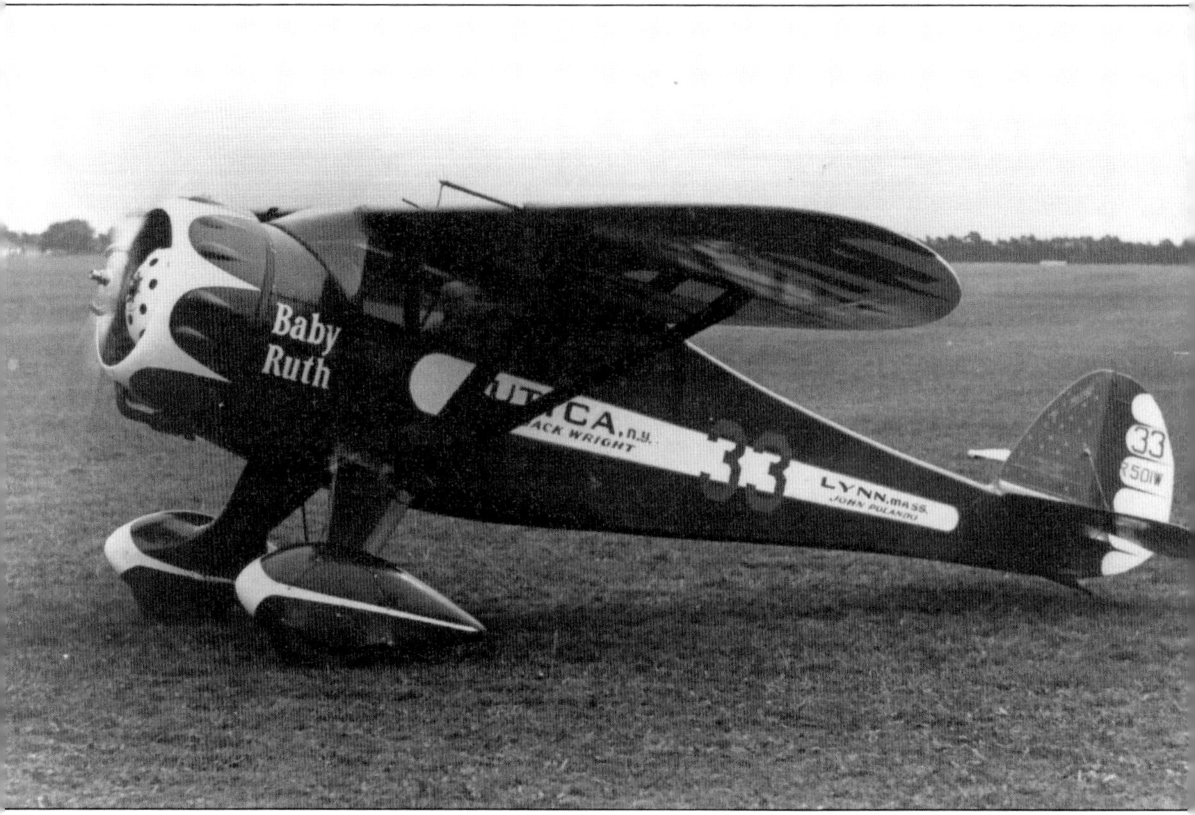

Jack Wright was the "dapper Dan" of Marcy airport. He was always well-dressed in business attire and played the part of the successful businessman very well. He was in the insurance business but flying was his passion. His private plane, called *Baby Ruth*, was entered in the London to Milbourn air race, but he had to make a forced landing in one of the Arabic countries. The plane was impounded, but after several weeks, it was released and flown back to Marcy.

Seven

Churches and Cemeteries

The early settlers were largely religious people. The first to organize in 1808 was a mission group. They originally met in member's homes and then in 1838, built the church of the Holy Cross on the top of Bell Hill Road in what is now Deerfield. The congregation grew to 400 or 500 people, especially during the times of the year roads were passable. In the next few years, several other churches were built by Methodists, Baptists, and Welch Presbyterians. The original Methodist church on Maynard Drive was built in 1839 at a cost of $925. This building was of such historic significance that it was dismantled piece by piece and rebuilt as part of the Erie Canal Village, a historic tourist attraction at nearby Rome.

Of equal importance are the Marcy cemeteries, which seem to correspond to the dates of the churches. Only one of the early denominations still exists, but the cemeteries are all well maintained and kept in very nice condition. In some of them, early headstones are in the Welch language and can be read only by Welch descendents. Unlike other stones, the Welch headstones contain a wealth of genealogical information such as where the person was born, parental information, and date of departure from Wales.

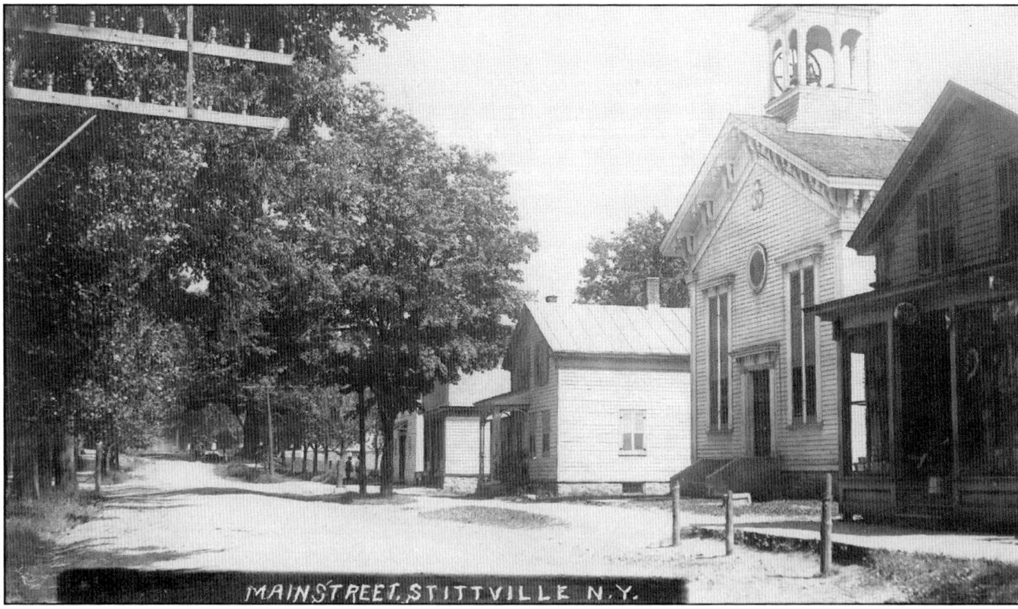

Main Street in Stittville was the site of the original Methodist church, organized about 1836.

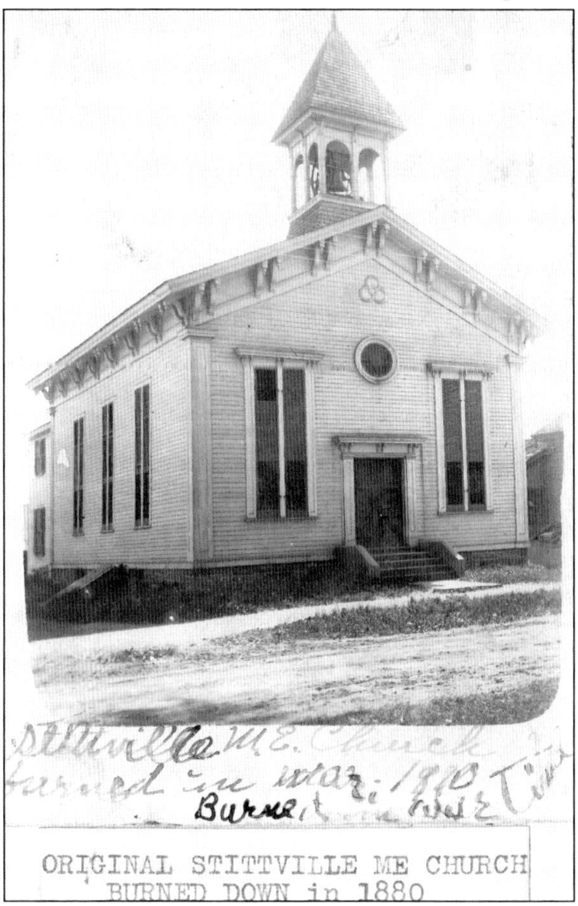

A front view of the Methodist church shows the fine architectural details. Shortly after, this building burned.

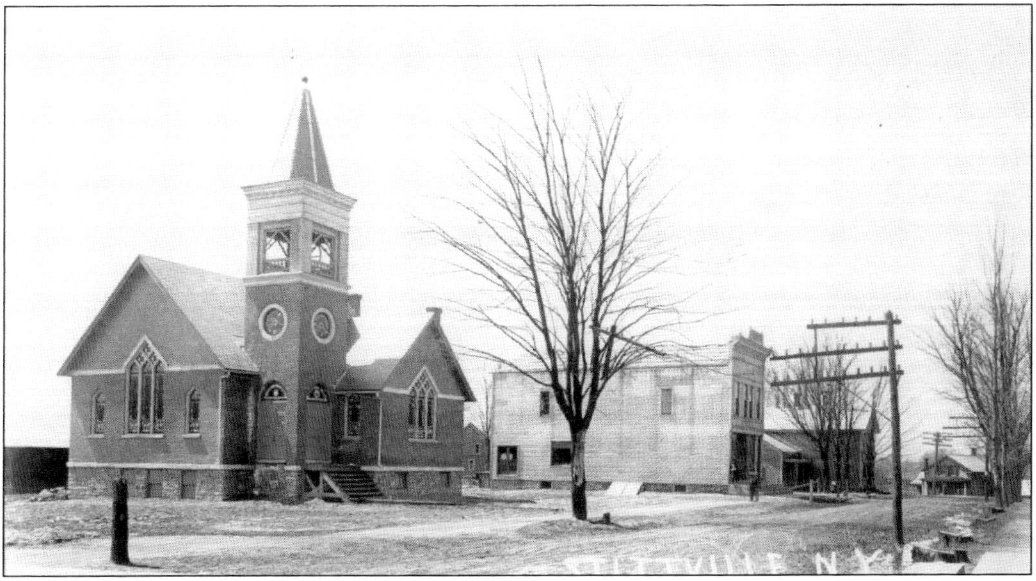

The Methodist Episcopal church was rebuilt with brick veneer siding, and it stands as of 2007.

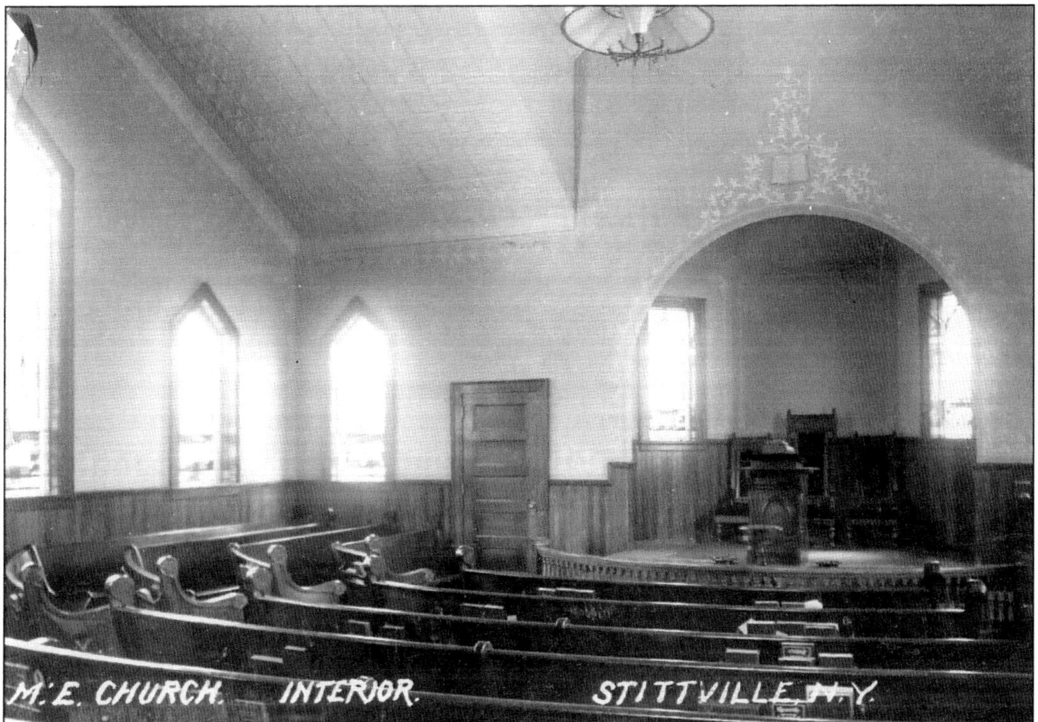

This is an interior view of the Methodist church.

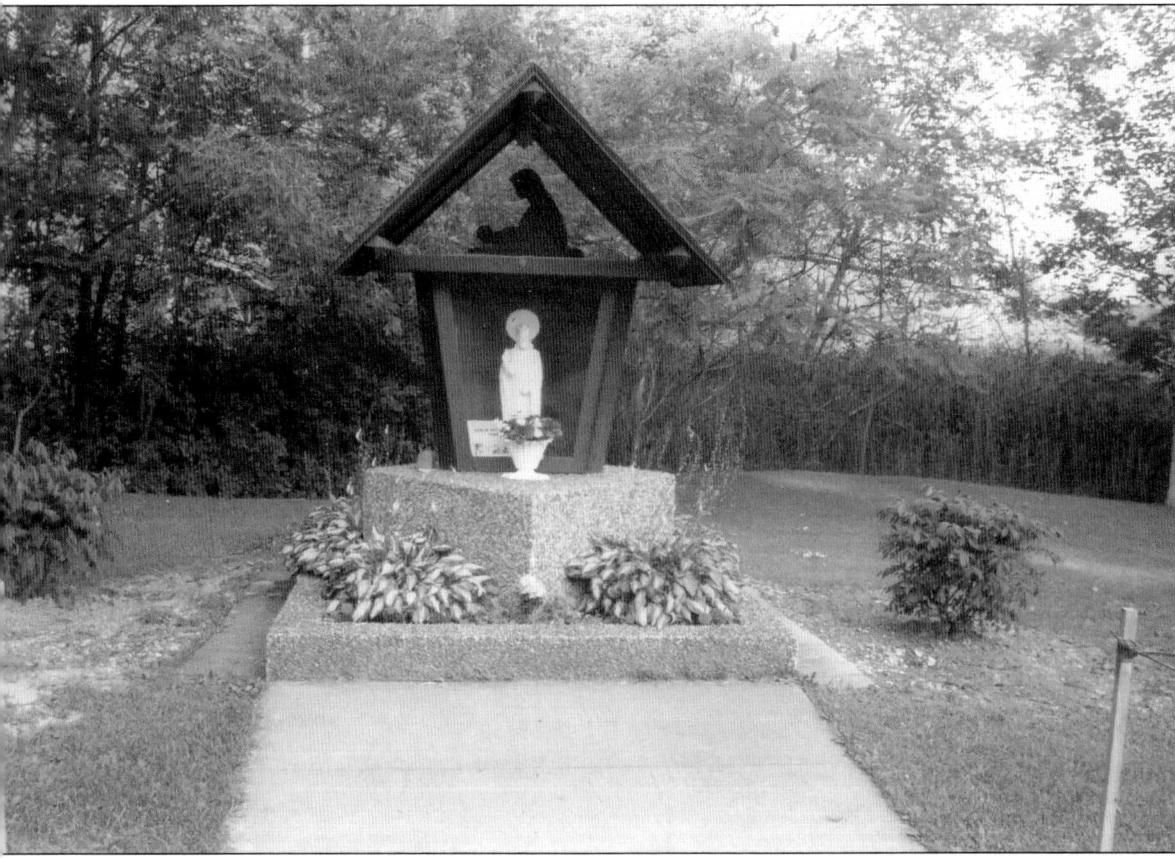

It is claimed that Jesus appeared on several occasions at this shrine in Marcy. The Catholic Church has not yet verified this, but it is on the agenda for future study.

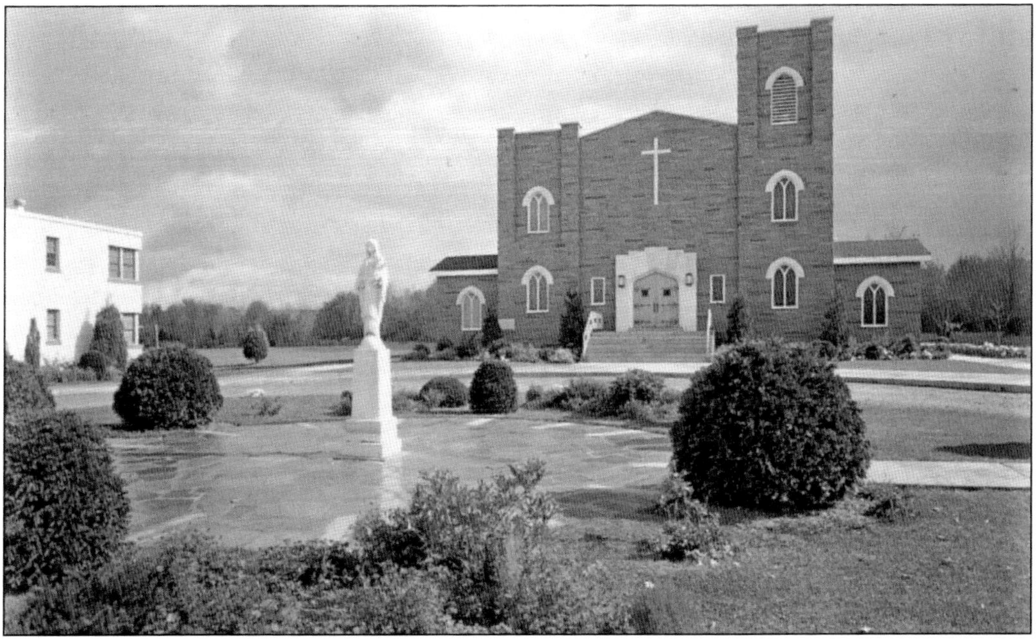

Chaminade Chapel of Chaminade Preparatory is pictured here. This organization was very active but closed down back in the 1970s due to a shortage of students who were interested in the seminary.

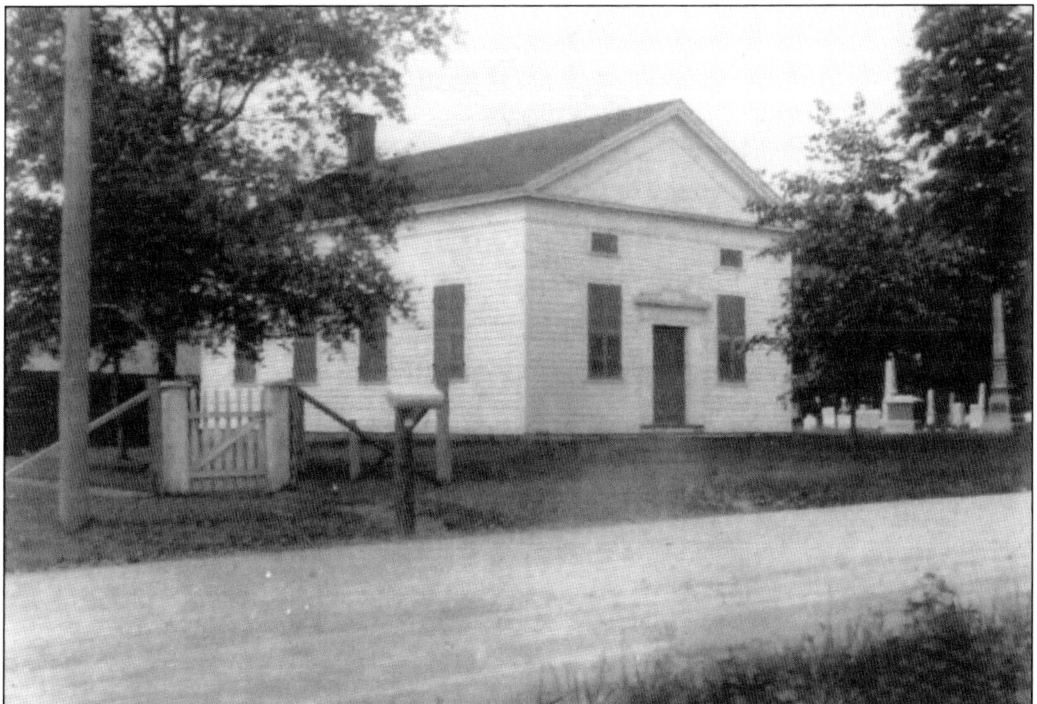

This was the original Methodist church built in 1839 in the area of Marcy now known as Maynard, thus the church was locally known as Maynard Methodist Church. The church has now been replaced with a more modern building.

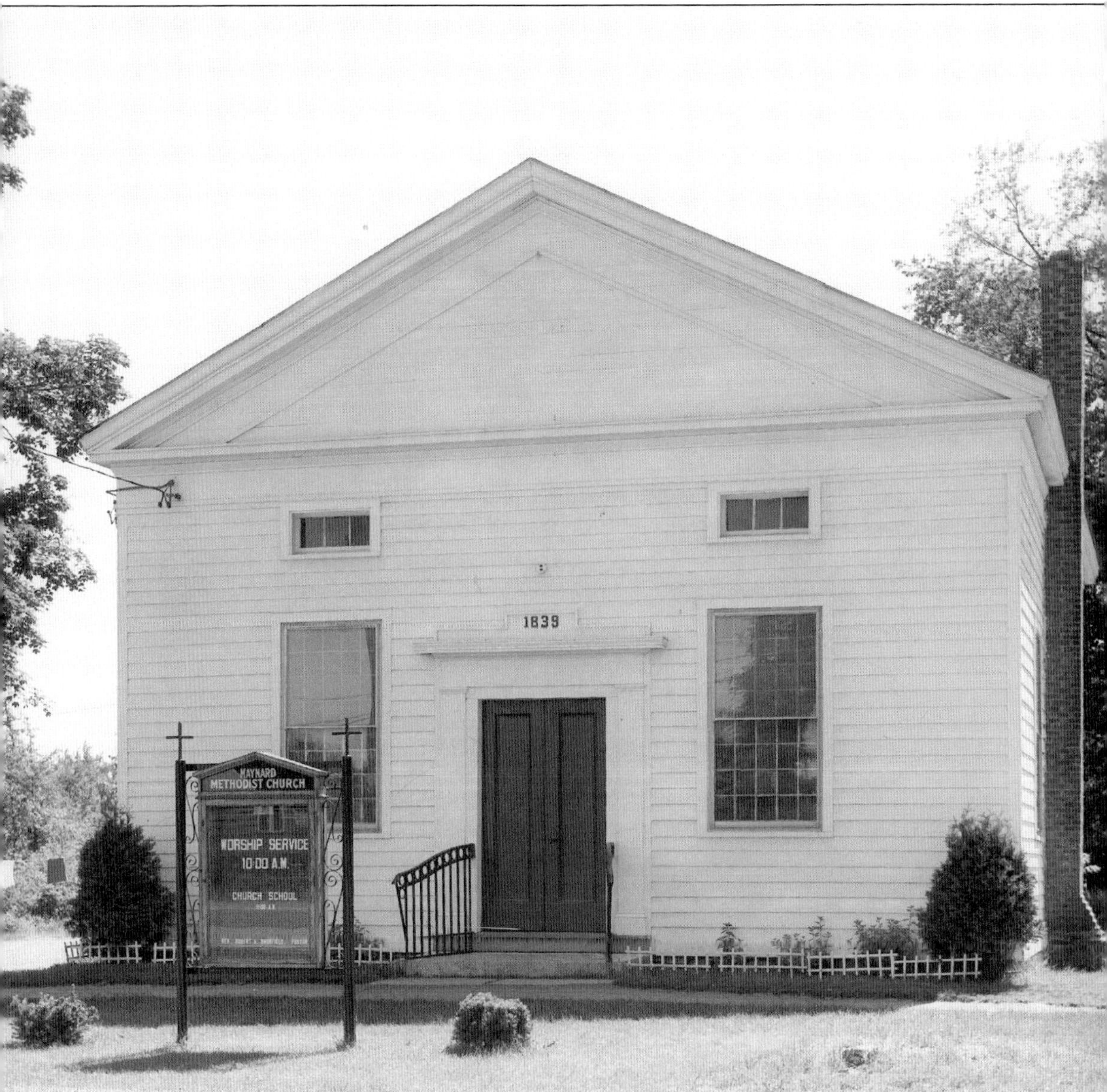

This is the original Maynard Methodist Church from Marcy. Built in 1839, it was dismantled piece by piece and taken to Erie Canal Village in nearby Rome, where it was reassembled and now functions as the village church in this re-created historic Colonial town.

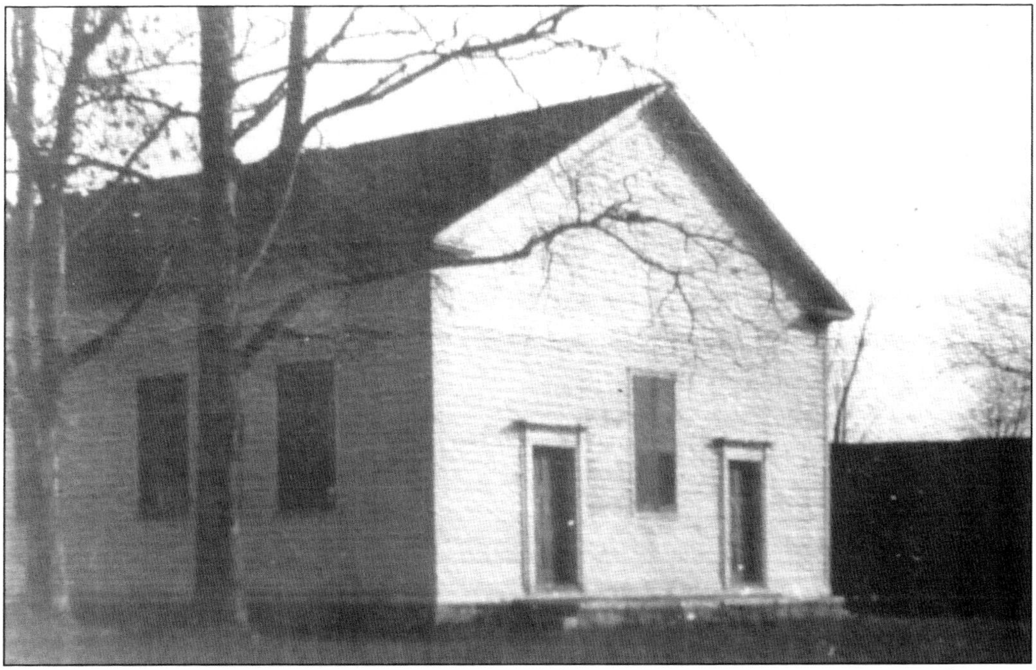

The Berean Baptist Church was built in 1844, and the congregation was very active in that part of Marcy. In more recent years, the building has been extensively modified, and it is now known as Marcy Community Church.

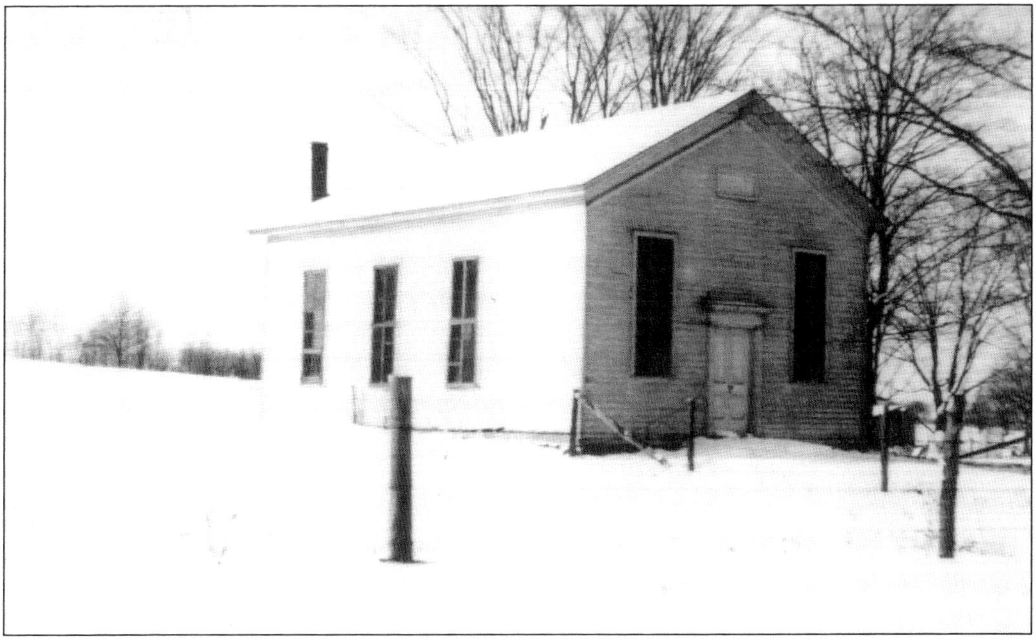

This photograph is a rare find. The original church was built in 1836 by the Calvinistic Methodist Church of Marcy. In 1840, it was sold to the First Welsh Congregational Society. In 1859, that church became too small so it was replaced with the one pictured. By 1910, as the Welch people moved from the area, the church was torn down, leaving only the cemetery. They left no records, so it is fortuitous to have found this only remaining photograph.

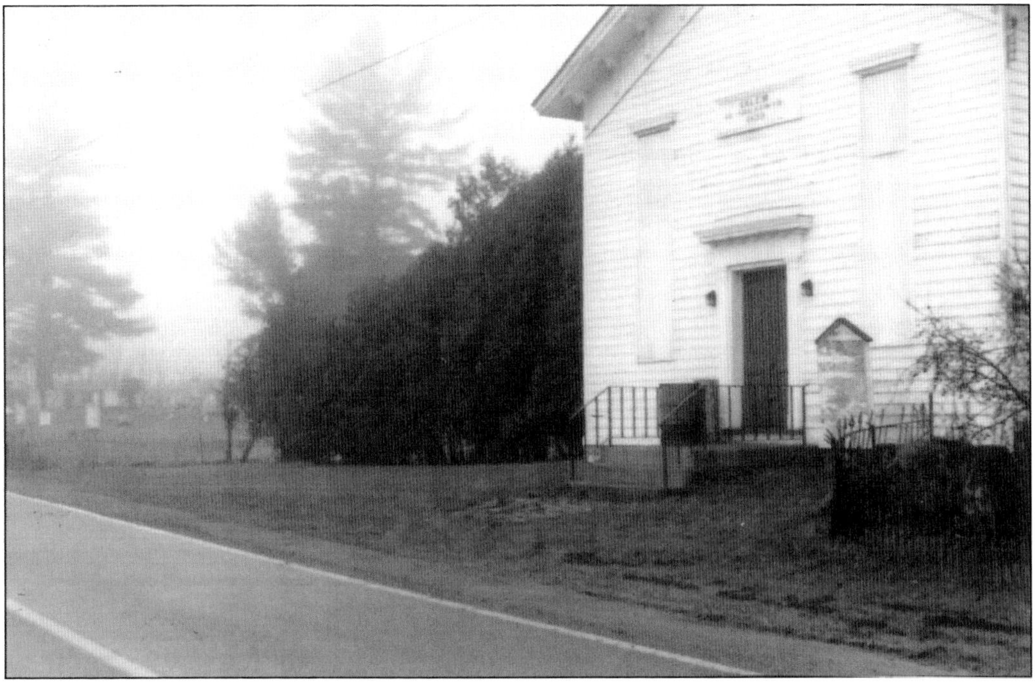

The land for this church and cemetery were donated by Cadwalader Richards from his farm in 1815. The church organization took place in 1830. It was called the First Welsh Congregational Society of Deerfield. In 1840, the name Salem was adopted. By 1859, the congregation had grown, and the original small church was moved and made into a cheese factory. It was replaced by the structure that now stands there.

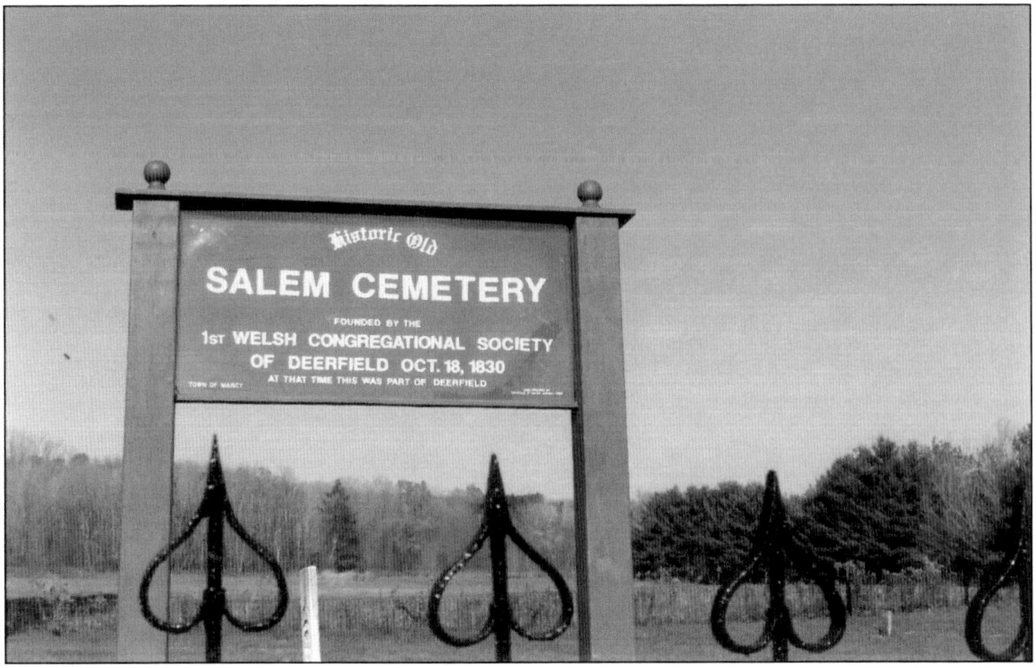

Salem cemetery surrounds the church and makes a proper background for this historic property.

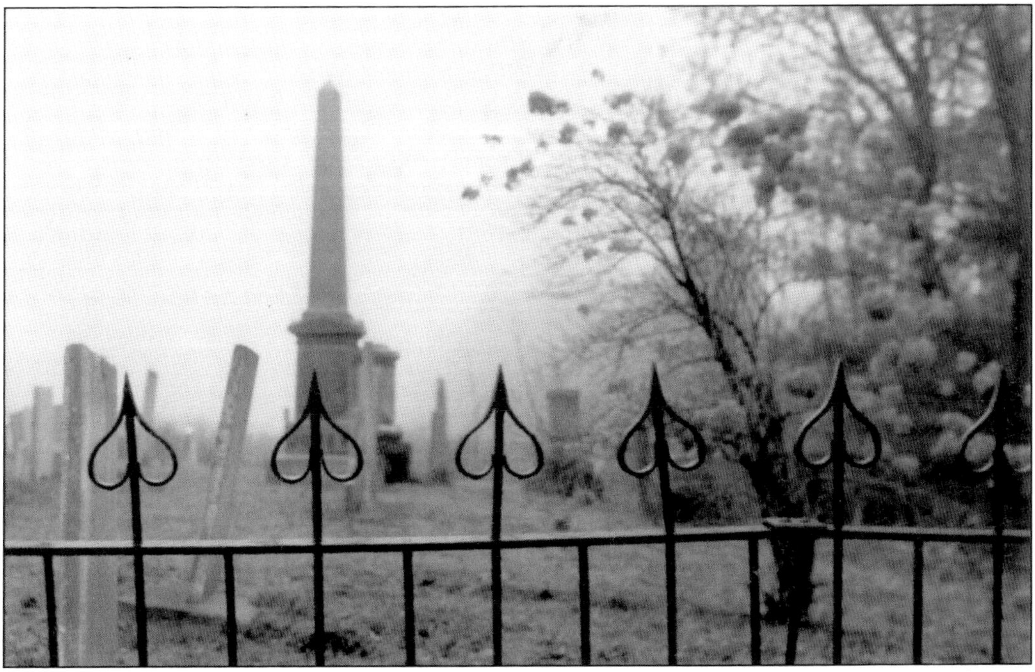

An early-morning photograph, when the fog is still on the hill, captures a weird effect and some say ghosts can be seen if one looks closely into the fog.

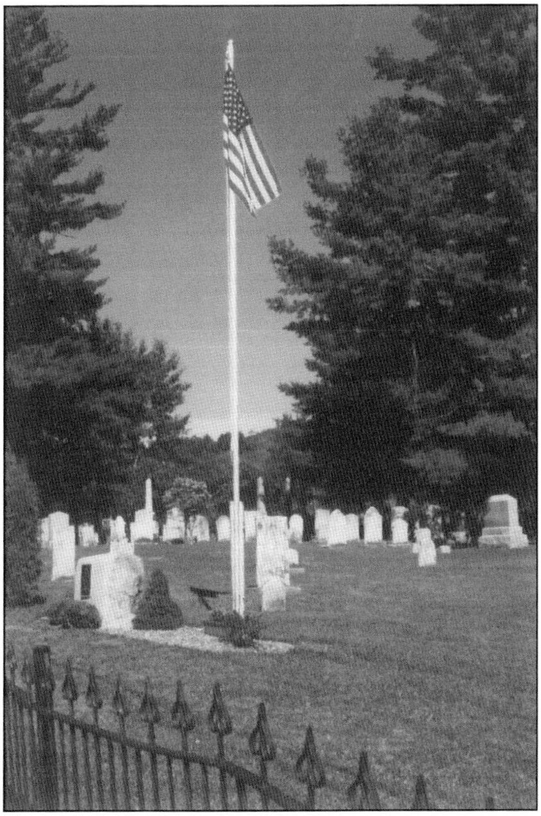

On the east side of the cemetery around the church are the average-type headstones typical of that time frame. On the west end of the cemetery, there appears to be more affluent headstones and family plots.

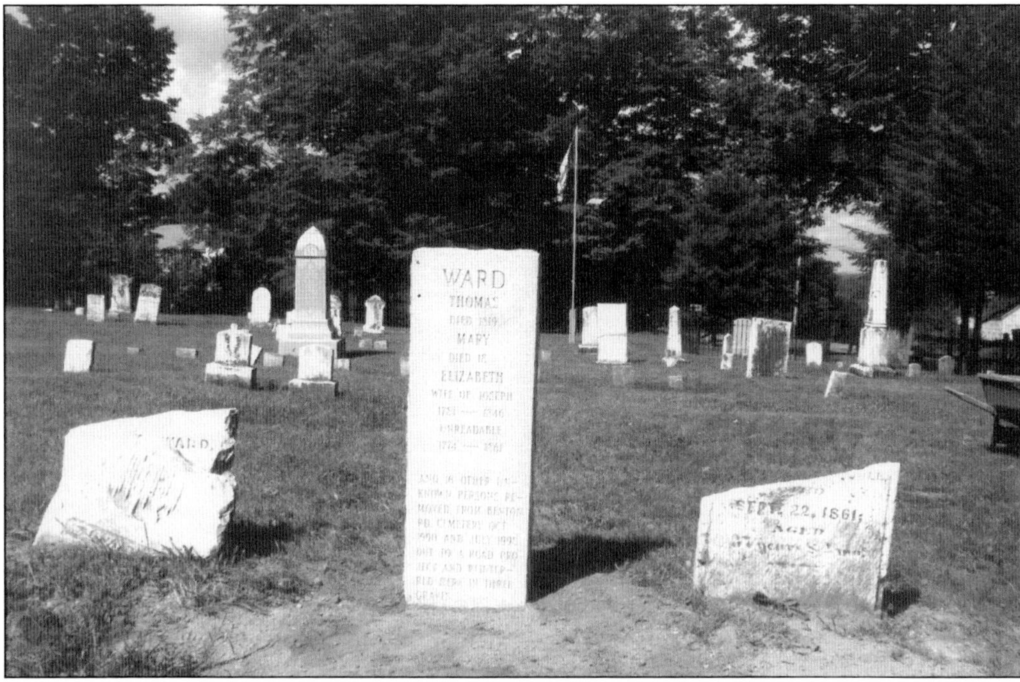

Bethania Church may be gone, but the cemetery remains. Reburied here are the remains of the Ward family and about a dozen others who were removed from the former Benton Road Cemetery when that plot was eliminated by a new road project in the 1990s.

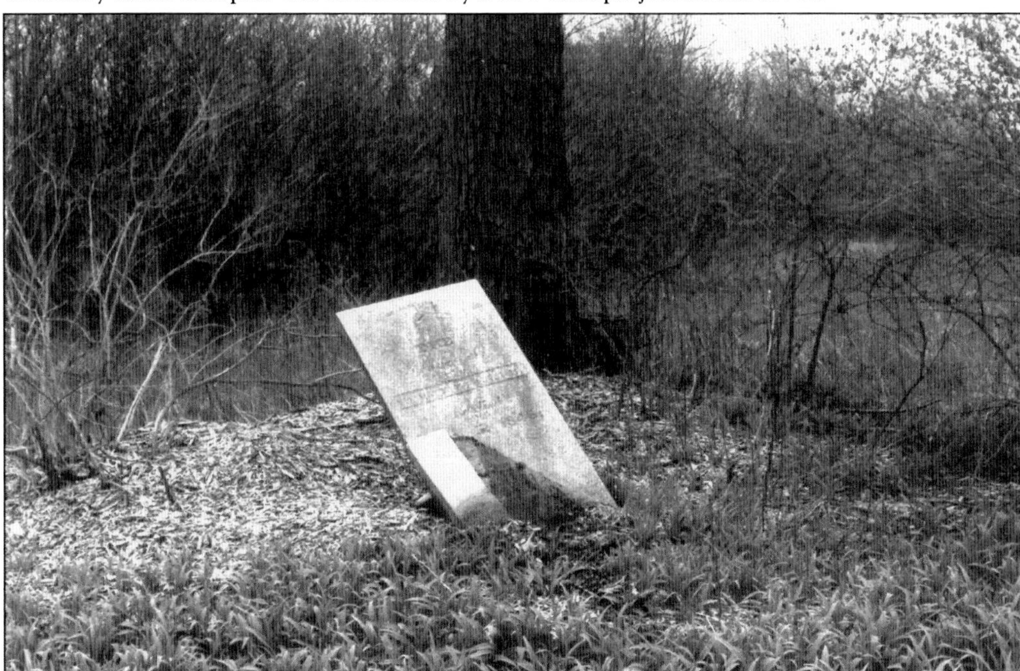

The Luther Hall plot of three graves sits 300 feet northwest of Crane Cemetery at the base of a large tree. Hall was part of the Crane family, but due to a family spat, he was isolated from the main plot.

This is the Cavana grave deep in the woods on Cavanaugh Road. Catherine died in 1848 at age 86. "Behold my friends as you pass by, / As you are now so once was I; / As I am now, so you must be, / Prepare for death and follow me."

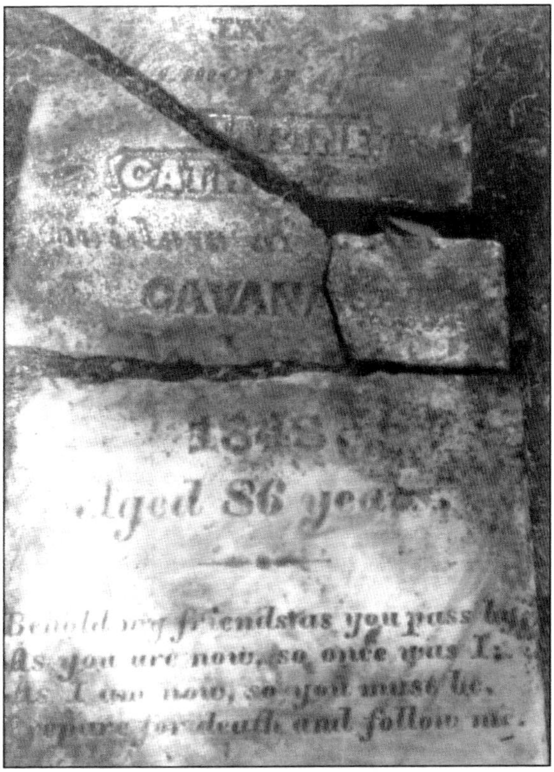

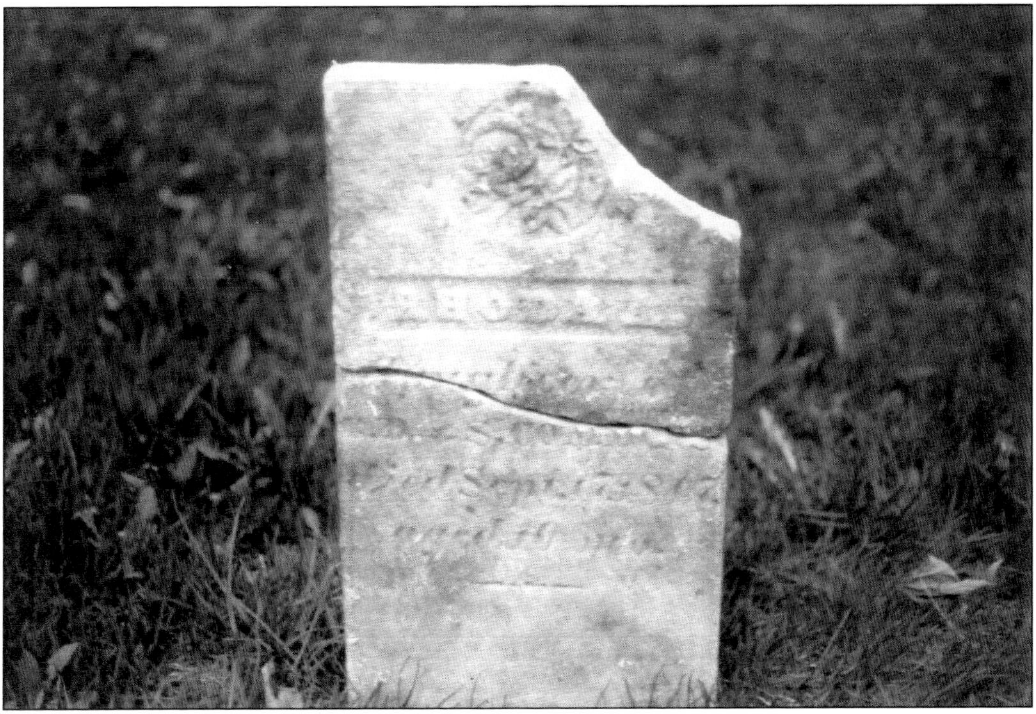

This is a small stone from site of Glassville, the community at the former glass factory. Rhoda A. died at age 10 in 1817.

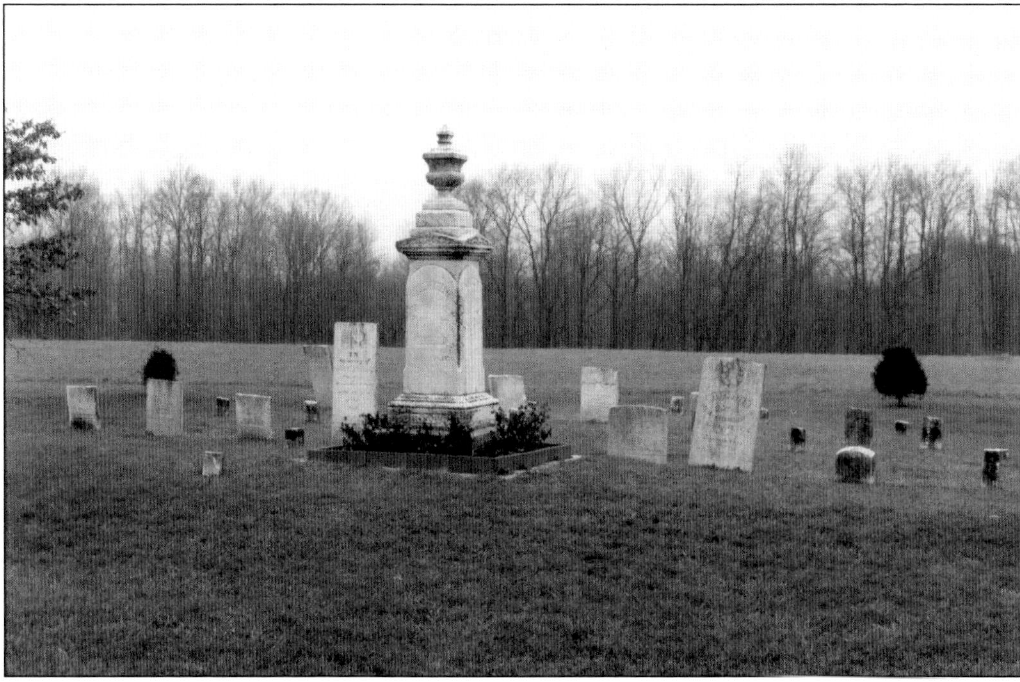

Most of the members of the Crane family are buried at the Crane Cemetery, with the exception of Luther Hall (see page 74). This plot is on top of the hill on Old River Road.

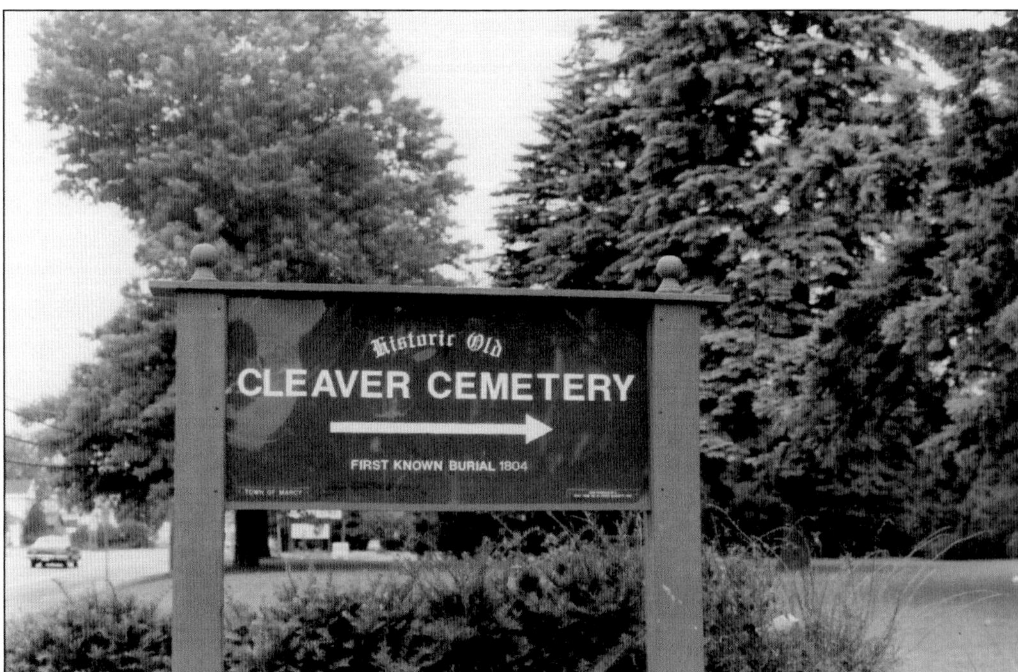

This sign appears at the entrance to historic old Cleaver Cemetery on River Road. The first burial in this cemetery occurred in 1804.

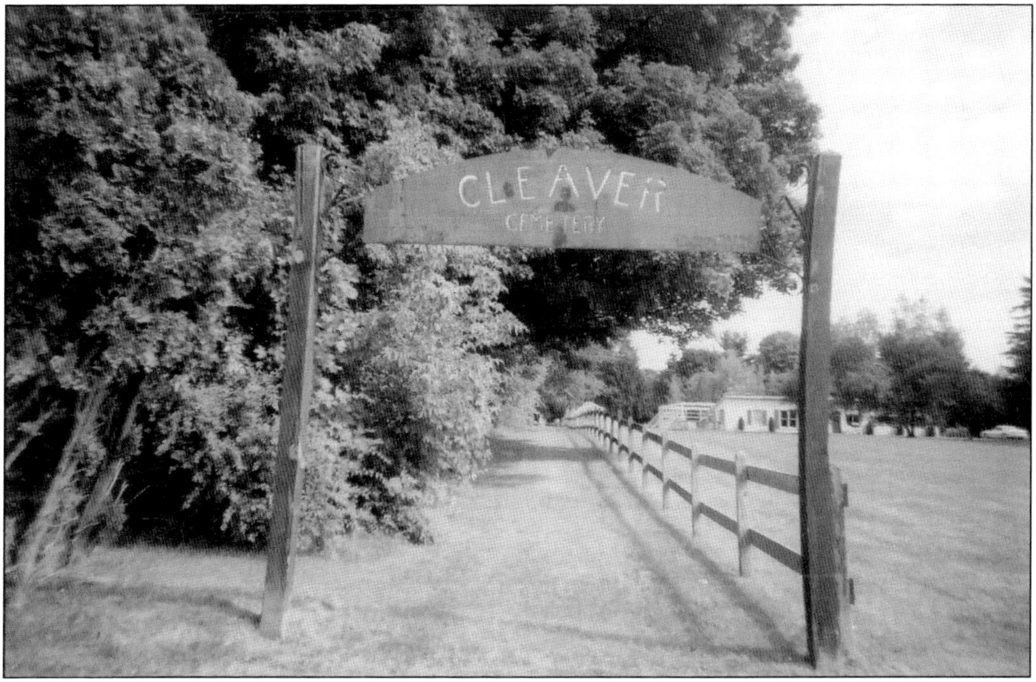

Cleaver Cemetery, the gateway of which is pictured here, is rumored to be the site where two Native Americans are buried, but this cannot be confirmed as the original record books are missing.

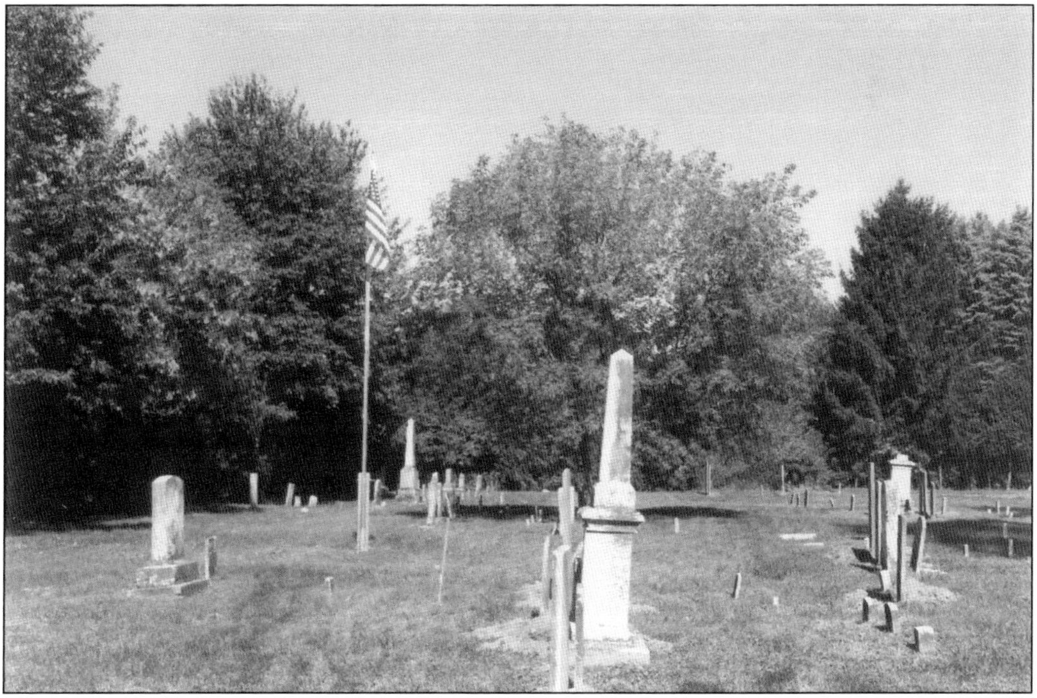

Most of the stones in Cleaver Cemetery are so old they can no longer be read.

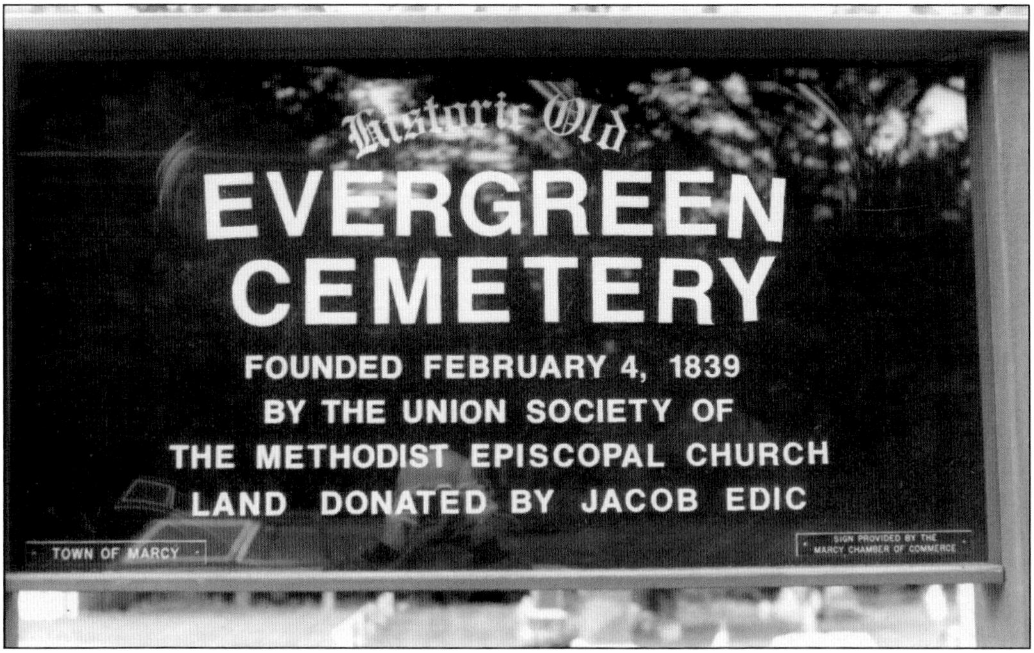

This sign appears at historic Old Evergreen Cemetery, which was founded in 1839 on Maynard Drive.

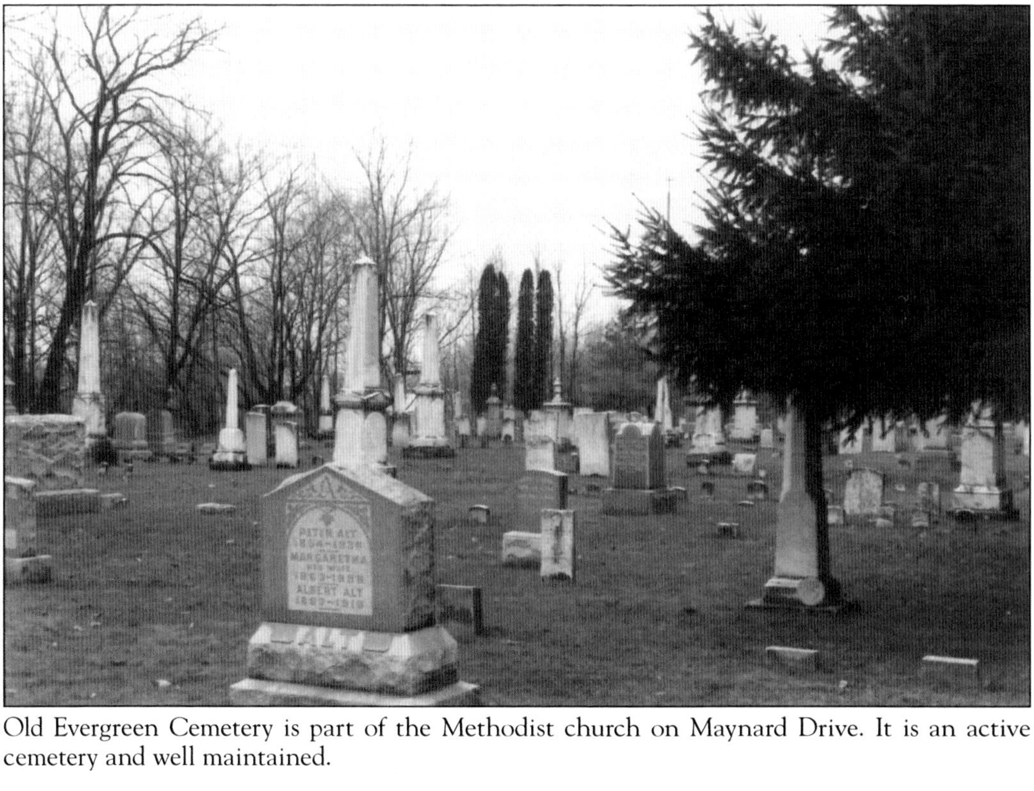

Old Evergreen Cemetery is part of the Methodist church on Maynard Drive. It is an active cemetery and well maintained.

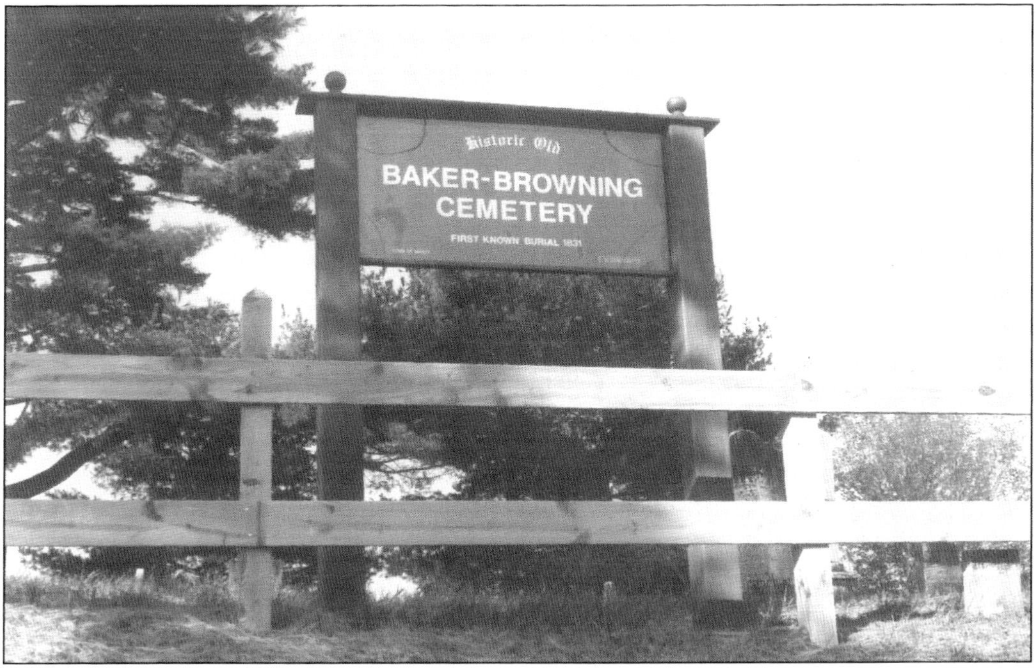

Founded in 1831, Old Baker-Browning Cemetery on Fox Road in Marcy is a small cemetery, but it contains a large amount of local history.

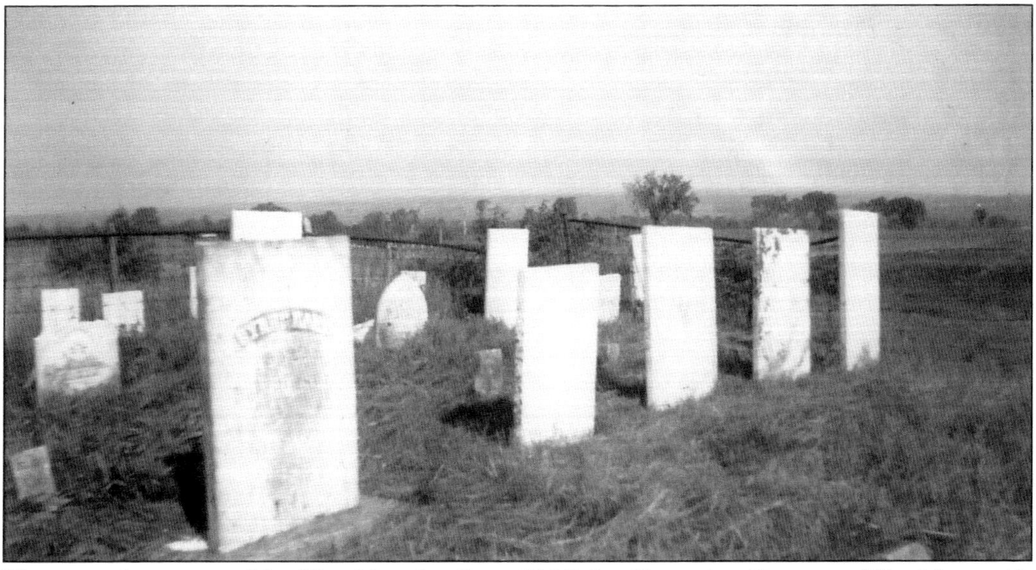

These are the graves of the Eliza Hart family in Old Baker-Browning Cemetery. Eliza Hart, with her husband, Rev. Henry Spalding, was the first woman to cross the Rocky Mountains on their way to Idaho to serve as missionaries to the Nez Perces native tribes (see page 84).

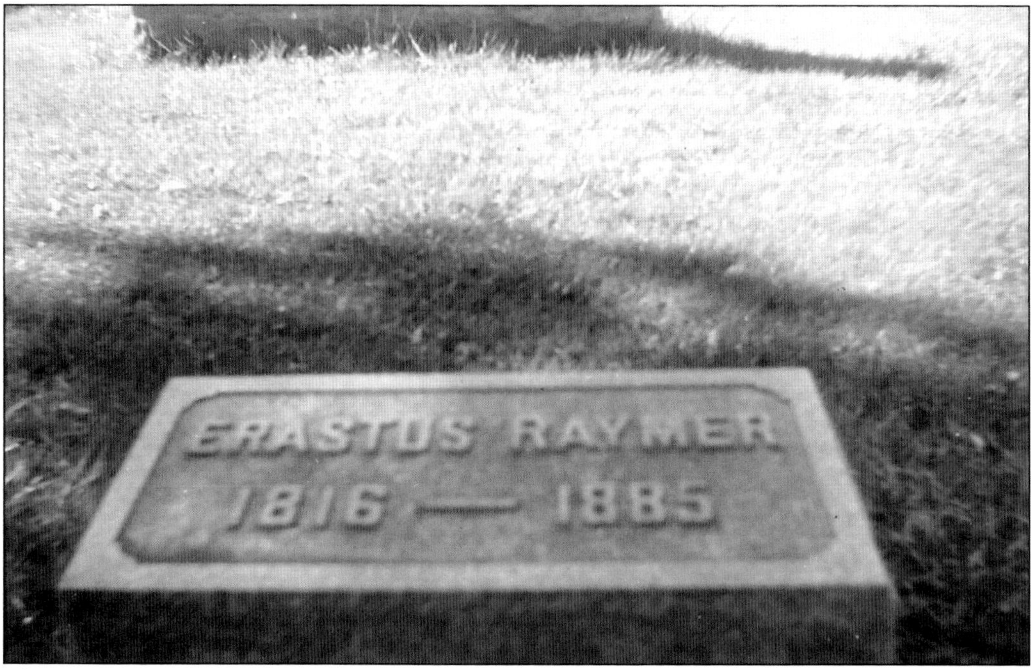

The Erastus Raymer monument is found at the front of the original Carr Cemetery near the highway. This was one of Marcy's pioneers, born in 1816.

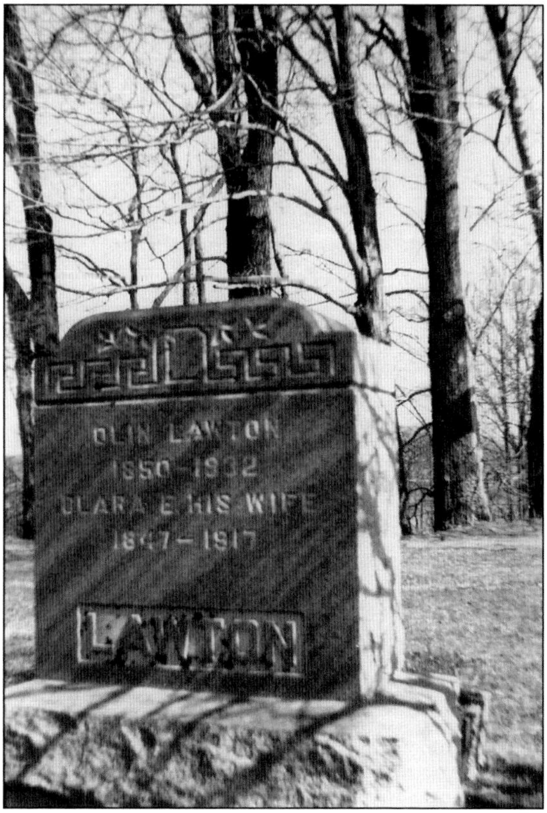

The graves of Olin Lawtor and his wife, Clara, from 1917 and 1932 are pictured here.

The records of John Stitt, the father of Robert Stitt, are uncertain due to the stone being worn, but the date looks like he died in 1821. His grave is in the Pittstown Baptist Church cemetery.

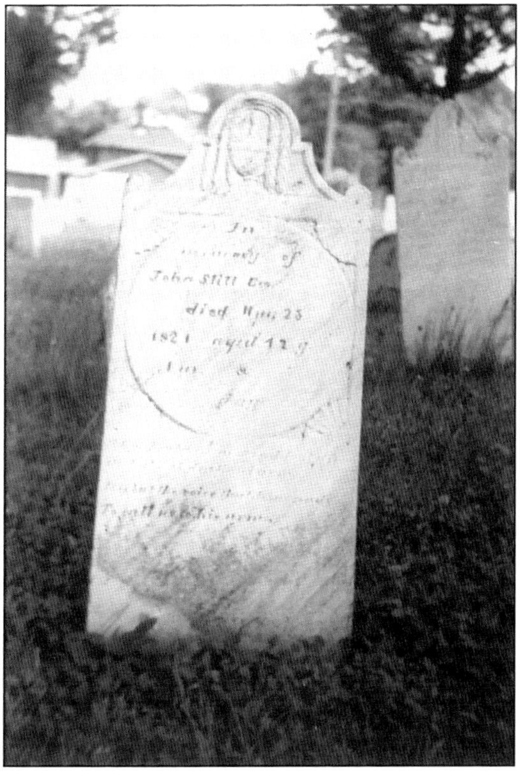

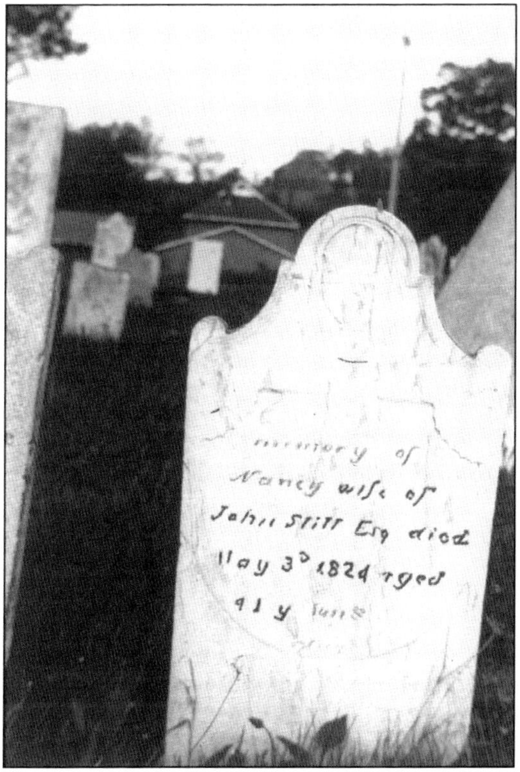

The headstone of John's wife, Nancy, is likewise badly worn, except the date of death can still be read as 1824.

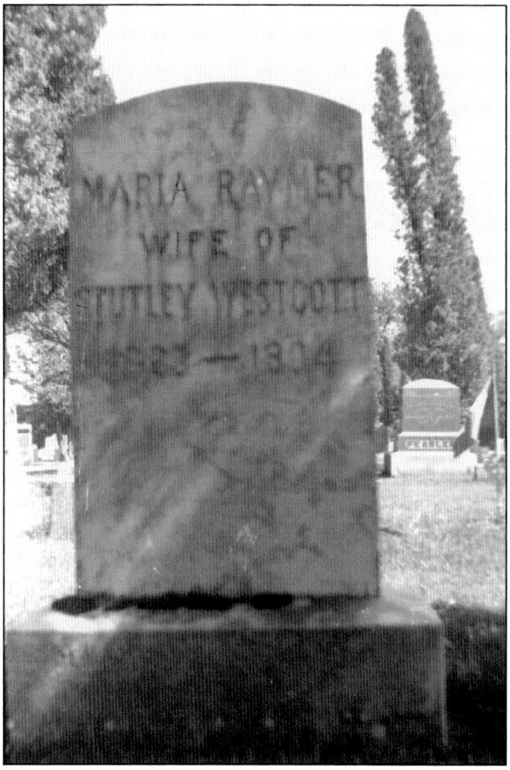

Maria Raymer was the wife of Stutley Wescot and lived from 1823 to 1904.

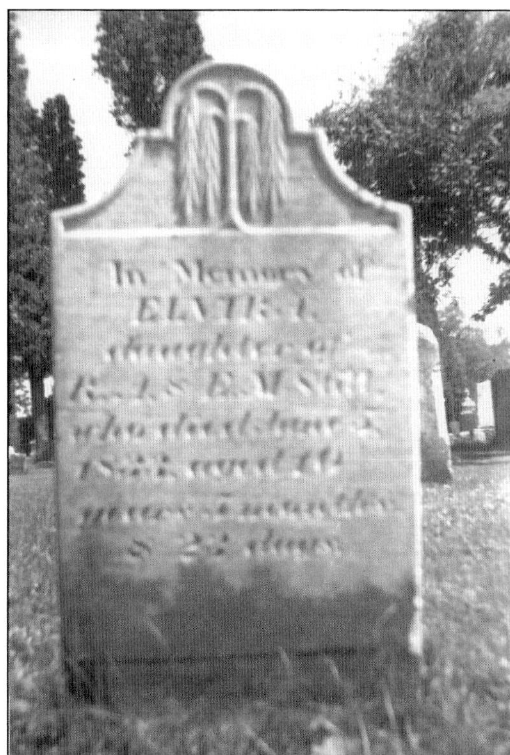

This stone reads "in memory of Elviry, daughter of R. A. and E. M. Stitt, who died June 5, 1833 at age 10 years, 5 months, and 23 days." This grave is in Townsend Cemetery in Stittville.

Abiah Agan, born March 18, 1747, and died June 7, 1802, was the grandmother of Robert A. Stitt. John Agan, her husband, was born June 16, 1747, and died April 22, 1801. He was the grandfather of Stitt.

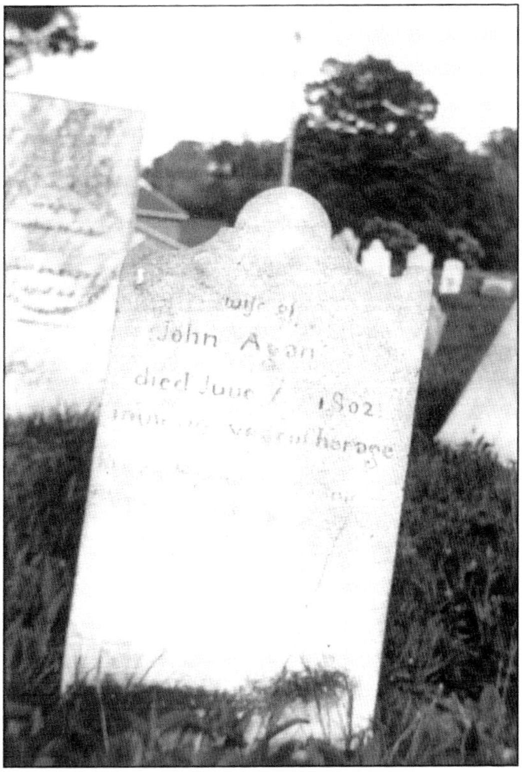

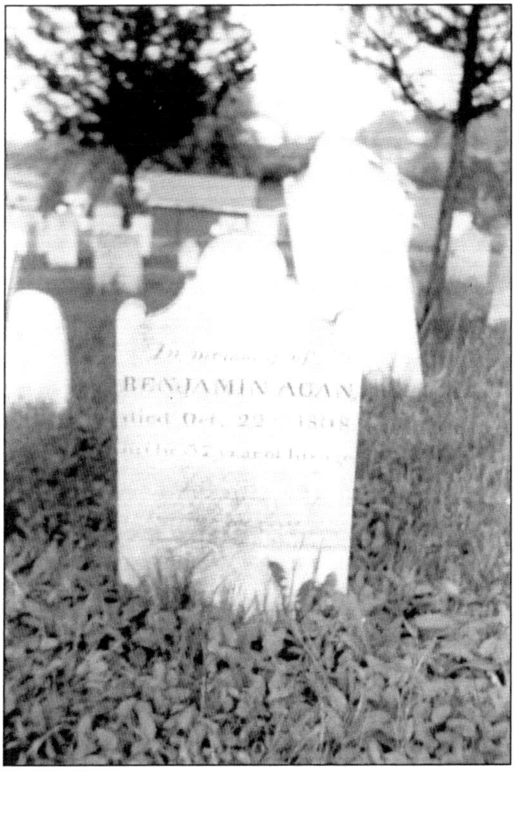

Benjamin Agan, the son of Abiah and John Agan, died in 1808 was an uncle of Stitt. The graves on this page are in Pittstown, at the old Baptist church.

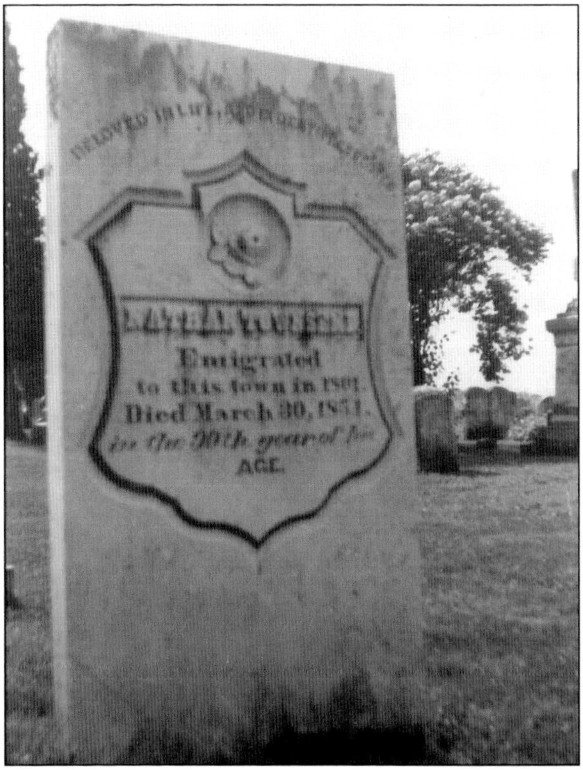

Nathan Townsend came to this town in 1801 and died March 30, 1854, in his 90th year. He is buried in Townsend Cemetery in Stittville. He was the second husband of Dolly (Rhoda) Haskin Cadwell, whom he married in 1814.

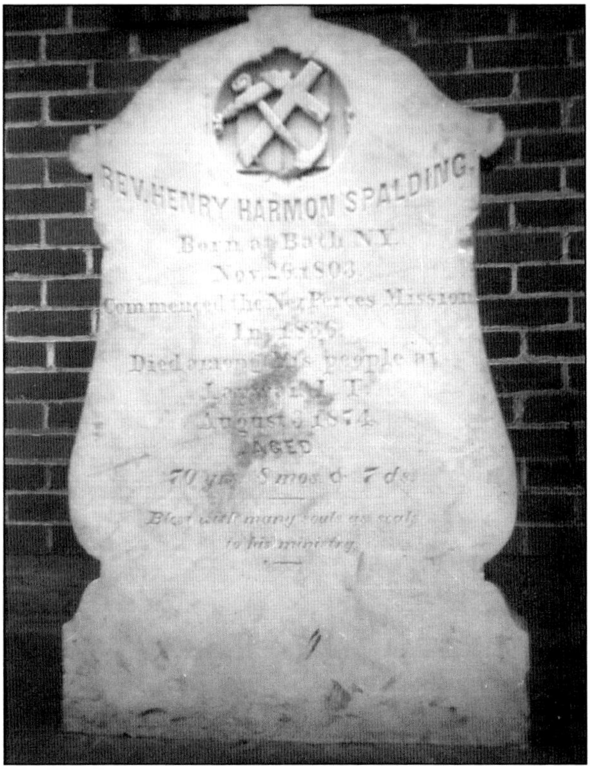

This is a monument to Rev. Henry Spalding and his wife, Eliza Hart, from Marcy. She was the first woman to cross the Rocky Mountains. They served as missionaries to the Nez Perces of Oregon.

Eight

BUSINESSES

Before the town was created, there were business operations in Marcy. An early sawmill turned out lumber in 1788, followed by a gristmill, a blacksmith, and other trades. The most impressive was a group of investors, who realized the need for window glass and put up the money to build such a factory. It was a big operation employing over 300 men and brought into the Marcy wilderness from nearby Utica. They built several factory buildings, large clay pots to melt the sand, cut thousands of trees for furnace fuel, and hauled tons of sand from a nearby sand pit. The business survived for about 25 years, supplying the local market and shipping as far as New York City. Of course farming itself was a business, and all that supported the farmer was business. But Marcy had other operations that were unique to the town. Several knitting mills operated, along with a silk cloth factory, several shoe factories, a vegetable canning plant, wood working shops, a fishing line weaving factory, a quarry of limestone products, machine shops, and in more resent times, a snowmobile manufacturer.

A wise man once said that a business is like a man: he comes along, he likes what he sees, and decides to stay awhile. But eventually he gets weary and goes away. So it has been with Marcy businesses; they also fade from the scene. As of 2007, all business in Marcy is confined to education, distribution, retail and service, and some remaining farming.

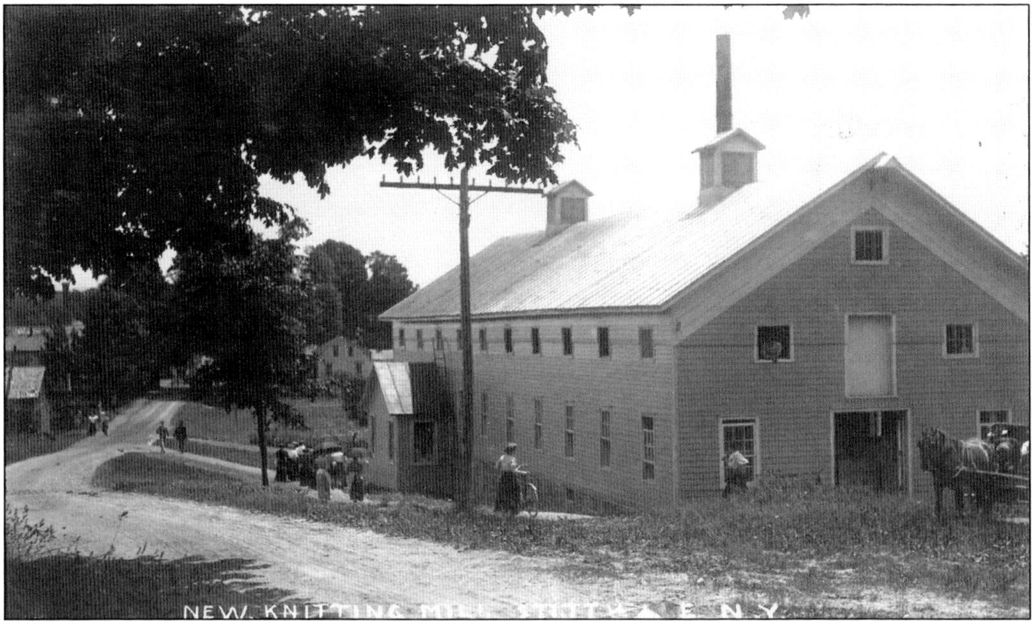

The knitting mill in Stittville is pictured here.

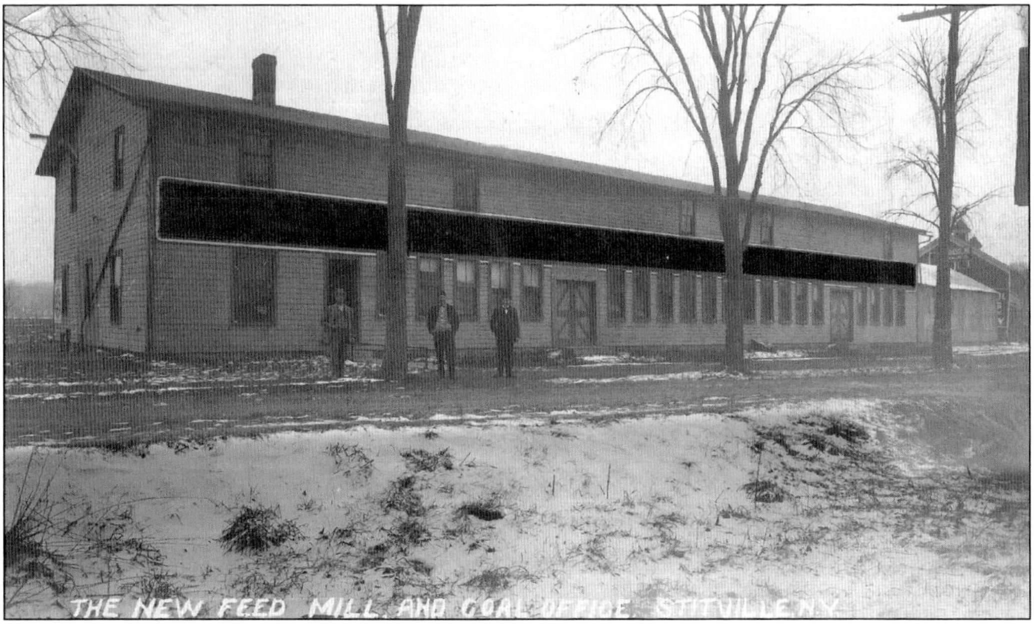

The feed store, also in Stittville, is pictured. The year of this image is unknown. The man on left is Clayton Payne and the other two are unidentified.

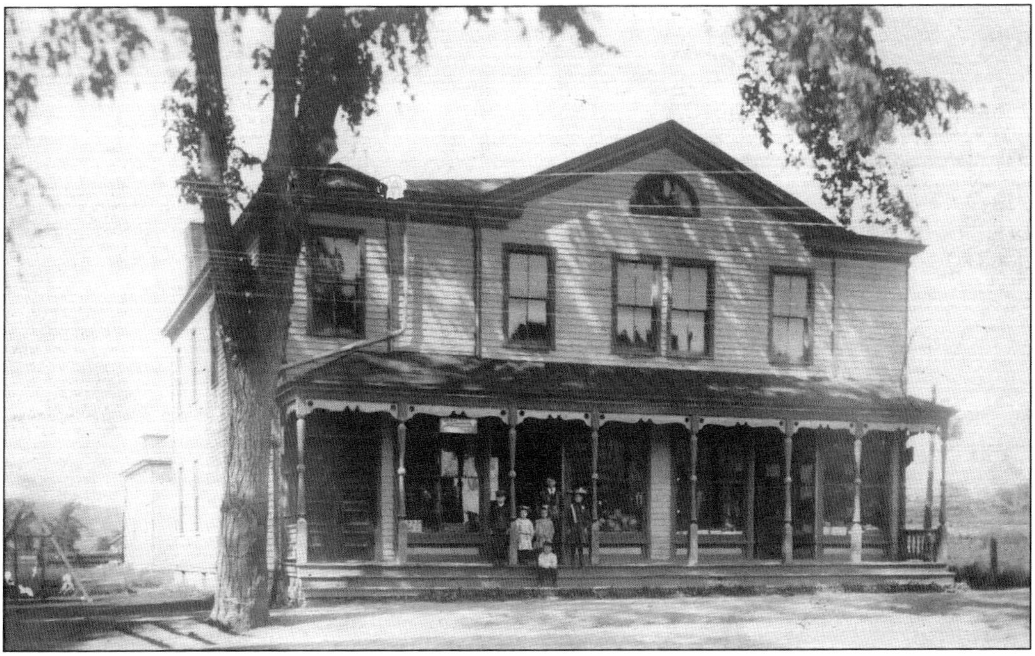

This was the original Owen G. Owens department store before it was destroyed by fire.

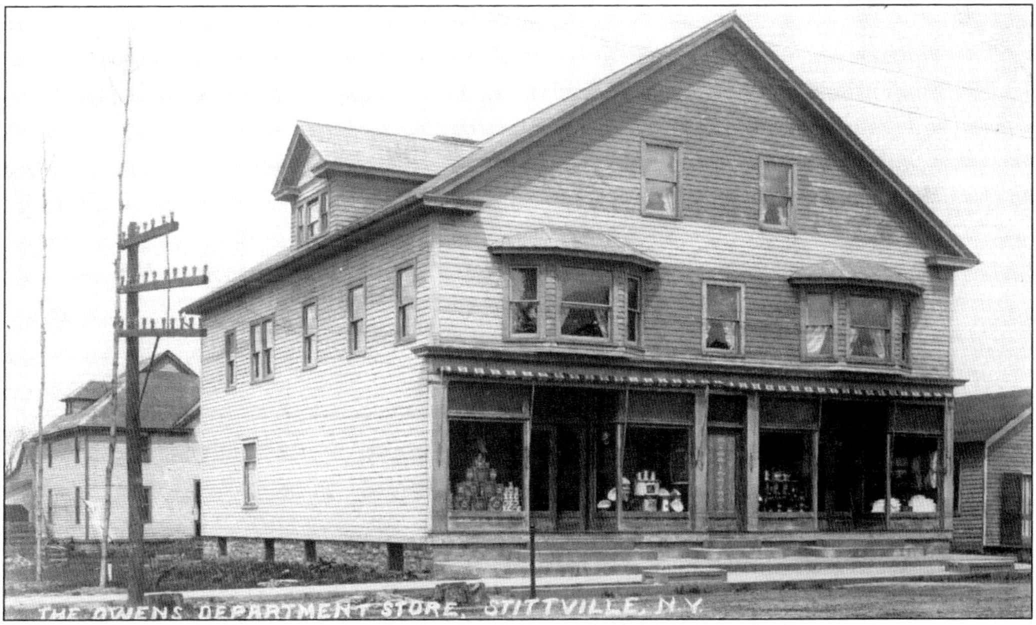

The new Owen G. Owens department store is pictured after it was rebuilt.

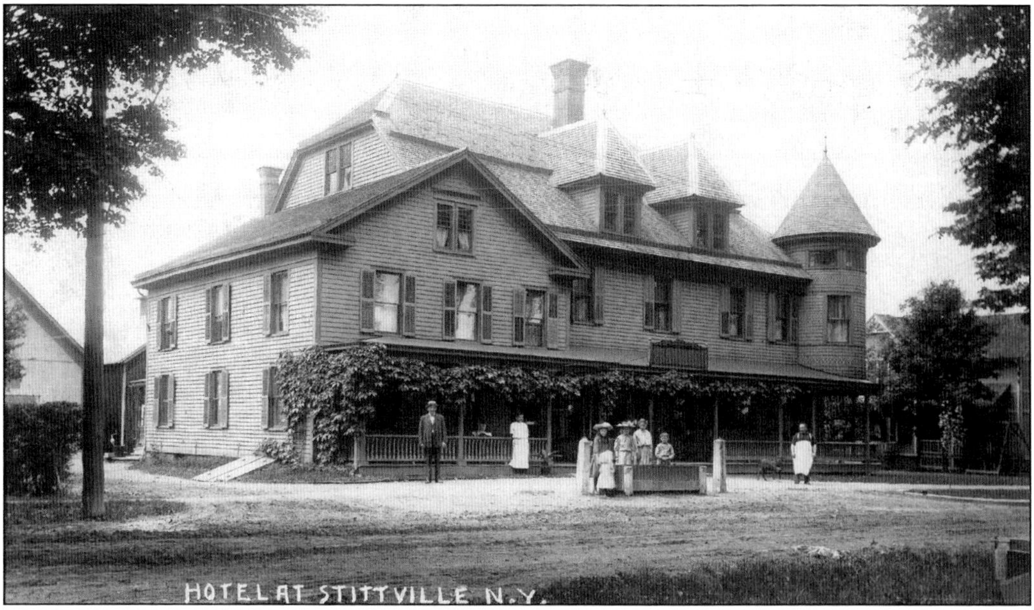

The hotel at Stittville was also called the Cottage Hotel.

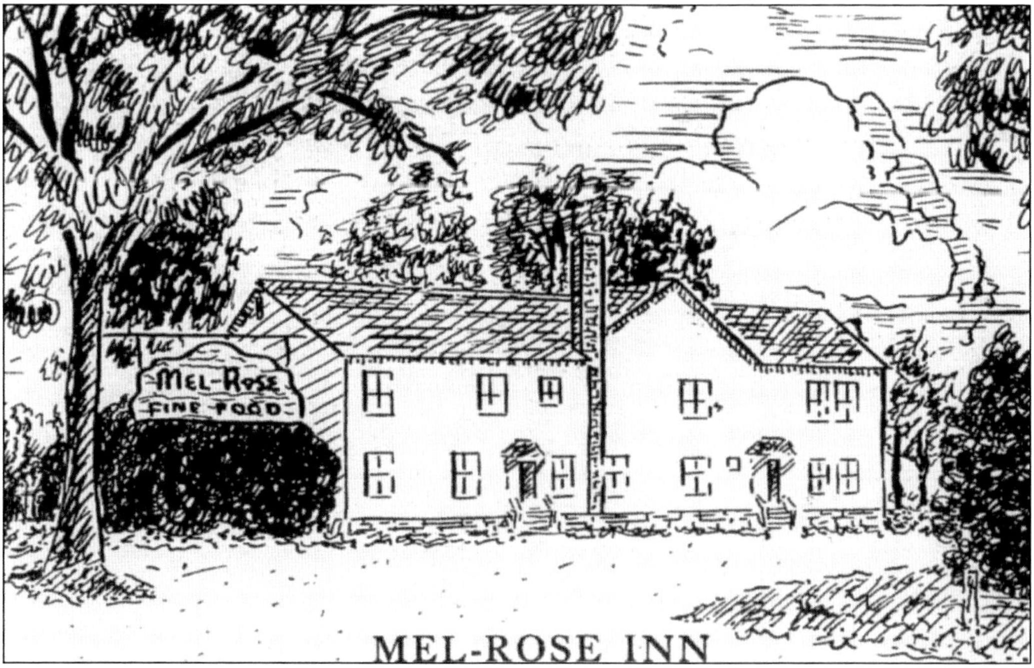

This hotel restaurant was called the House of Pentland, but was more commonly called Mel-Rose Inn. It was noted for fine food. It was situated on the bank of Nine Mile Creek

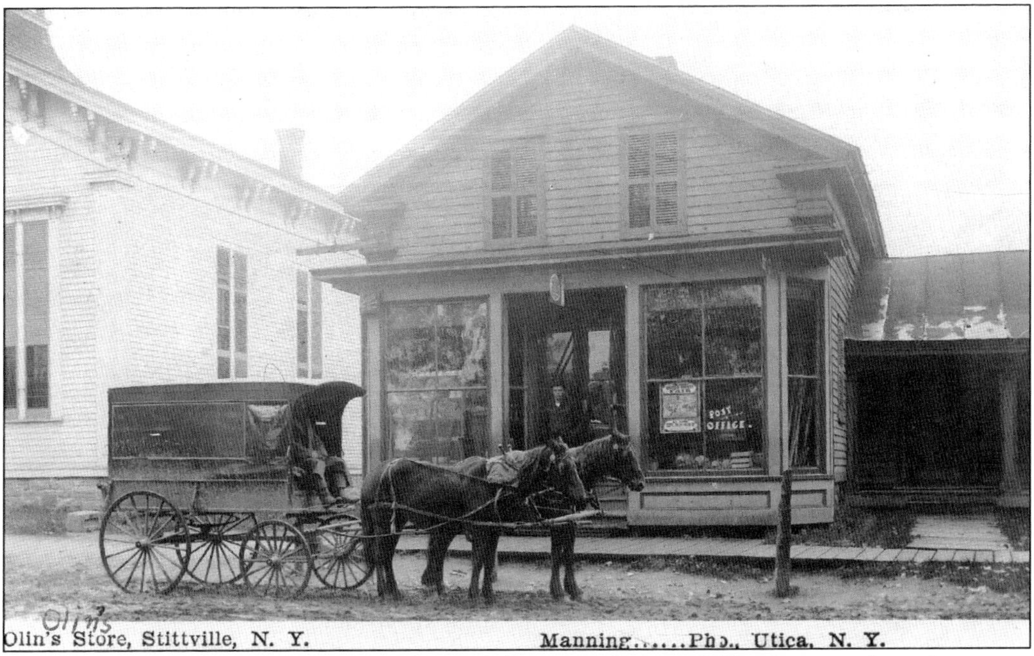

Olin's General Store in Stittville also housed the Stittville Post Office for a number of years.

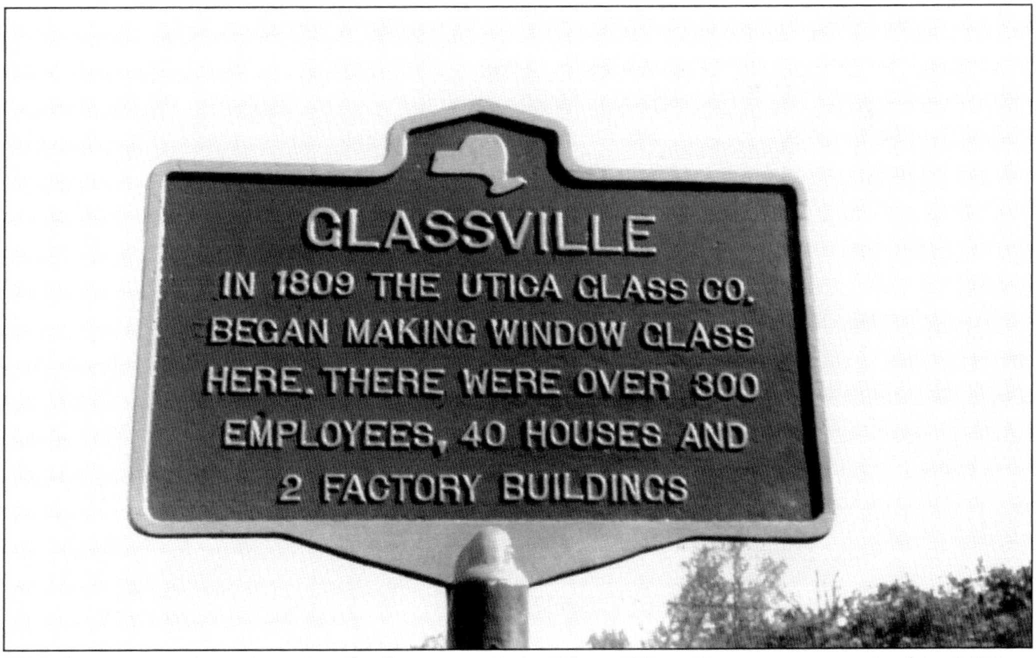

This historic marker identifies the location of the Utica Glass Company, organized in 1809 to make window glass. It operated for almost 25 years and gradually went out of business due to having to travel further to get sand and wood to burn and not being near the Erie Canal for shipping the glass.

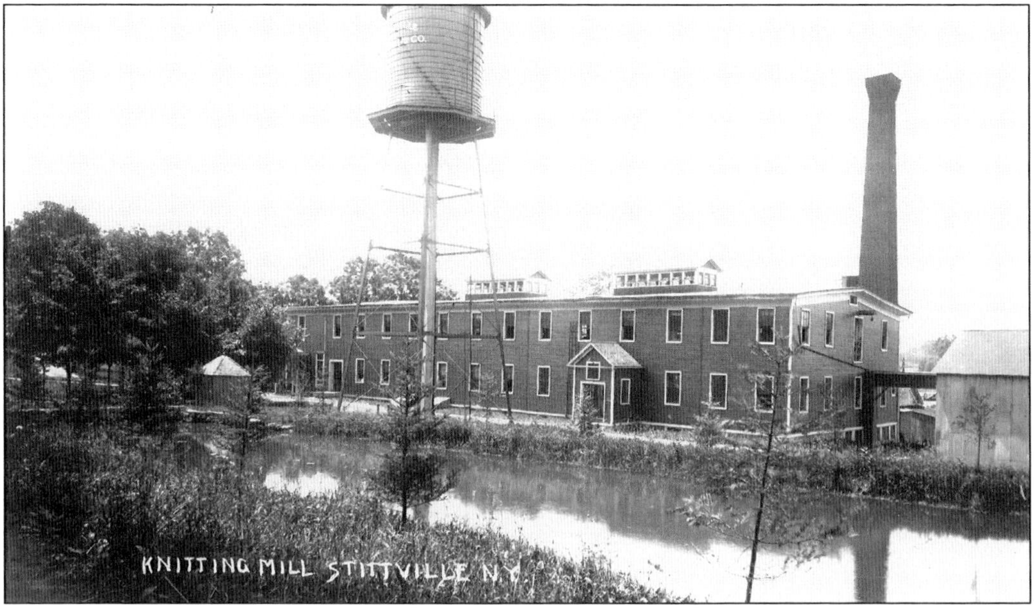

The knitting mill in Stittville got its power from water from this millpond. The water was pumped up into the tank, from which it could fall with significant power.

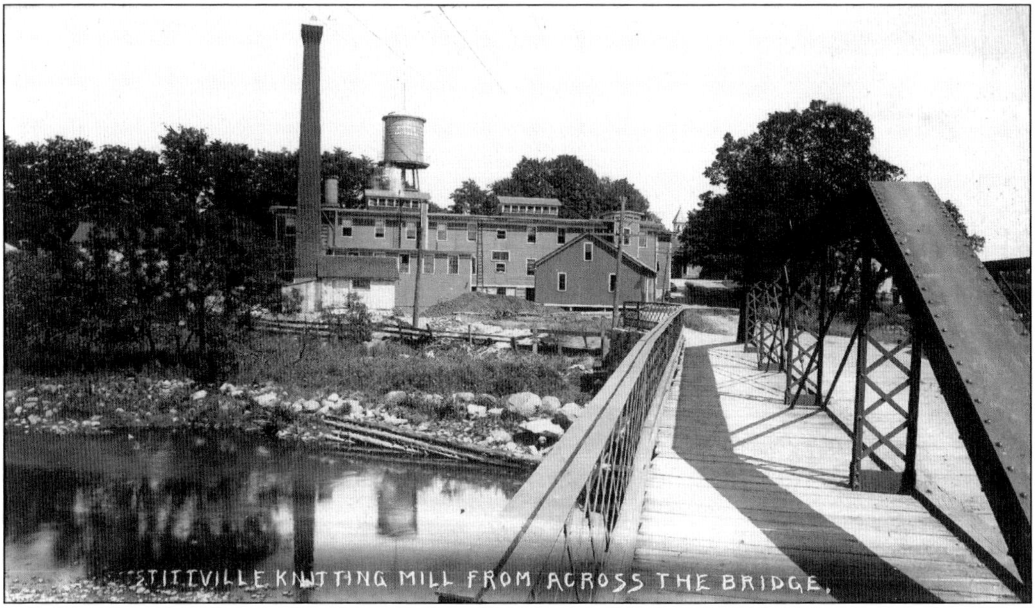

The backside of the mill faced the Nine Mile Creek.

Nine

Fires and Firemen

Many communities have had an event that could be considered historic. Few have had a tragic event that would lead to national headlines and a place in history. Such was the great Stittville fire of April 1910, which burned a large part of the village right to the ground. The fire started in a large meeting room over the general store, where a school dance had been held that evening. The fire spread rapidly from one building to the next and across the street. Residents stood by helplessly and could do nothing because there was no water and no fire department. One of the knitting mills had a millpond and a hose but could not help with the disaster. In the next few years, more fires would bring more disasters and great loss.

By 1925, it was realized something had to be done. The first volunteer fire department was organized and purchased a used Ford truck. Since then, both Stittville and Maynard have consistently grown in size and kept up in obtaining the latest equipment.

A part of life in any small community is the holding of events to raise money to improve the firehouses and buy new fire trucks. These include events such as ham dinners, fish fries, field days, beef dinners and roasts, and the like. Indeed these events are not only fund-raisers but an opportunity to socialize for the whole community.

The fire departments are people organizations made-up of volunteers whose services have been available to the area through the unselfish efforts and dedication of those who care.

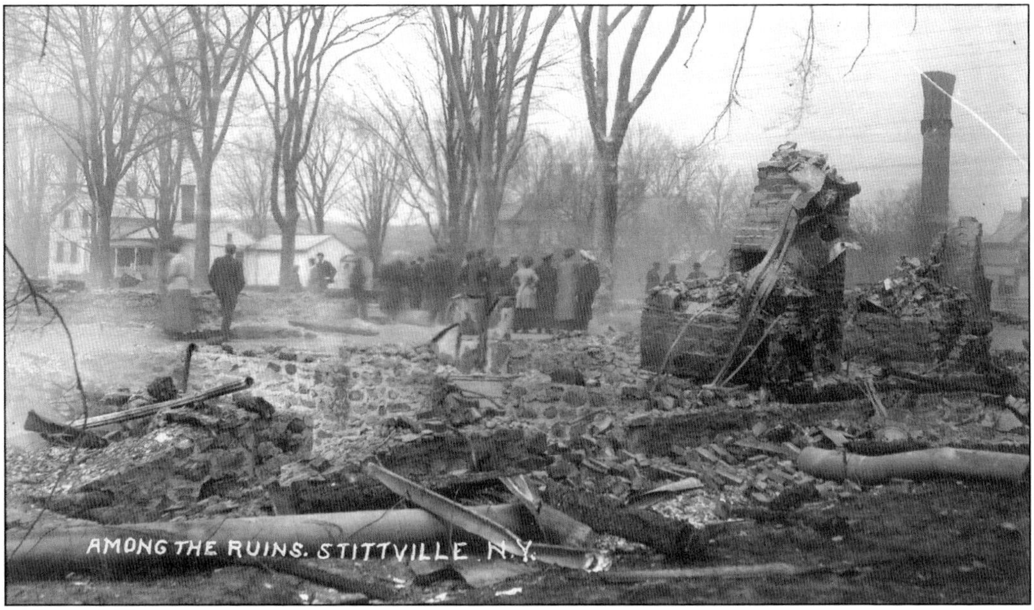

The great fire at Stittville burned out a large part of the entire village.

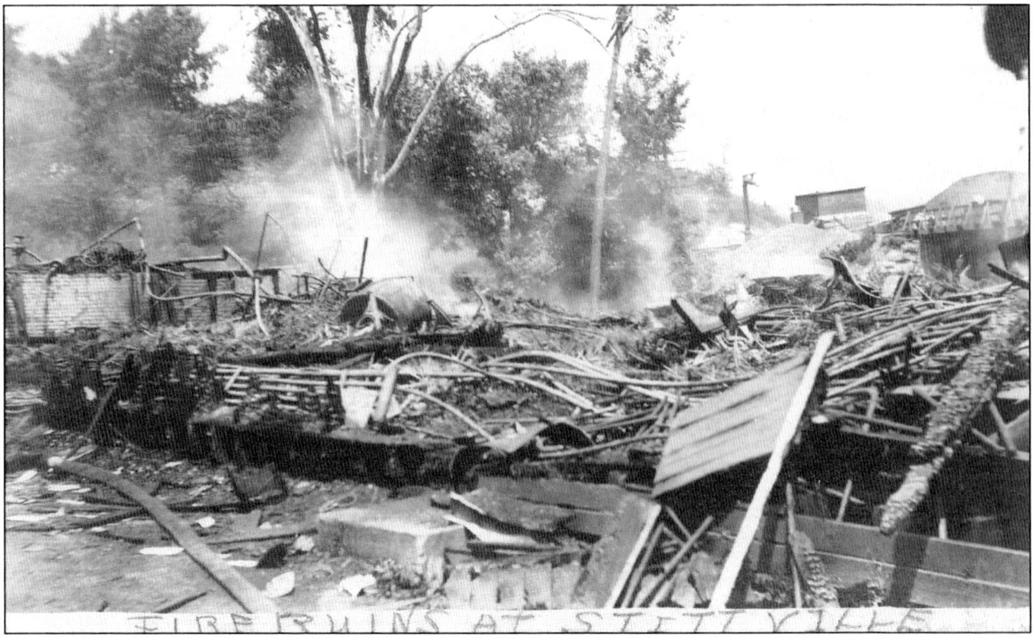

The meat market shown here was nothing but ruins the morning after the fire.

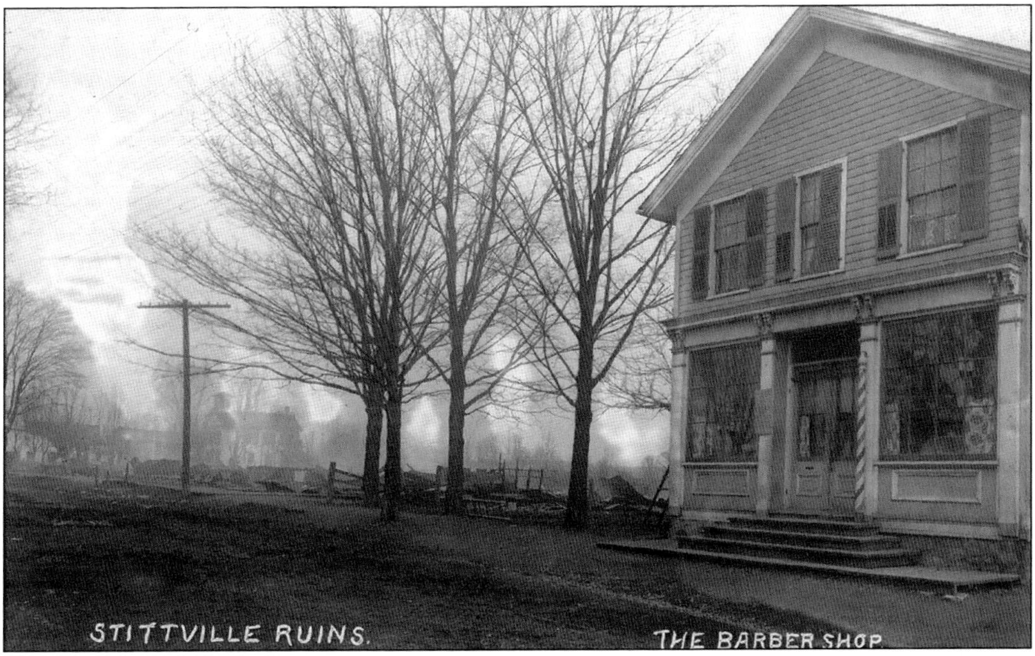

The barbershop survived the flames although everything to the left was completely gone.

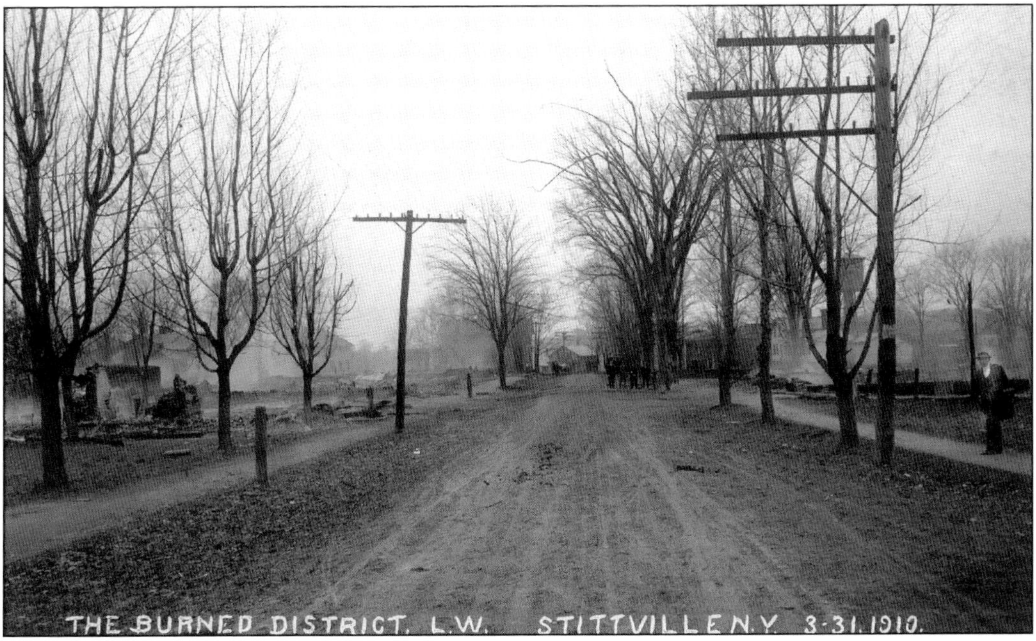

Looking down Main Street everything on both sides is burned right to the ground. March 31, 1910, was a time to remember.

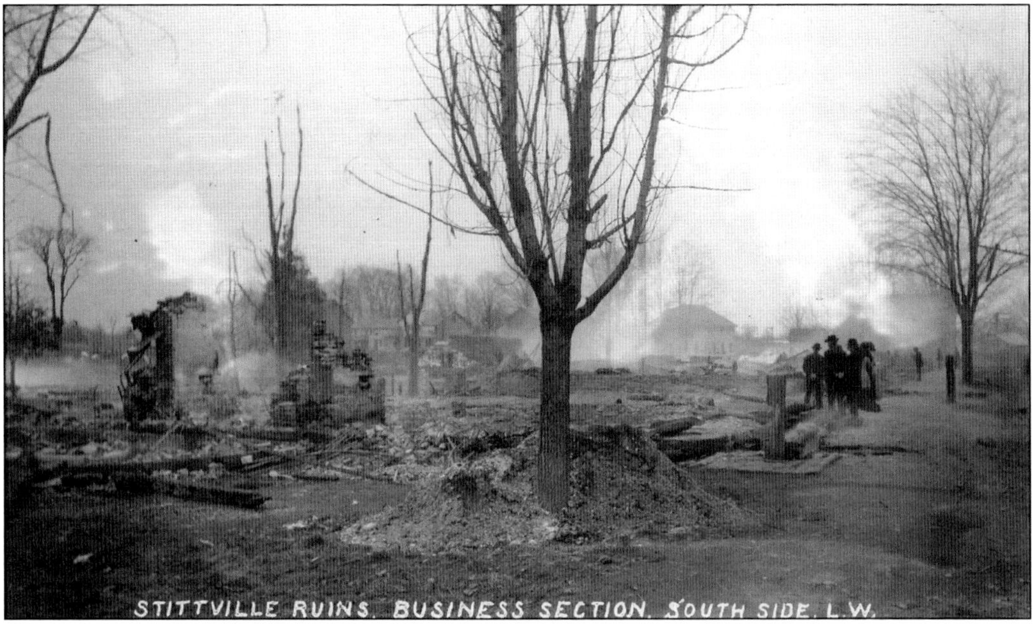

On the south side, the business section is completely gone. The smoke hung over the village for days, and the smell lasted for weeks.

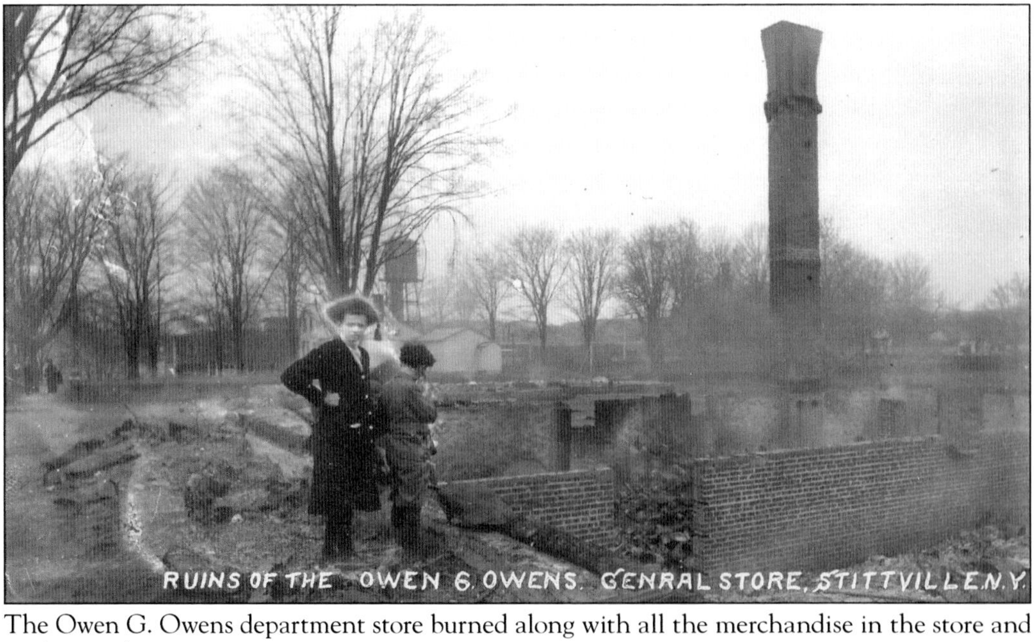

The Owen G. Owens department store burned along with all the merchandise in the store and in the warehouse.

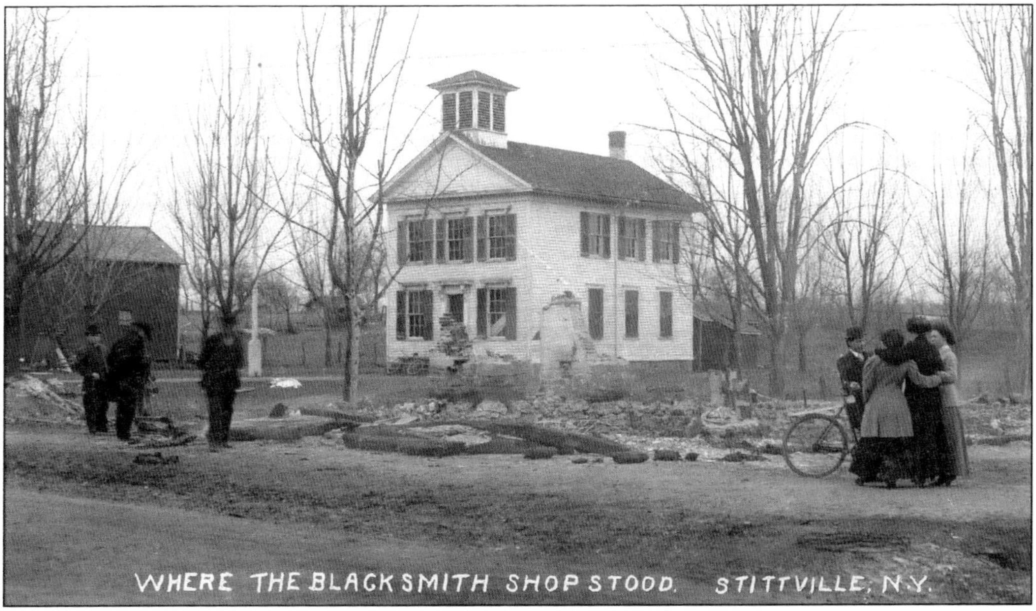

The blacksmith shop was reduced to ashes but the Graded Schoolhouse survived the great fire.

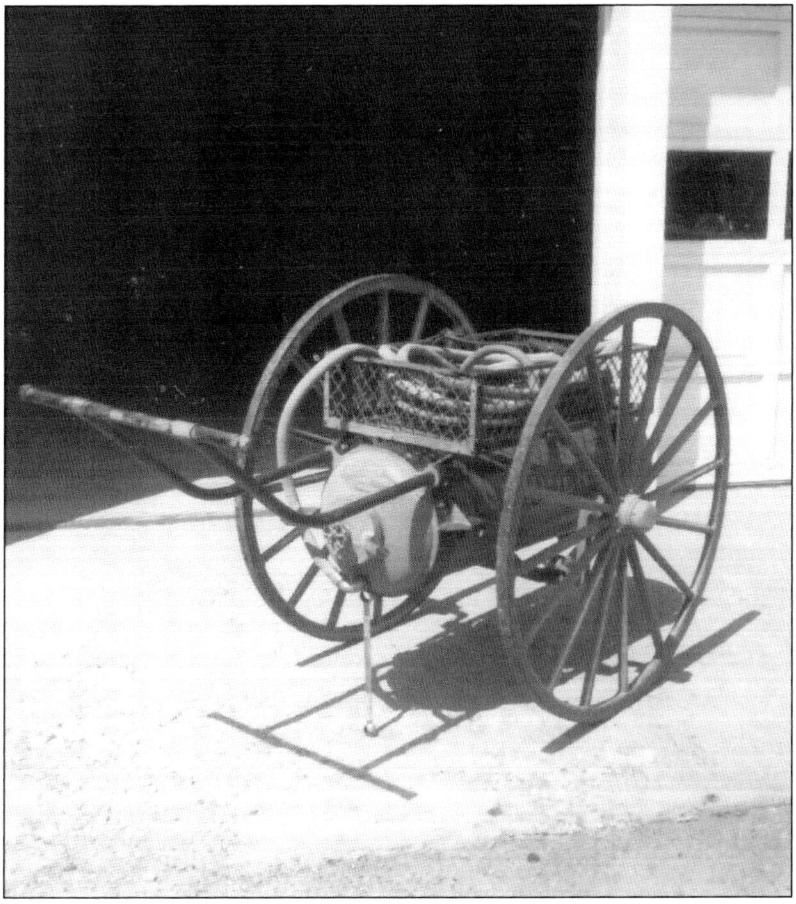
One of the first new hand pumps purchased after the fire is seen here. It rolled on big wheels and had a 50-foot hose.

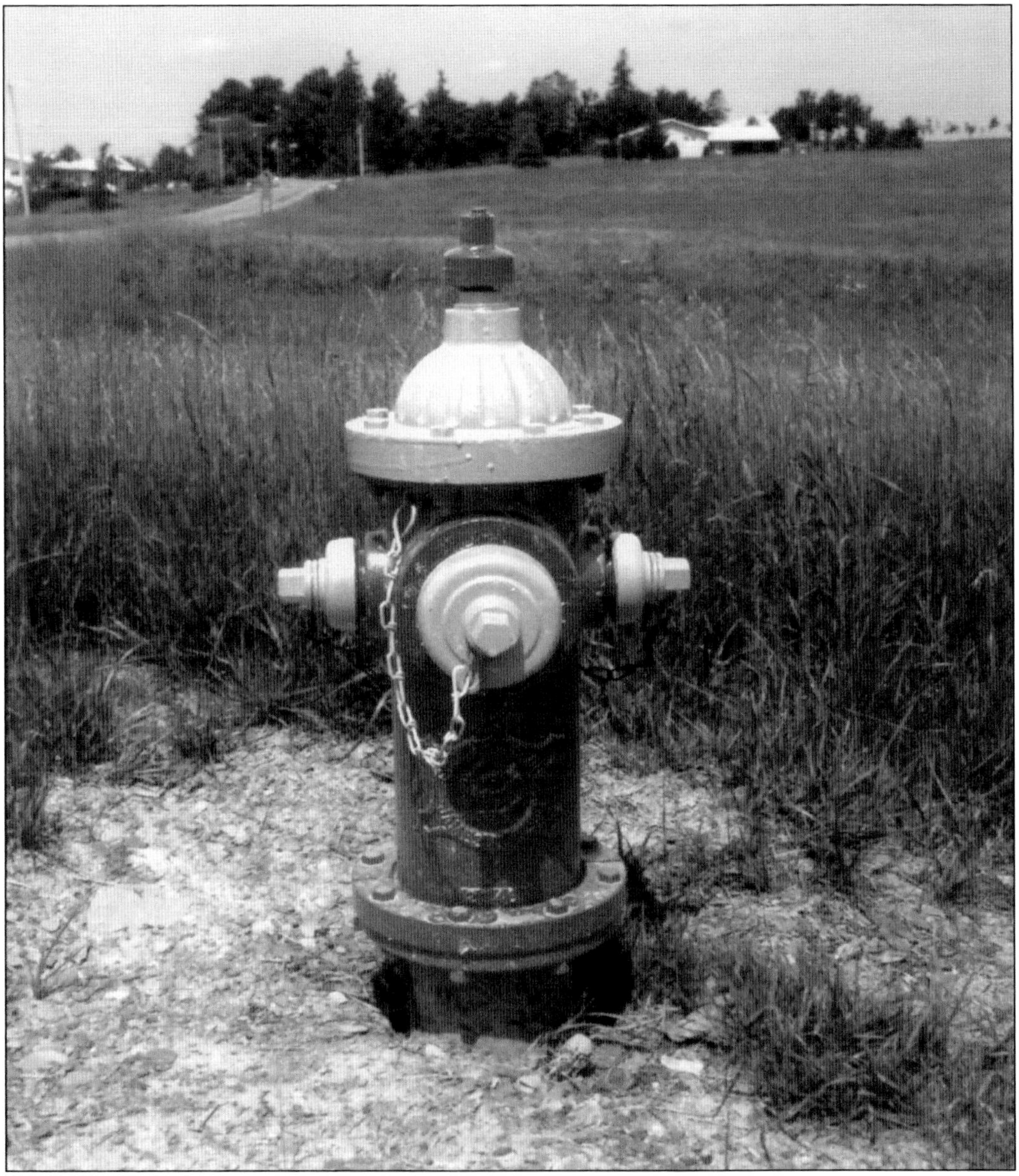

The water hydrant is a great symbol to a village that was almost burned off the face of the earth. It took almost 70 years for the first city water to be installed, but now there is city water with great pressure on almost every street and rural road in the town of Marcy and its many hamlets. To the people of Stittville who lost their village because of no water, this red and yellow hydrant has great meaning.

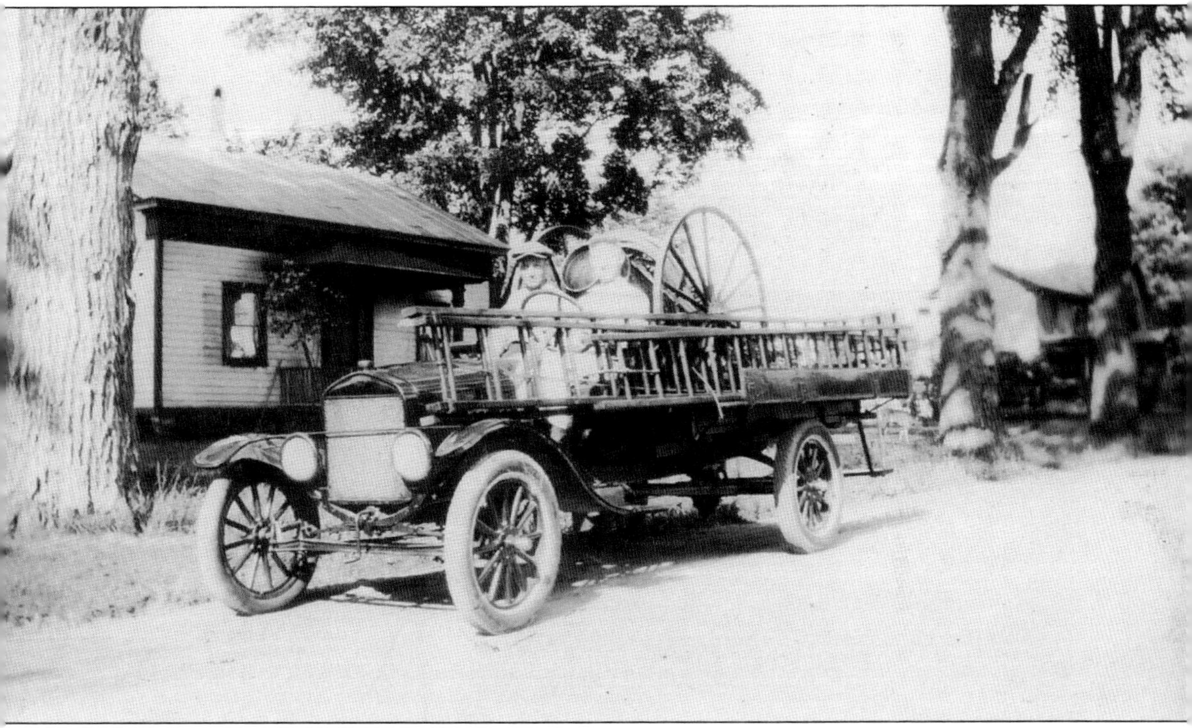

After the big fire, the first fire department was formed. This was the first fire truck put in service in 1927. It was purchased used for $100 and remodeled under direction of H. J. Brown. It had ladders, ropes, pails, and assorted tools. It was housed in Orendorf's Stittville garage and fire calls were received at the W. F. Blust store and then relayed to the members by telephone. Orville Brown and Harold Simons are pictured in the seat.

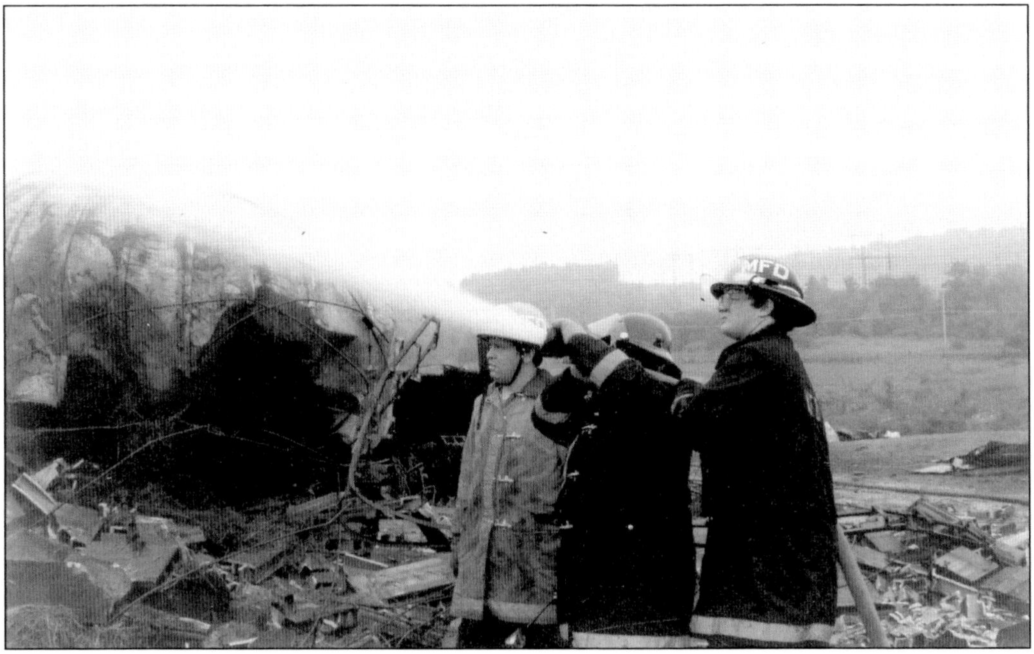

One of the biggest fires in Marcy in recent memory was that at the Marcy Riding Stables. Over 60 horses and saddles and riding equipment were saved.

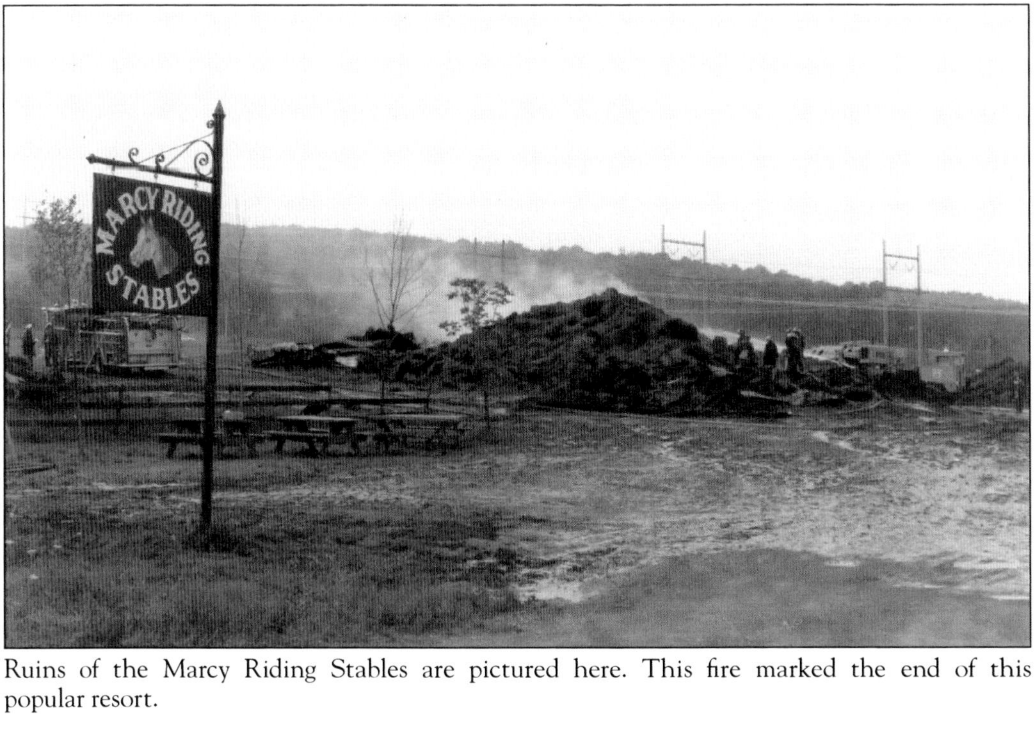

Ruins of the Marcy Riding Stables are pictured here. This fire marked the end of this popular resort.

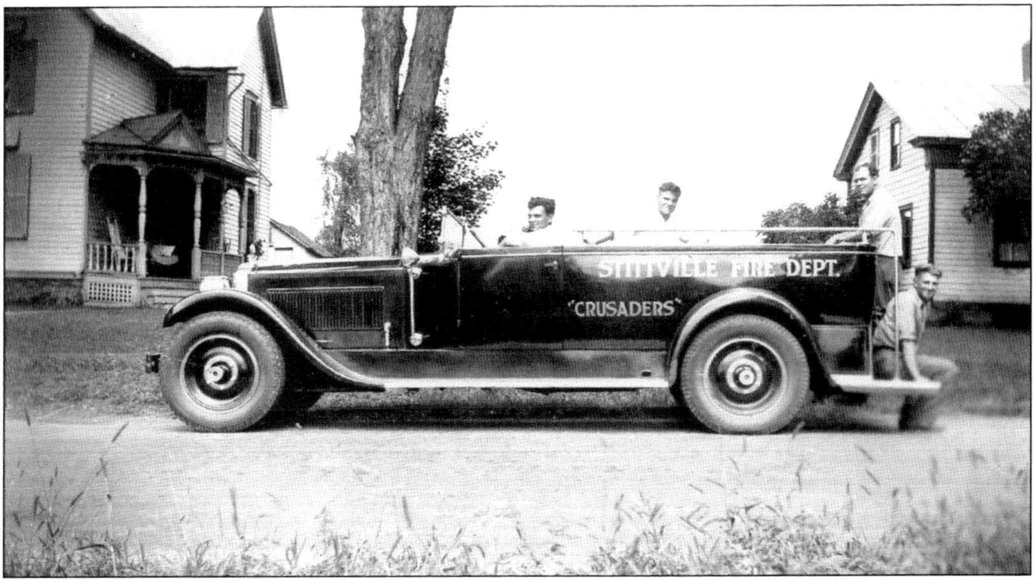

All fire departments usually obtain an open vehicle that they modify to carry team members to parades and open events and sometimes even use in firefighting, such as the Stittville Fire Department's squad car.

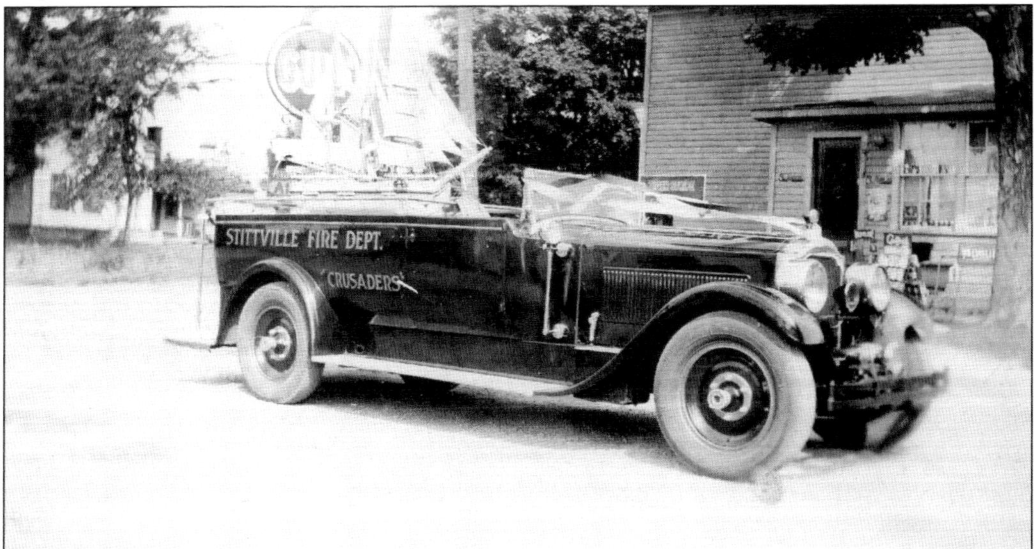

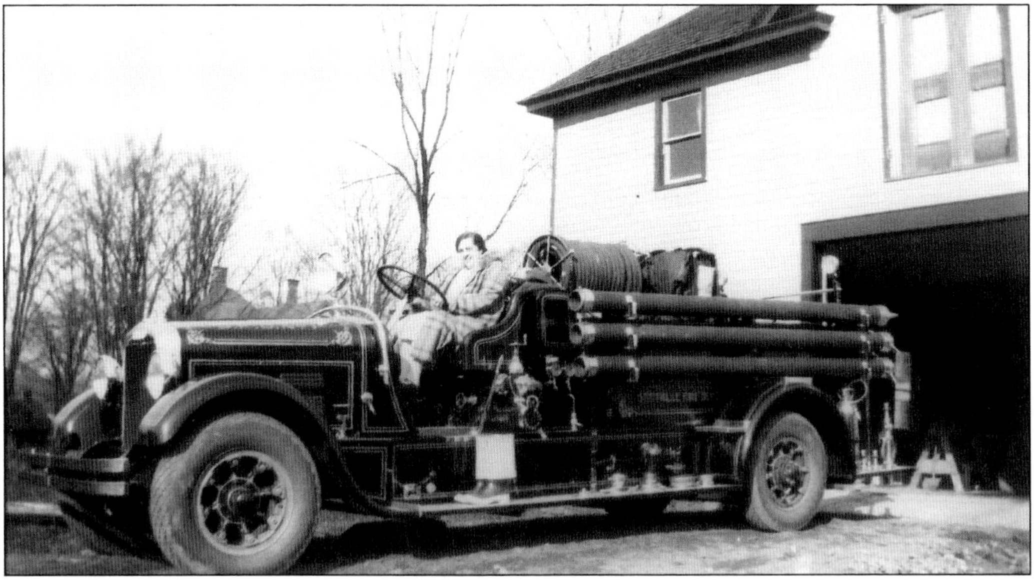

The Stittville pumper is pictured in front of the old firehouse.

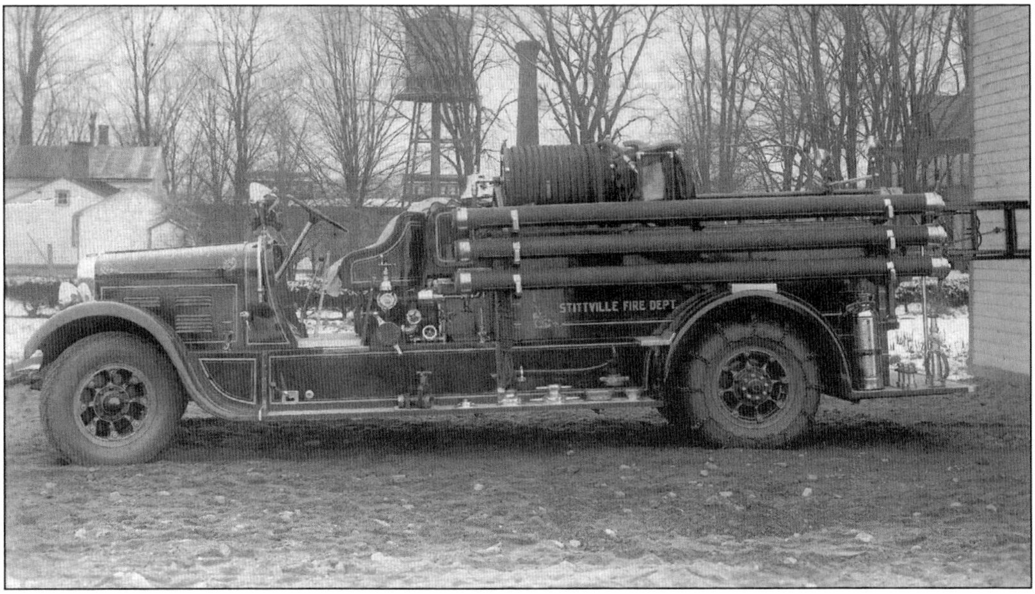

In winter, the pumper was always outfitted with chains to be ready for any weather.

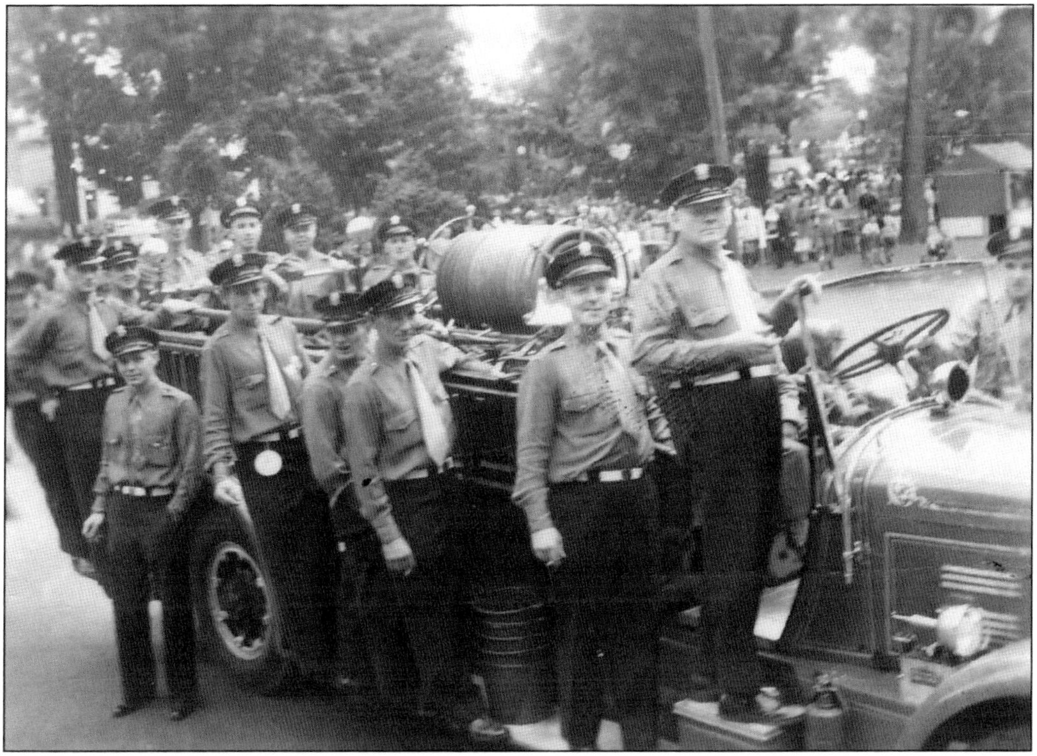

Wearing their best uniforms, the team was always ready for a parade in 1933.

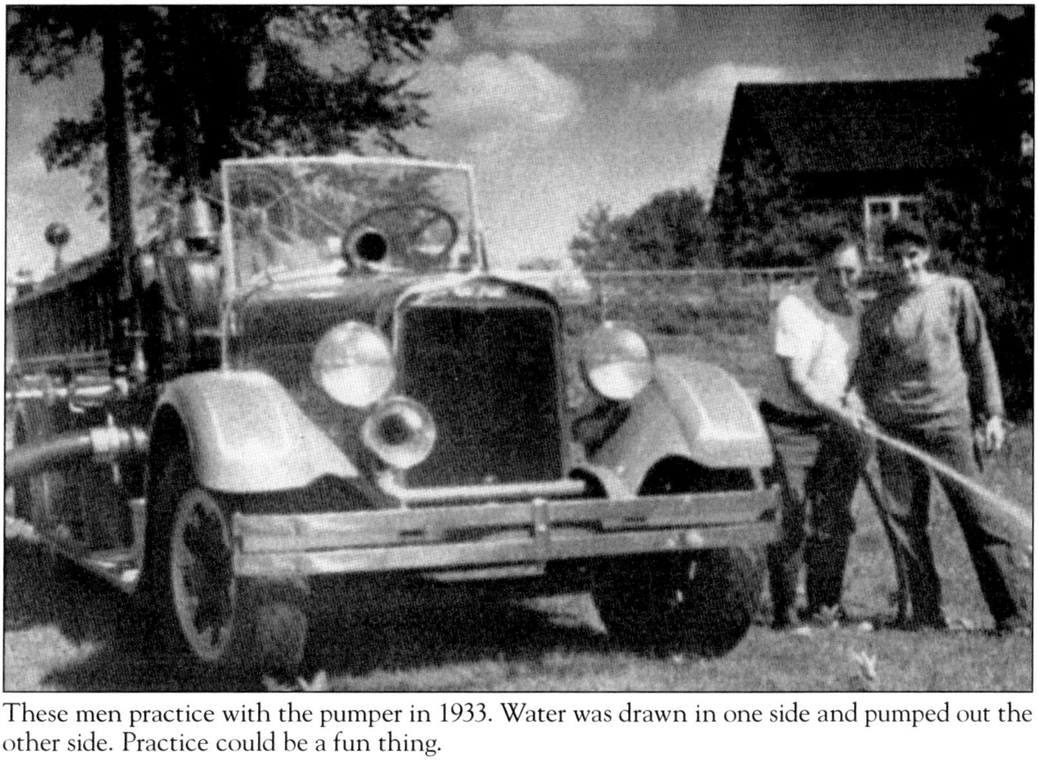

These men practice with the pumper in 1933. Water was drawn in one side and pumped out the other side. Practice could be a fun thing.

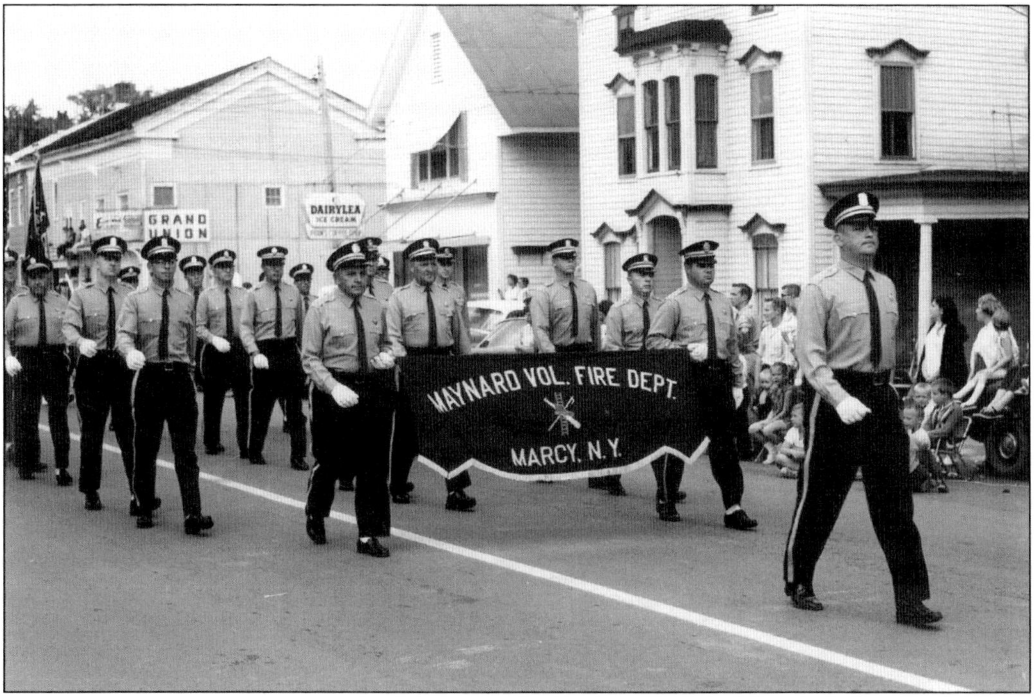

Parades are always a time for residents to strut their stuff and show off their pride in the community.

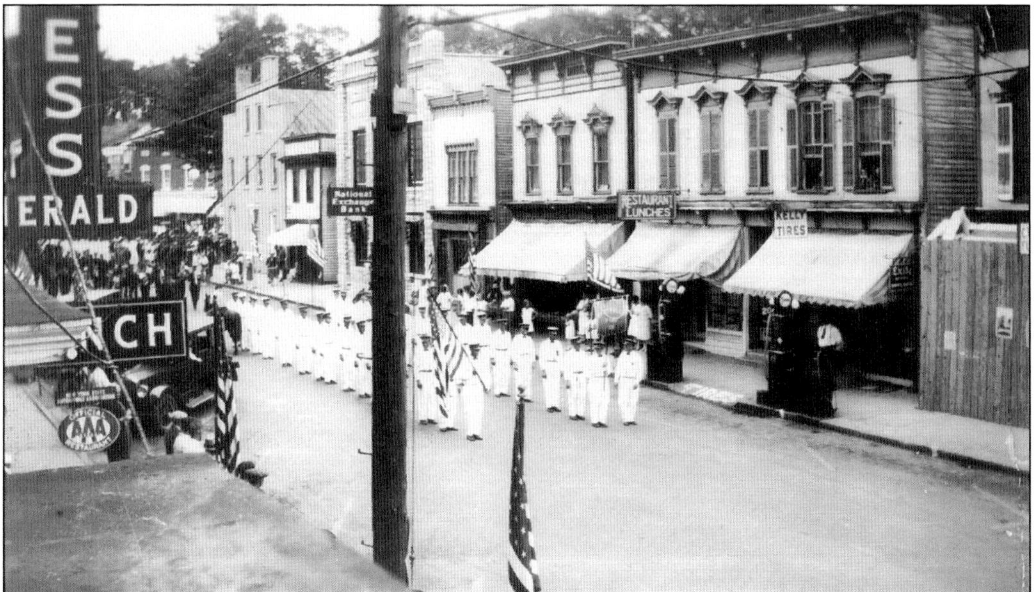

Every small town loved the firemen's convention and parade. For many, it was the highlight of the summer.

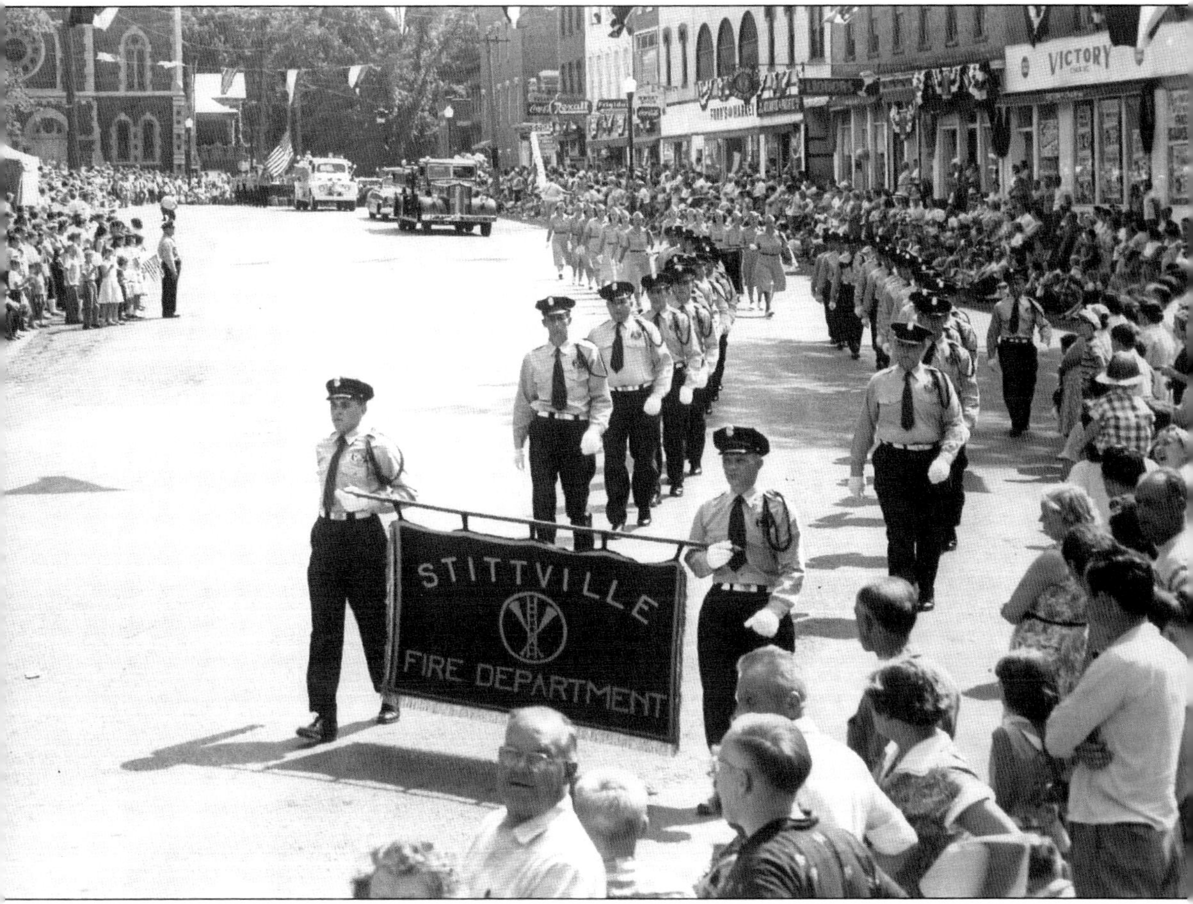

The Stittville fire department, ladies auxiliary, and even the trucks are seen coming around the curve in downtown Clinton.

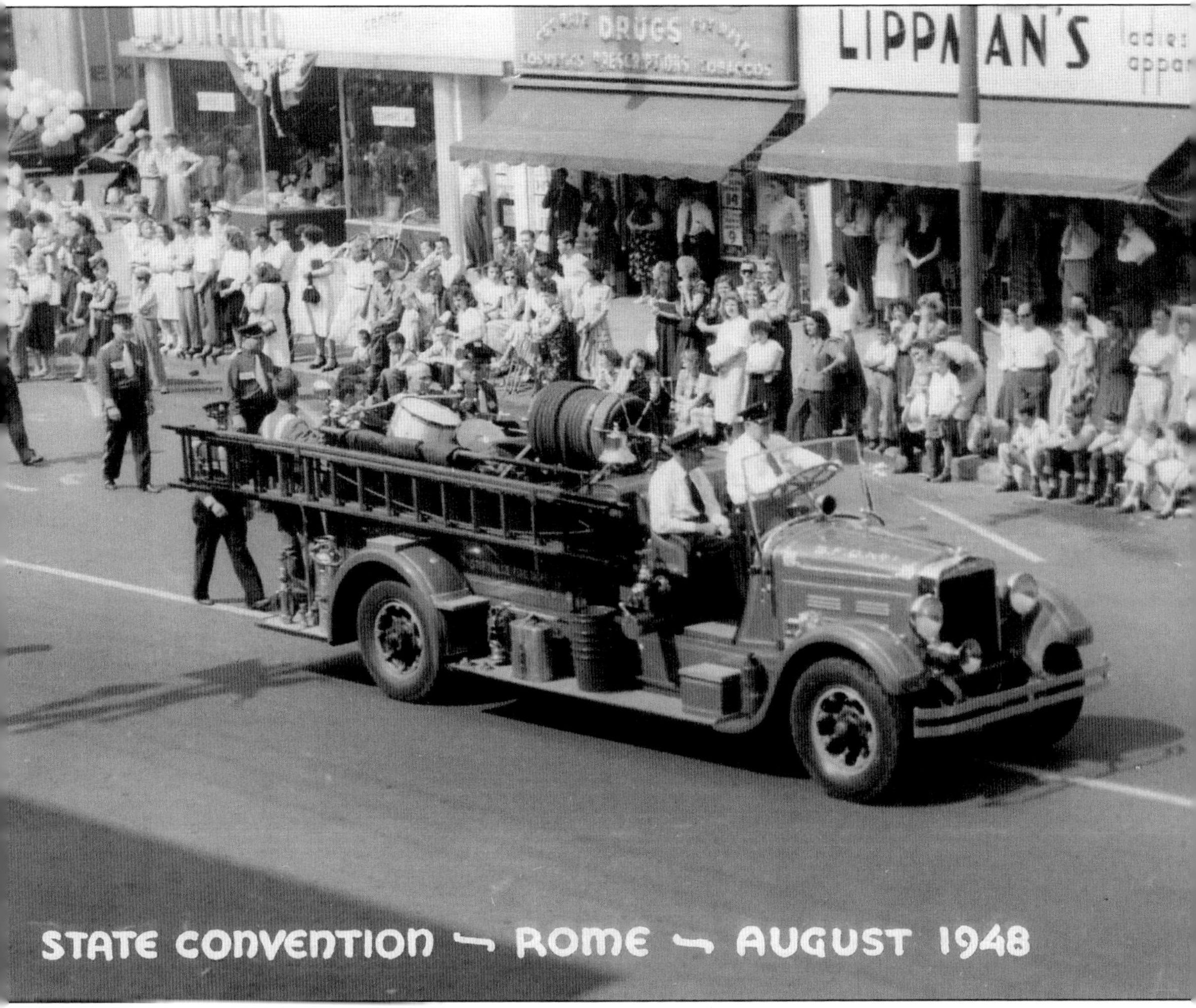

The year is 1948. World War II is over and the place in this image is Rome. What better time and place to celebrate than by holding a state firemen's convention. Stittville received high awards.

Ten

Schools, Colleges, and the Future

Schools and education have always been important in Marcy, ever since the first classes were conducted in homes. The first school was erected on the old River Road about one half mile east of Nine Mile Creek. That schoolhouse burned to the ground. In 1816, the settlers decided to replace it with a stone school, which they reasoned, although the roof would burn, at least the walls would be left. This building did last a long time, in fact, up to the early 1950s when it was torn down to make way for a new prison.

There were 10 school districts in Marcy and one in Stittville. Each district built its own school at prices from $127 to as much as $400, not including the land. Heat was supplied by a wood stove, and a year's supply of wood was as high as $15.50. In some cases, when the money could not be raised, each pupil would bring in a chunk of wood for the daily fire. Teachers were paid $50.86 for teaching for six and a half months. By 1891, the rate of pay was up to $5.50 per week and sometimes included room and board in a nearby farmhouse. Some districts even threw in a bolt of cloth so that the teacher could make her own dresses.

In 1940, consolidation began, and the one-room schools vanished. Over the years, Marcy has had a school of aviation and now even the Erie Canal School Boat.

Perhaps Marcy's greatest educational achievement is the new State University New York Institute of Technology, with over 2,000 students.

Marcy does have a great future, and that future is in the schools, colleges, and students. As the educational system grows, so does the town's future.

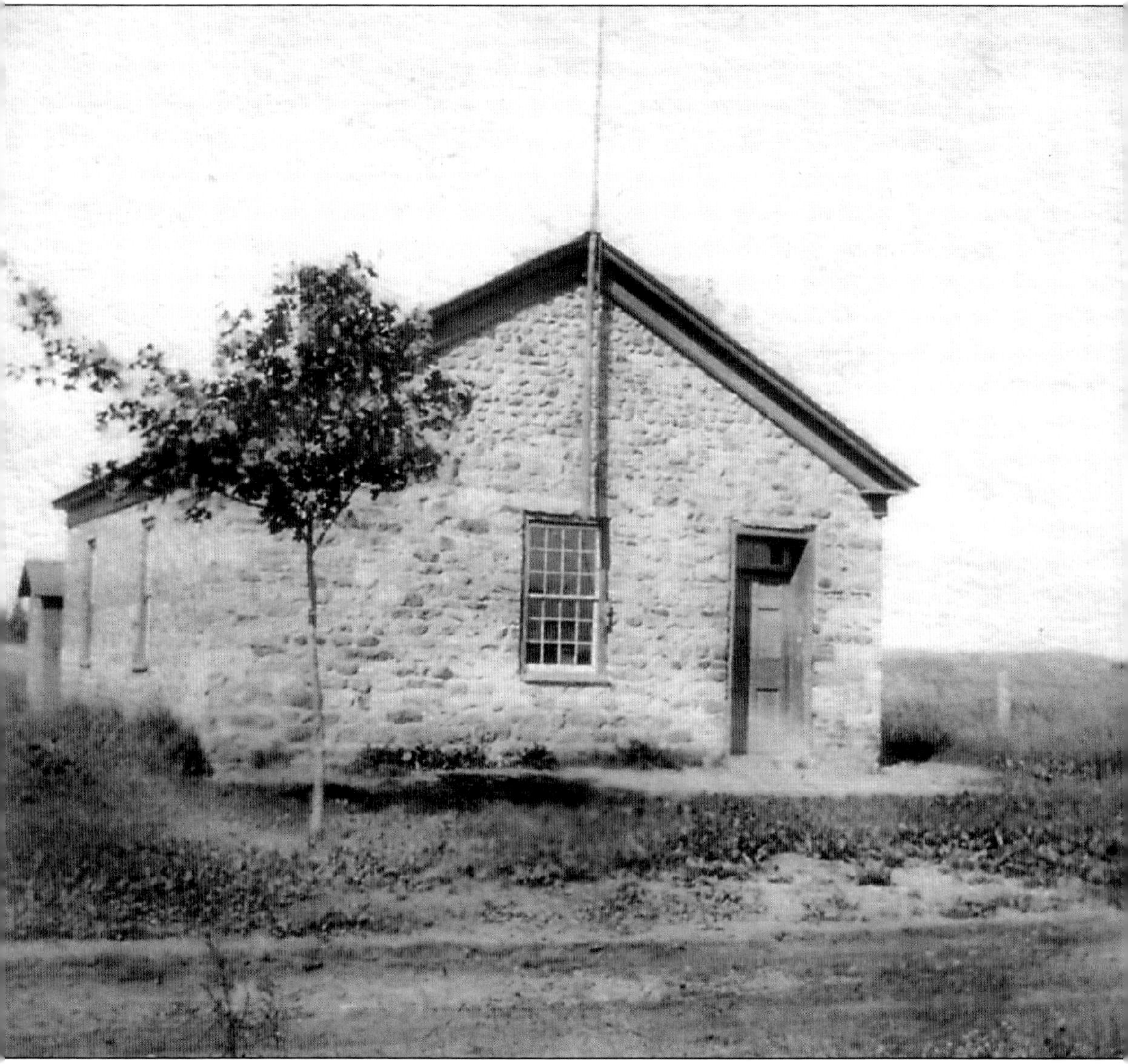

The original schoolhouse, built in 1814, burned to the ground. The settlers reasoned that if they built a new one of cobblestone, it might burn but at least they would have the walls left. The idea was right—this school did burn in 1816 and after the surviving walls received a new roof, the building was in use for about 120 years. It was the only cobblestone schoolhouse in New York State. This little school has turned out doctors, lawyers, judges, political people, and various businessmen.

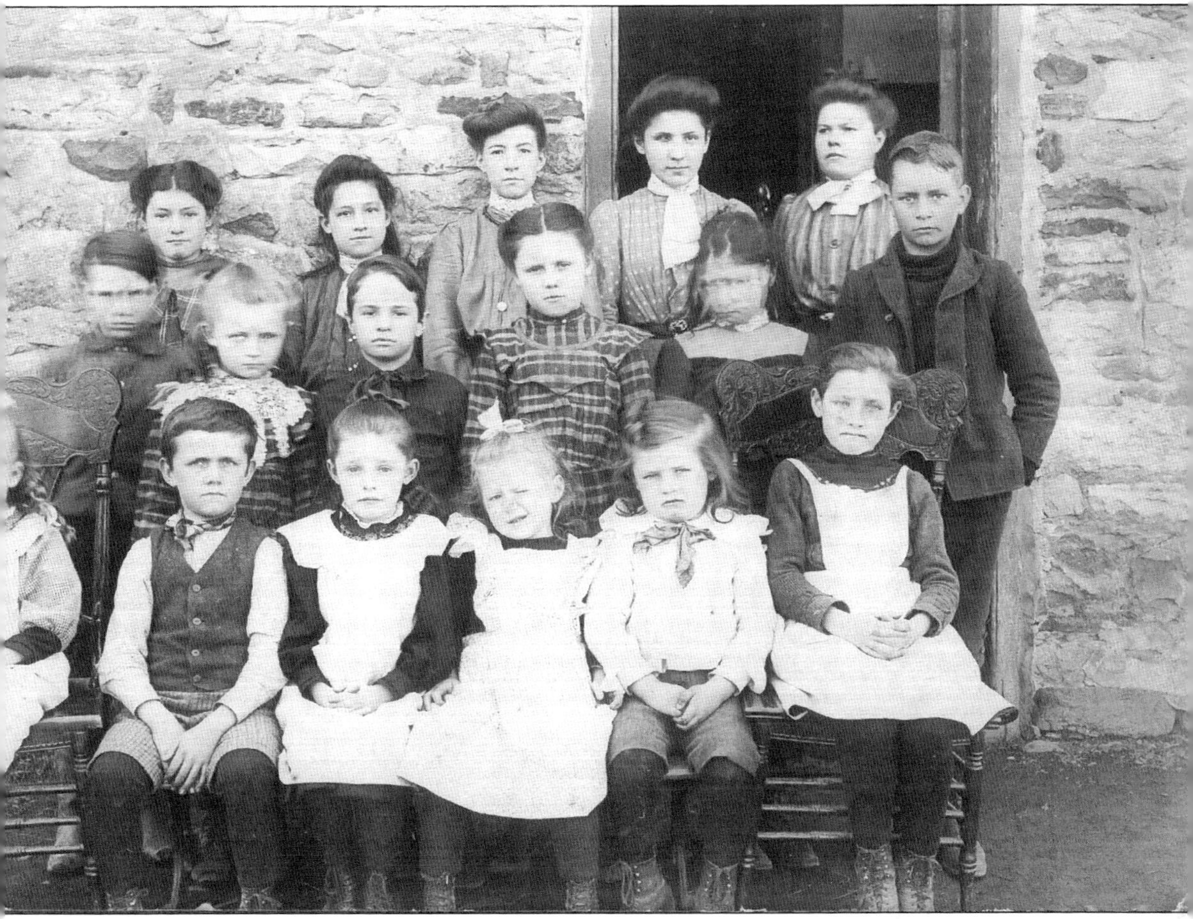

The class of 1896 at the cobblestone schoolhouse, Marcy District No. 3, is pictured here. They are, from left to right with teacher Ema Richards, (first row) Mary Marson, Ernest Davis, Jean Marson, Jullia Dingman, George Fryer, and Erma Griswald; (second row) Leslie Thomas, Minnie Fryer, Harold McClemens, Grav Fryer, Mary Carver, and Dewey Carver; (third row) Jennie Williams, Mary Williams, Serene Roberts, and Anna Thomas.

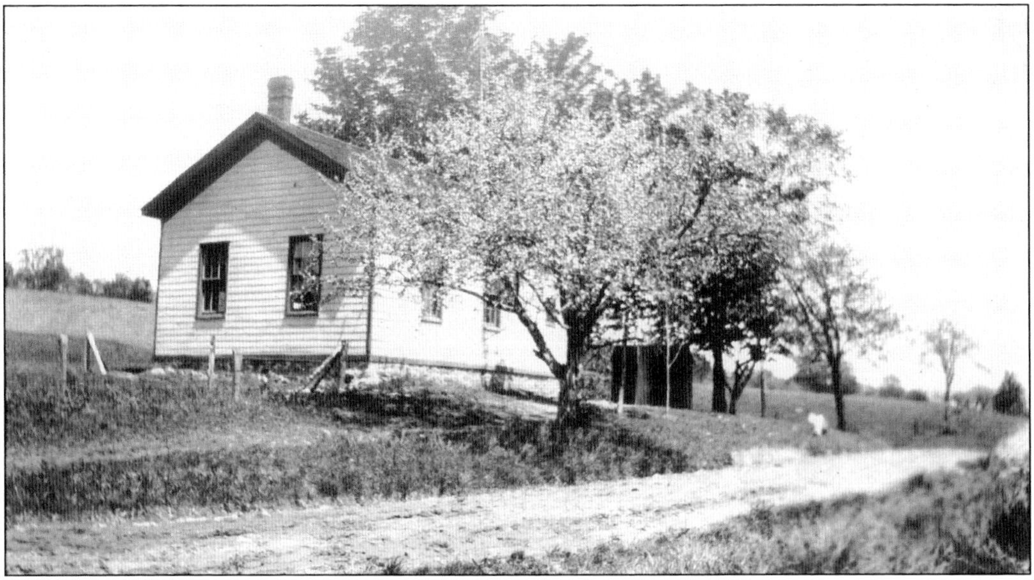

The one-room Doyle Road schoolhouse is a pleasant place to be in nice weather.

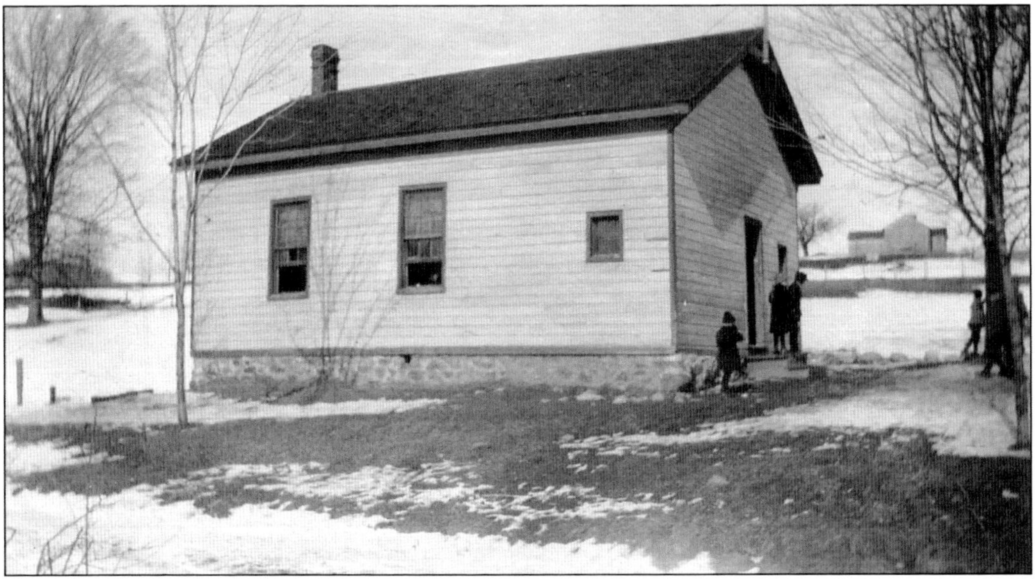

Seen here is the same schoolhouse in wintertime; it could have bad weather, making it a not-so-pleasant place to be.

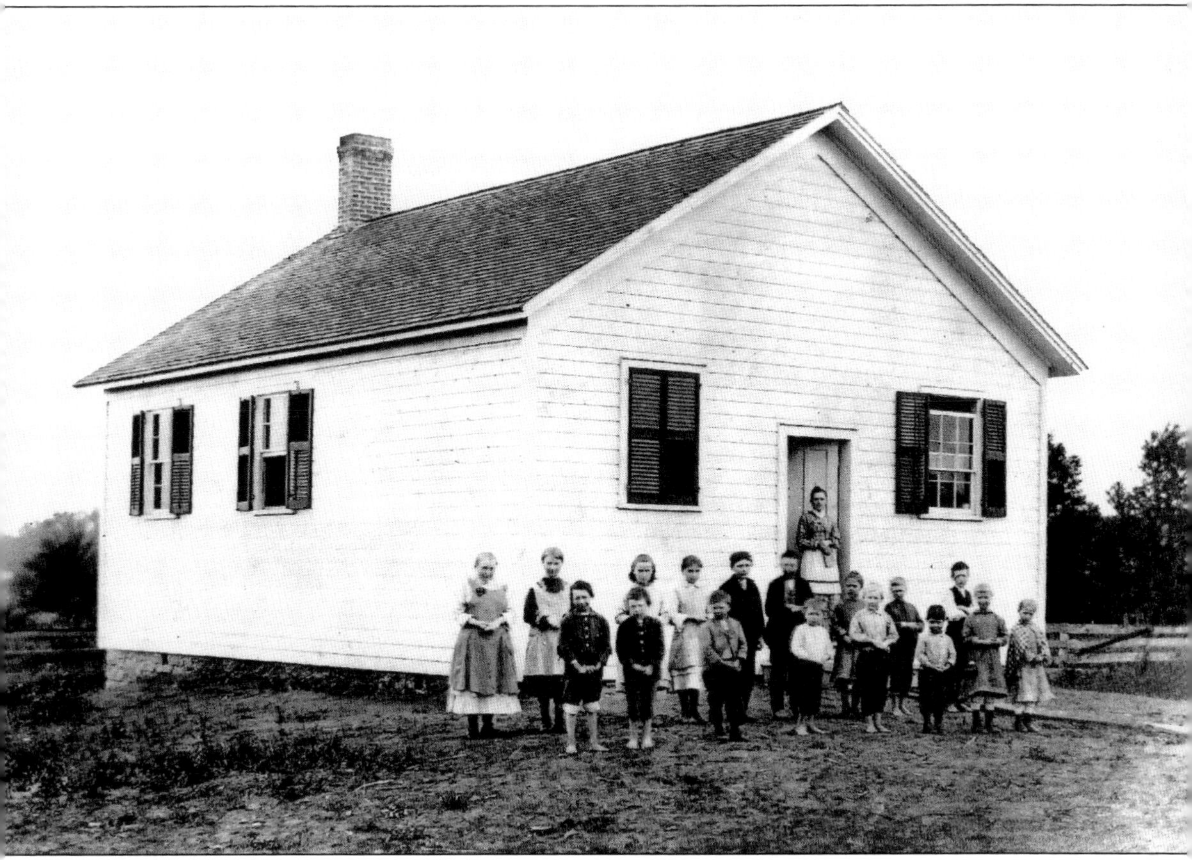

One of the newer one-room schoolhouses was in District No. 4 on Benton Road. After consolidation, this school was sold and converted into a home.

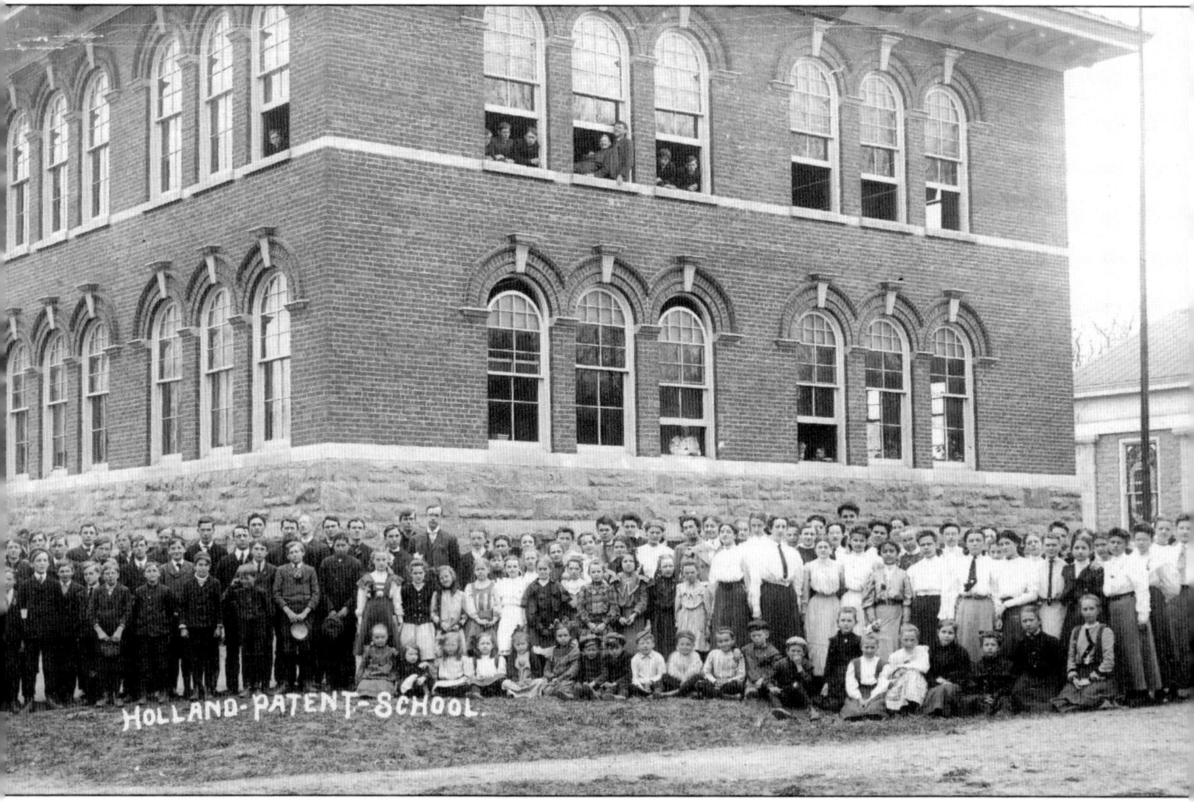

Holland Patent High School was in the next town beyond Stittville. When Stittville students reached high school age, they were brought here for their high school years.

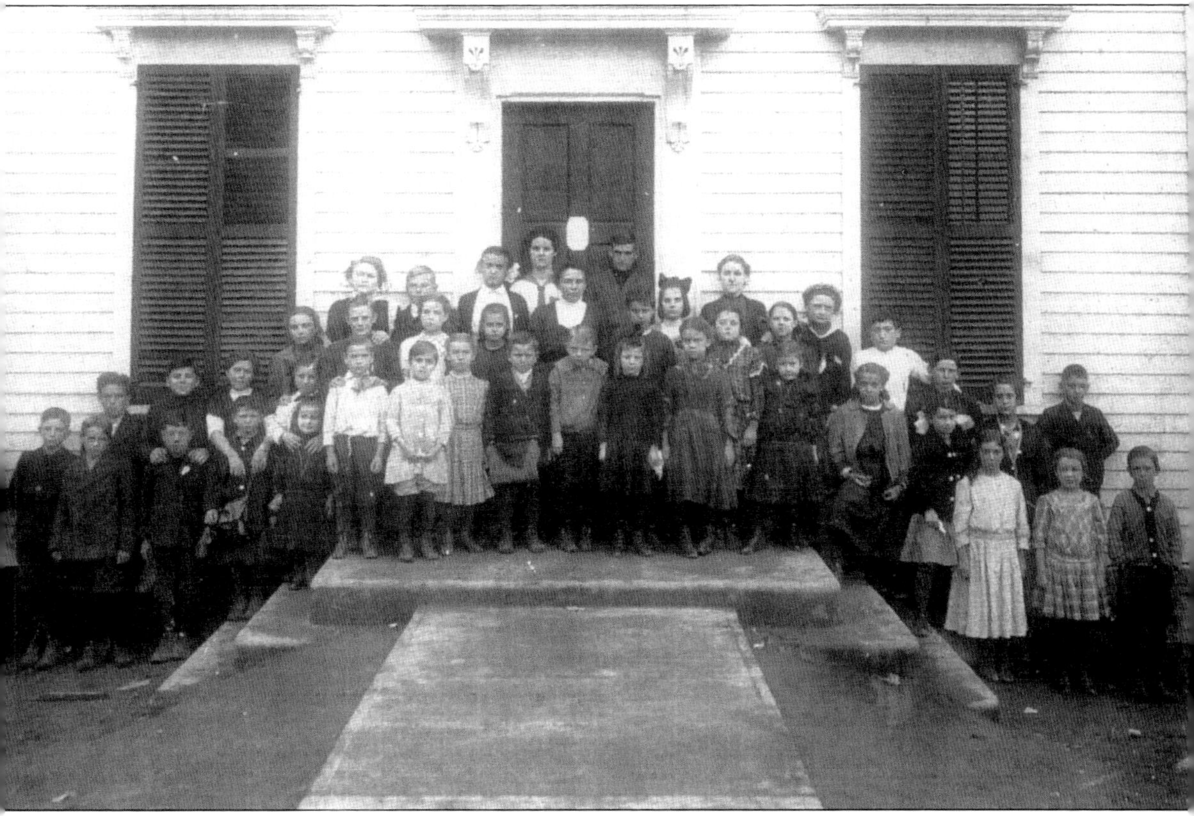

Unlike the one-room schoolhouse, this four-room graded school at Stittville had many more students of all ages, as shown in this 1912 photograph.

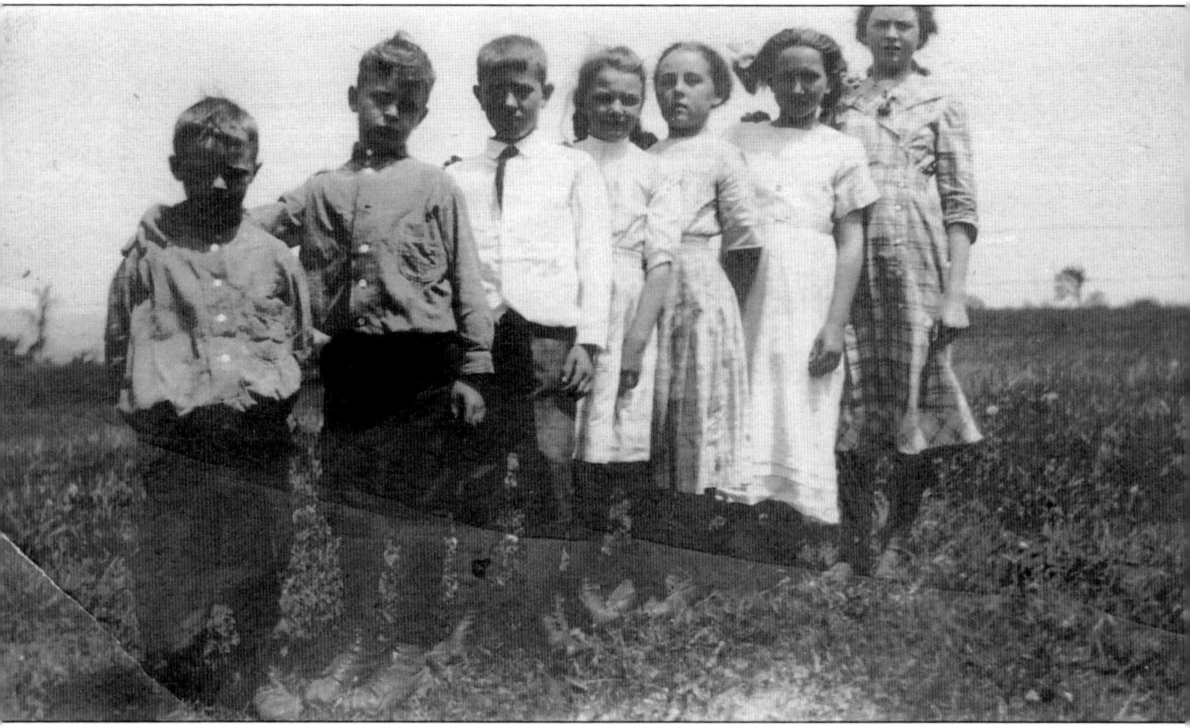

The light attendance in class at the Doyle Road school in 1916 included only the teacher and six students.

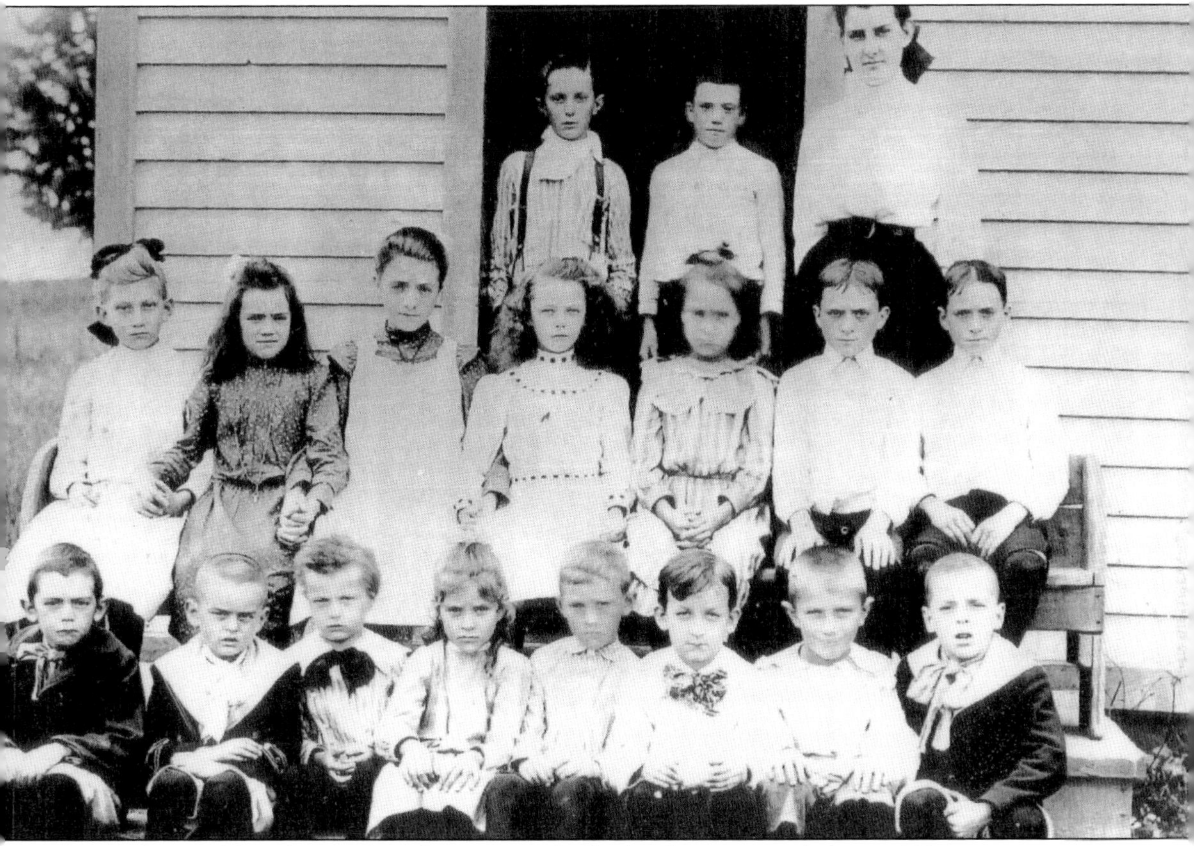

The teacher and her class at the Glass Factory Hill school are pictured about 1920.

STITTVILLE

Graded School,

Stittville, Oneida Co. N. Y.

FACULTY.

JOHN G. WILLIAMS, A. M., PRINCIPAL,
Classics, Mathematics, Nat. Sciences and German.

———— ———— PRECEPTRESS.

MISS FLORA A. UTTER, PRIMARY DEPARTMENT.

MRS. JOHN G. WILLIAMS,
Ornamental Branches.

MISS IDA M. CRANE,
Instrumental Music.

REFERENCES.

A. McMILLAN, SUPT. SCHOOLS, UTICA, N.Y.
WM. H. COMSTOCK, TRENTON, N.Y.
D. A. CRANE, M.D., HOLLAND PATENT, N.Y.
PORTER BUELL, STITTVILLE, N.Y.
REV. JAMES BUCK, FLOYD, N.Y.
JOHN. S. CAPRON, UTICA, N.Y.

CALENDAR.

FOR THE ACADEMIC YEAR, 1873-74.

FALL TERM begins, Monday, Sep.	1, 1873, and ends Friday,	Nov. 28, 1873.
WINTER " " "	Dec. 8, 1873, " "	Mar. 13, 1874.
SPRING " " "	Mar. 30, 1874, " "	June 26, 1874.
ANNIVERSARY................................. "		June 26, 1874.

This pamphlet for the Stittville Graded School indicates the faculty, references, courses of instruction, tuition costs, and other boarding expenses. Primary school cost $4 per term.

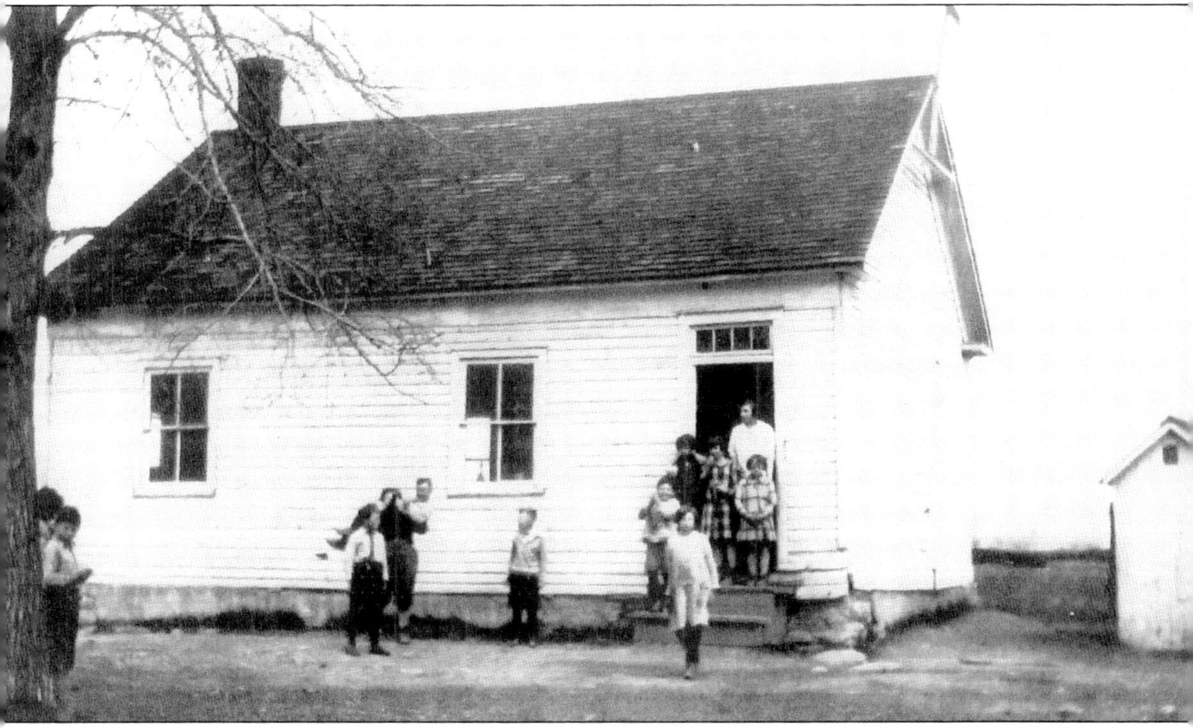

The schoolhouse on Cooms Road in upper Marcy is pictured here. The boy being held is future senator Jim Donovan.

Common School No. *One.*

Town of *Marcy.*

Report for the Term ending *Dec. 19,* 1893

Miss Clalista M. Edie

Spelling,	9	Arithmetic, { Class Standing / Examination	8
Reading,	10	Geography, { Class Standing / Examination	
Writing,	9½	Grammar, { Class Standing / Examination	9
Declamation,	7	:o:	
~~Composition,~~ *Dictation*	9½		
Drawing,	9½	Deportment,	8
Mapping,	—	Times Tardy,	14
History,	8	Days Absent,	0
~~Physiology,~~ *Civil Government*	8	Attendance,	72

☞ Parents or Guardians are requested to examine the report, and approve or disapprove, as the case may require.

John R. Pugh, Teacher.

SCALE--10 Denotes Perfect.

This is an actual report card from December 19, 1893.

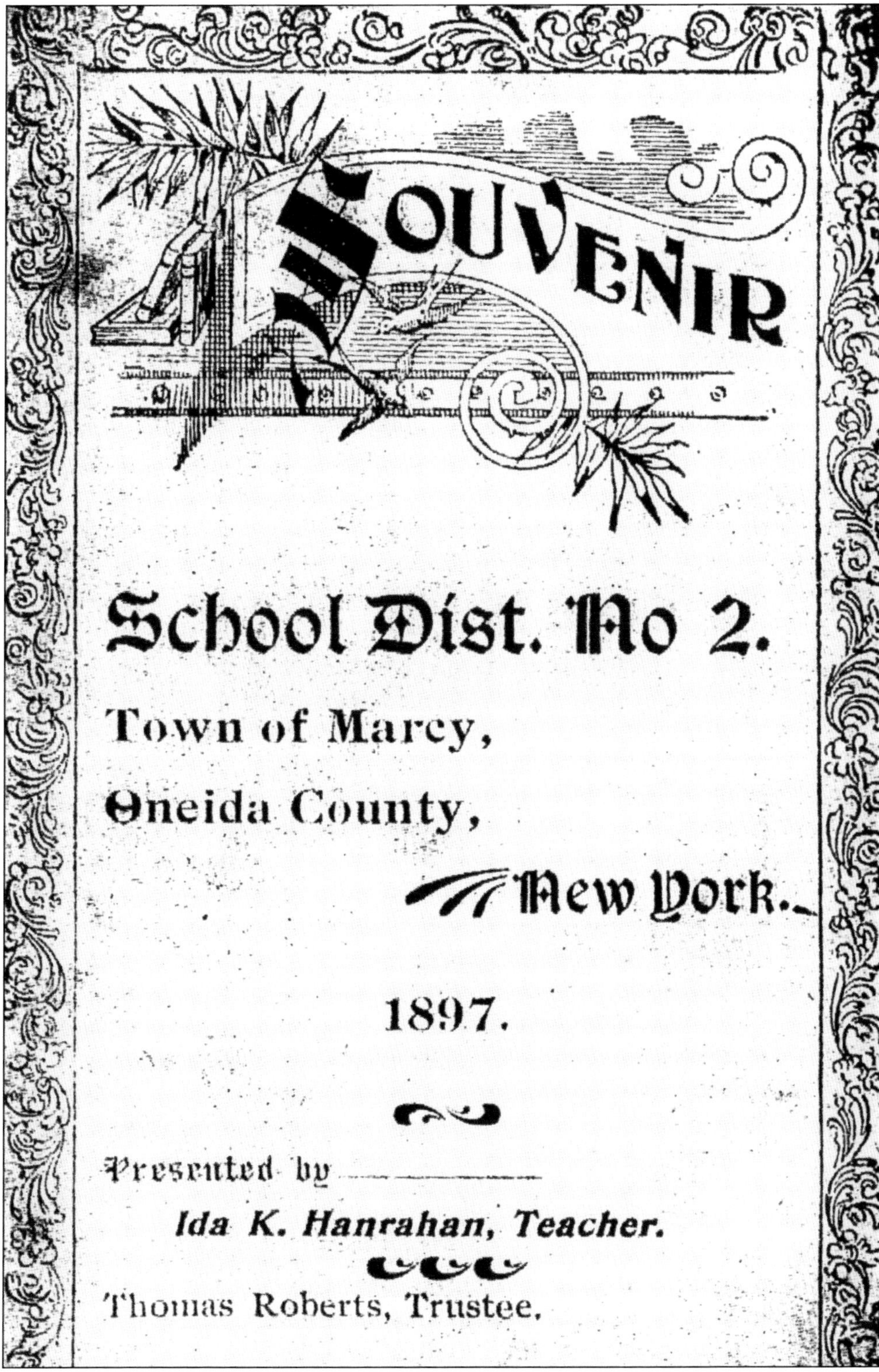
SOUVENIR

School Dist. No 2.

Town of Marcy,

Oneida County,

New York.

1897.

Presented by ____________

Ida K. Hanrahan, Teacher.

Thomas Roberts, Trustee.

An 1897 souvenir card is pictured here.

Names of Pupils.

Paul Bock

William Bock

Emma Carrier

George Edgar

Hayes Evans

Marian Evans

Hattie Edwards

Ada Hutchinson

Nettie Jones

Daniel Kane

Thomas Kane

Wallace Hulbert

Margaret Roberts

Pictured here is another view of an 1897 souvenir card.

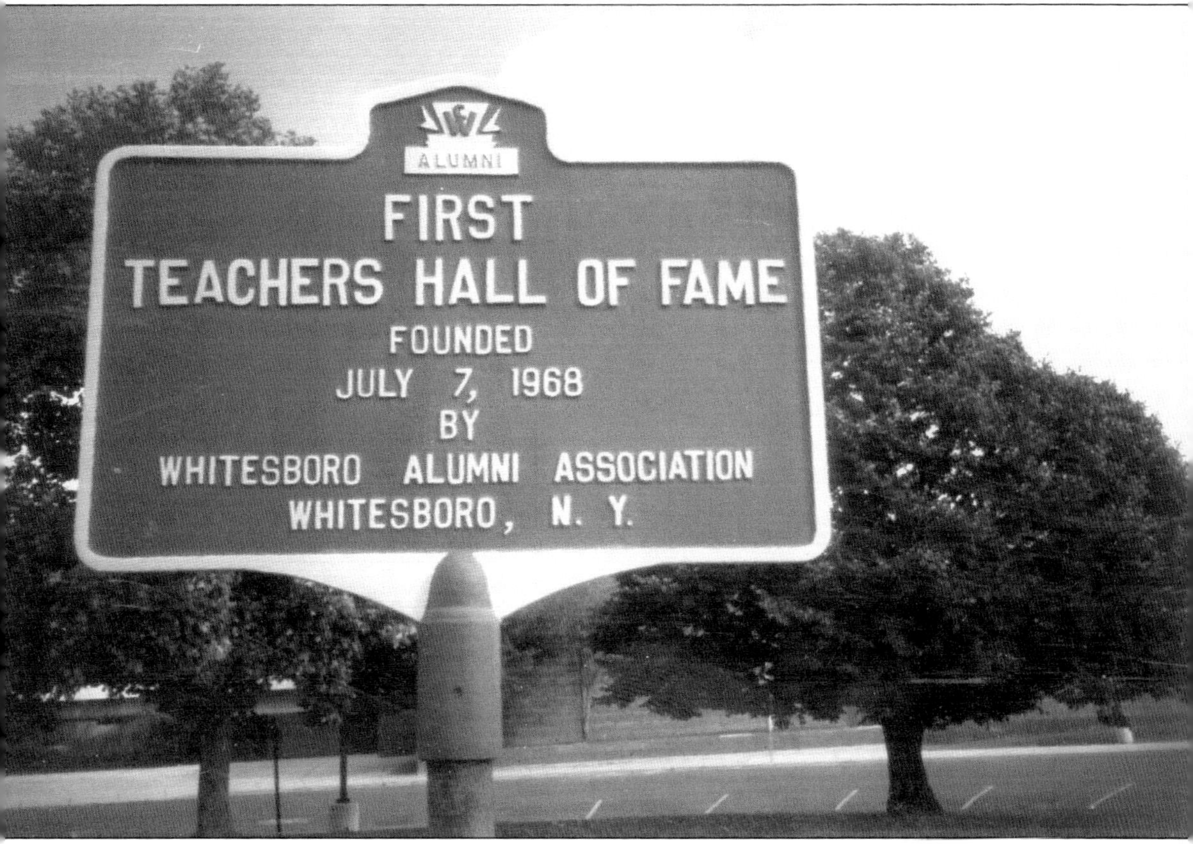

This historic marker is located in front of the Whitesboro Senior High School, which serves the entire district. The school is on the right-hand side of Route 291, about a mile north of Route 49 in the town of Marcy.

TOWN OF MARCY,

To WM. WOOLCOTT, Overseer of the Poor, Dr

1861	March 25th, Mr. Glisbie one sack Flour,	$1.50
	For getting and delivering the same,	1.50
	April 16th, Mr. Glisbie, to Veal, 21 pounds	1.05
	May 16th, Mr. Glisbie two sacks Flour	3.62
	For getting and delivering the same,	1.50
	June 20th, one day to Mrs. Miers	1.50
	June 21st, 6 pounds Sugar	.36
	1 pound Tea	.63
	2 sacks Flour for Mr. Glisbie	4.00
	For getting and delivering the same,	1.50
	July 1st, one day to Mrs. Miers,	1.50
	August 9th, 1 day getting Coffin for pauper,	1.50
	August 9th, paid for said Coffin,	2.50
	August 10th, for digging grave for pauper,	.50
	August 10th, for attending funeral of said pauper,	1.50
	August 13th, Mr. Glisbie, one sack Flour	1.38
	For getting and delivering the same	1.50
	September 2nd, Mr. Glisbie, one sack Flour	1.38
	For getting and delivering the same	1.50
	September 3rd, one day to Mrs. Miers	1.50
	October 8th, Mr. Glisbie one sack Flour	1.38
	For getting and delivering the same	1.50
	October 15th, Mr. Glisbie, to Beef 148 lbs. at 4 cts.	5.92
	For getting and delivering the same	1.50
		$42.22

	Brought Forward,	$42.22
	Nov. 27th, for meeting Supervisors,	1.50
	Nov. 29th, for meeting Supervisors,	1.50
	December 6th, for meeting Supervisors,	1.50
	December 17th, Mr. Glisbie, one sack Flour	1.63
	For getting and delivering the same,	1.50
	December 24th, helped Mr. Cassals' wife to boots and dress goods,	5.00
	For getting and delivering the same,	1.50
1862	January 9th, Mr. Glisbie, one sack Flour,	1.63
	For getting and delivering the same,	1.50
	January 18th, Mr. Glisbie 98 pounds beef at 4 cts.	3.92
	For getting and delivering the same	1.50
	January 31st, Mr. Glisbie, one sack Flour	1.63
	For getting and delivering the same	1.50
	February 3rd, helped the Glisbie family to Groceries	5.00
	For getting and delivering the same	1.50
	February 11th, helped Gains Barrett	10.00
	For ordering the same	1.50
	February 15th, for counsel with Collins	1.50
	February 26th, Mr. Glisbie, one sack Flour	1.56
	For getting and delivering the same	1.50
	March 3rd. Mr. Carstins, two bushels meal,	1.25
	For getting and delivering the same	1.50
		$93.36

ONEIDA COUNTY, as: TOWN OF MARCY—William Woolcott; being sworn, says that the items of the annexed account are correct; and that the disbursements and services charged therein have been in fact made or rendered; and that no part thereof has been paid or satisfied. WILLIAM WOLCOTT.

Sworn before me, this 13th day of Nov. 1862, E. T. MARSON, *Justice.*

This is the report of the overseer of the poor from 1861. Notice the costs recorded; for instance, a pound of beef cost 4¢.

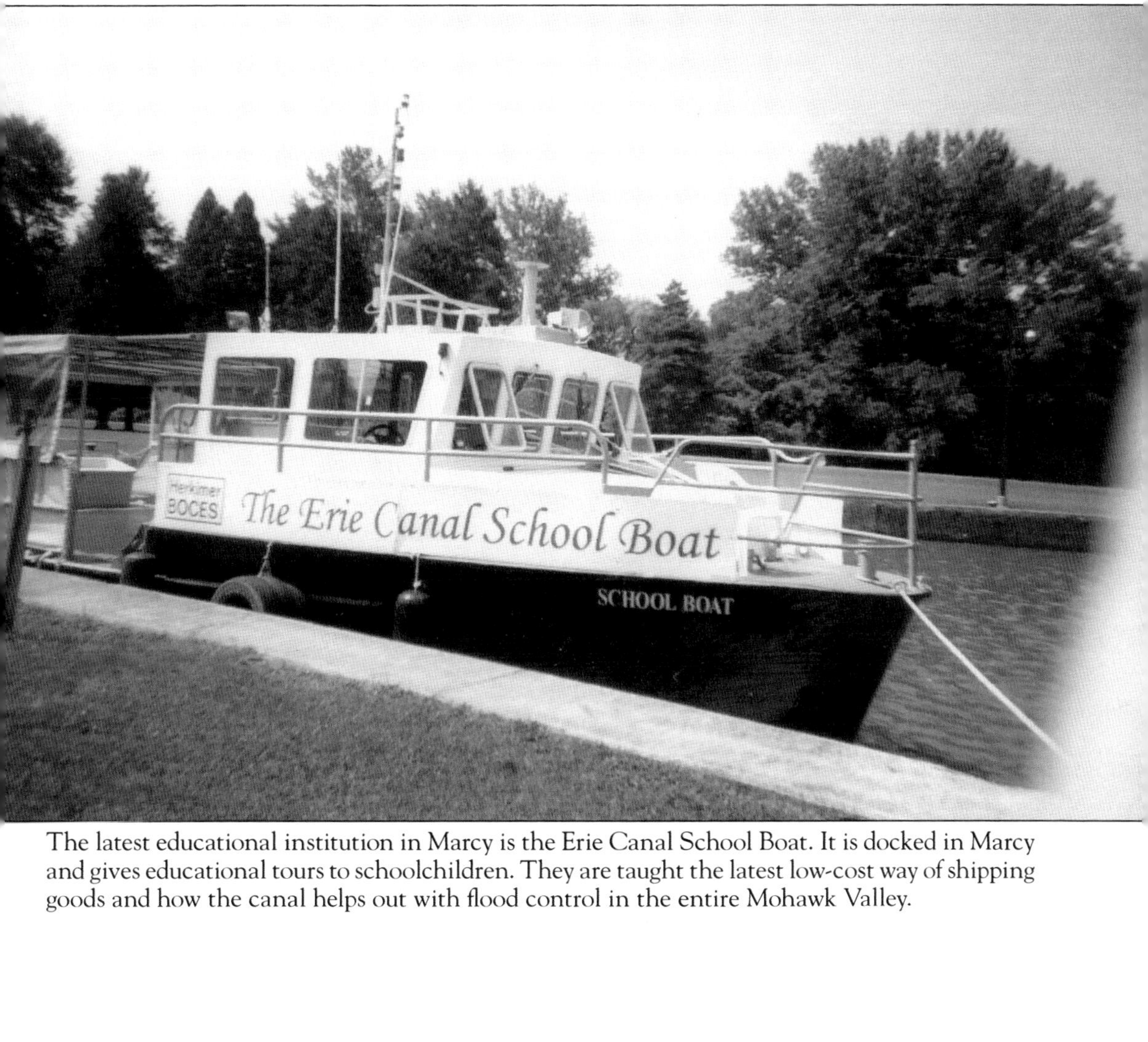

The latest educational institution in Marcy is the Erie Canal School Boat. It is docked in Marcy and gives educational tours to schoolchildren. They are taught the latest low-cost way of shipping goods and how the canal helps out with flood control in the entire Mohawk Valley.

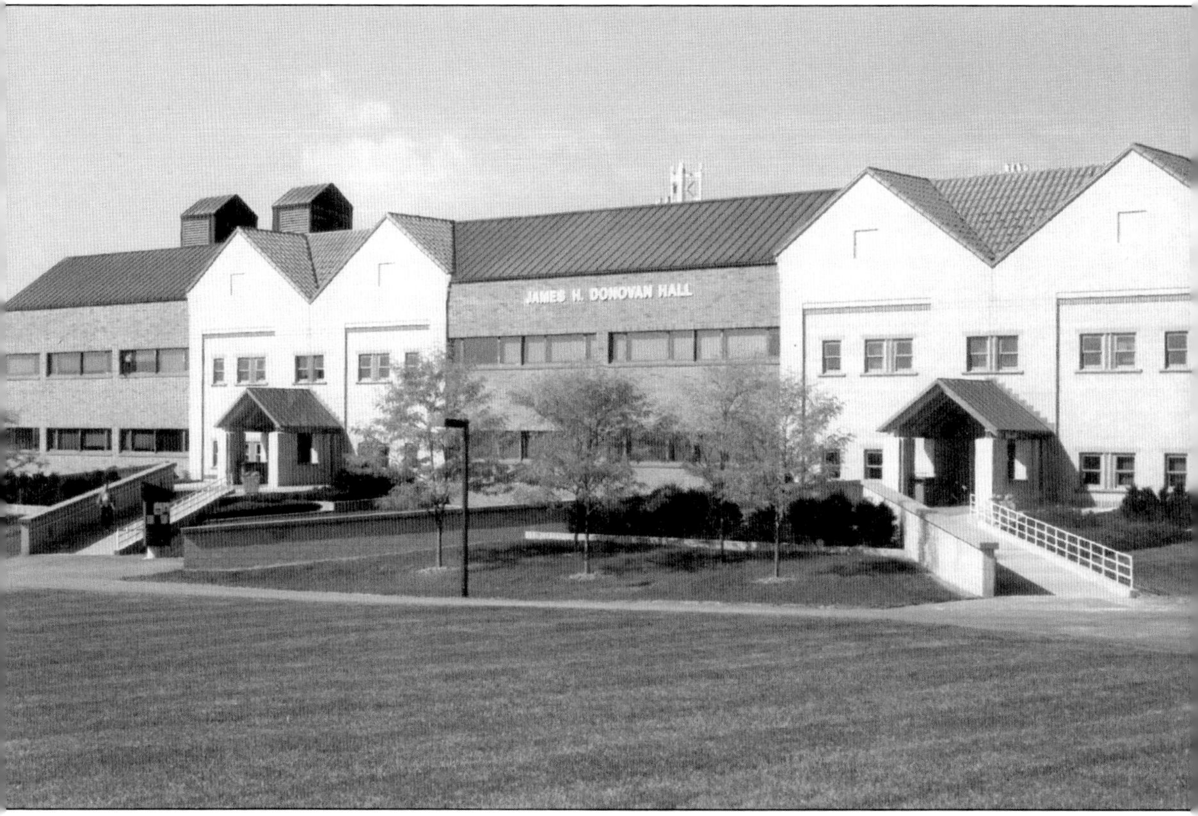

The future now looks different than it did 150 years ago. The new State University of New York Institute of Technology is already changing everything. From beautiful new buildings to several thousand students, the appearance of Marcy is forever changed.

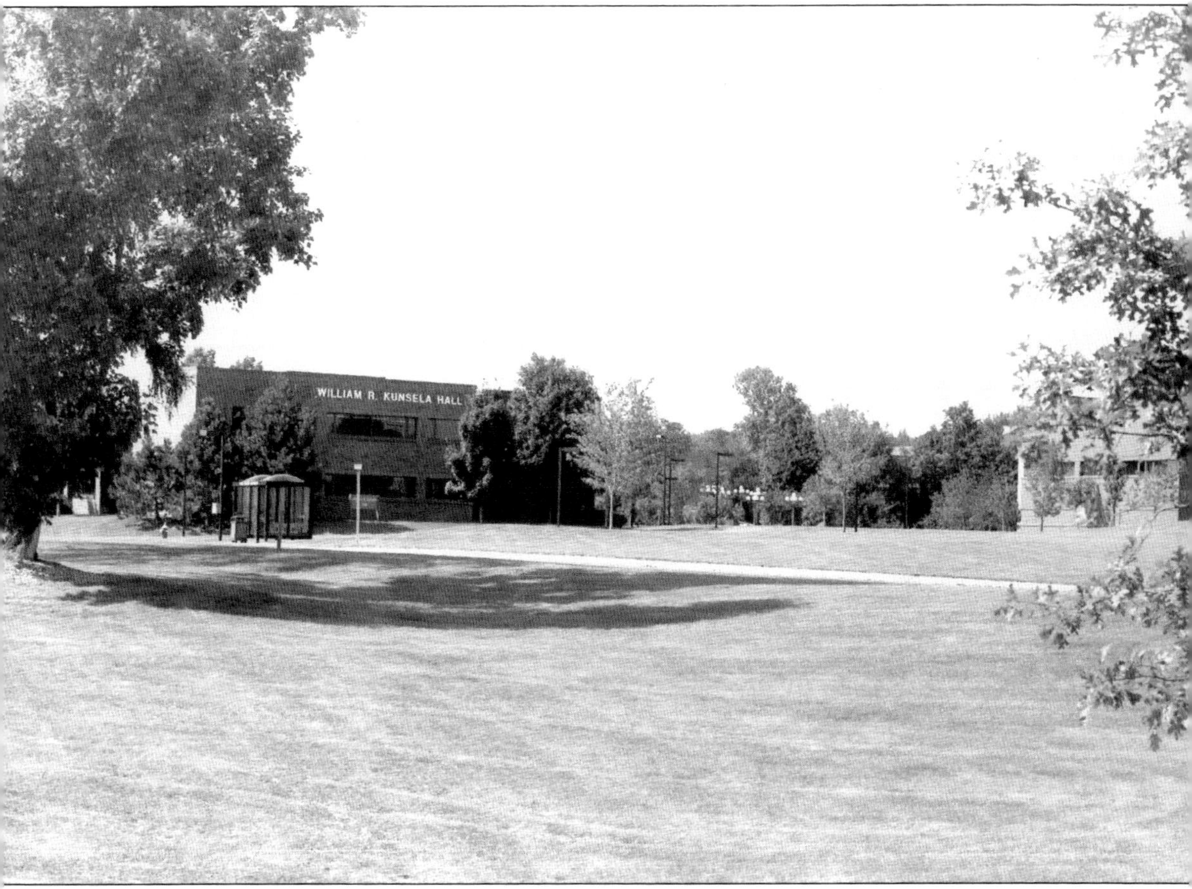

The main building and campus grounds of Marcy College are pictured here.

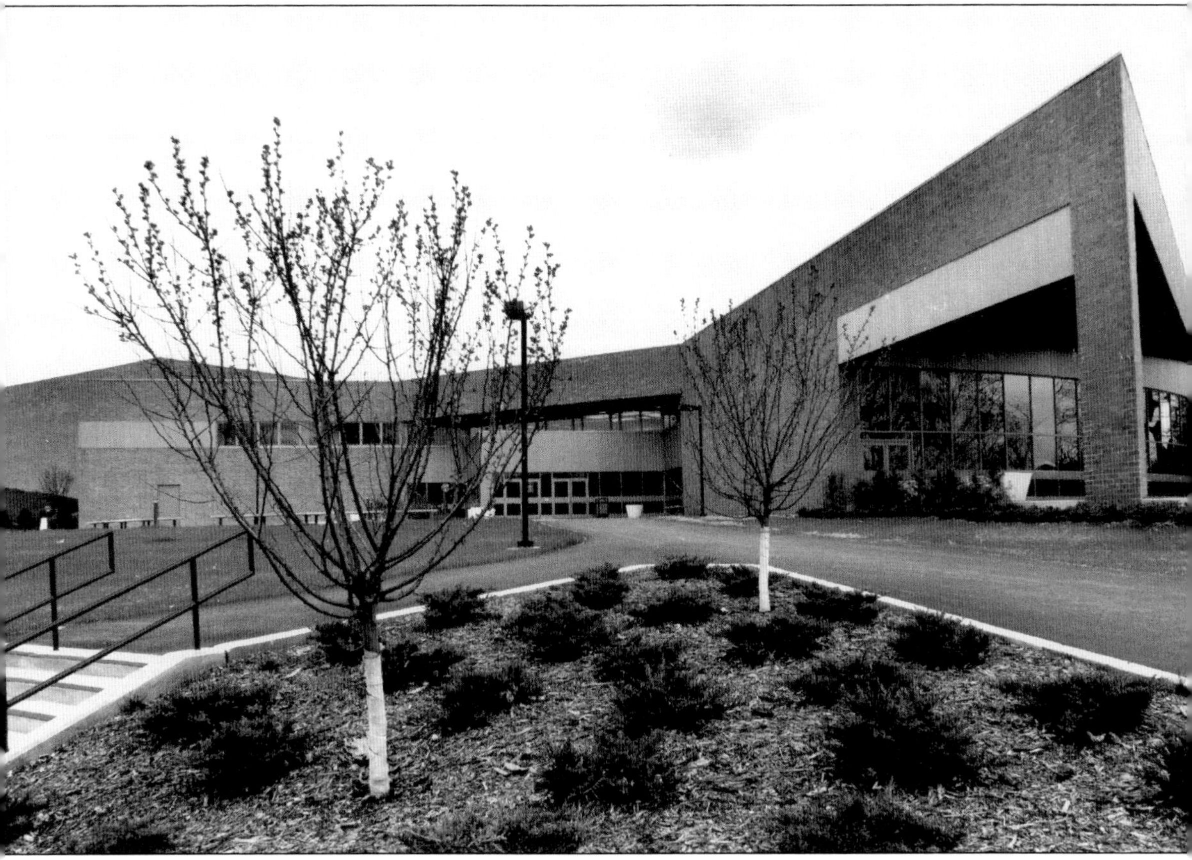

The new gymnasium, classrooms, and lunch facilities of Marcy College are pictured here.

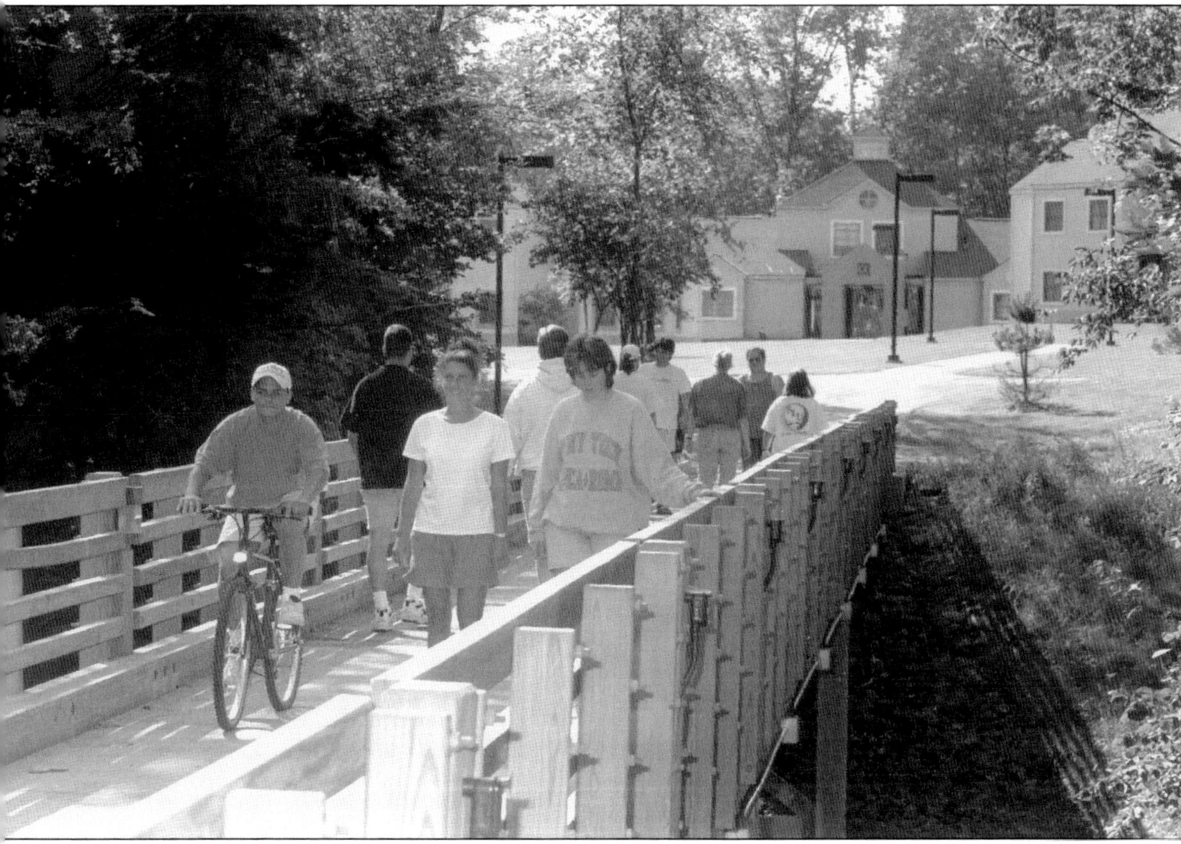
The bridge to the future, from dormitories to classrooms, is seen here; this is the future of Marcy.

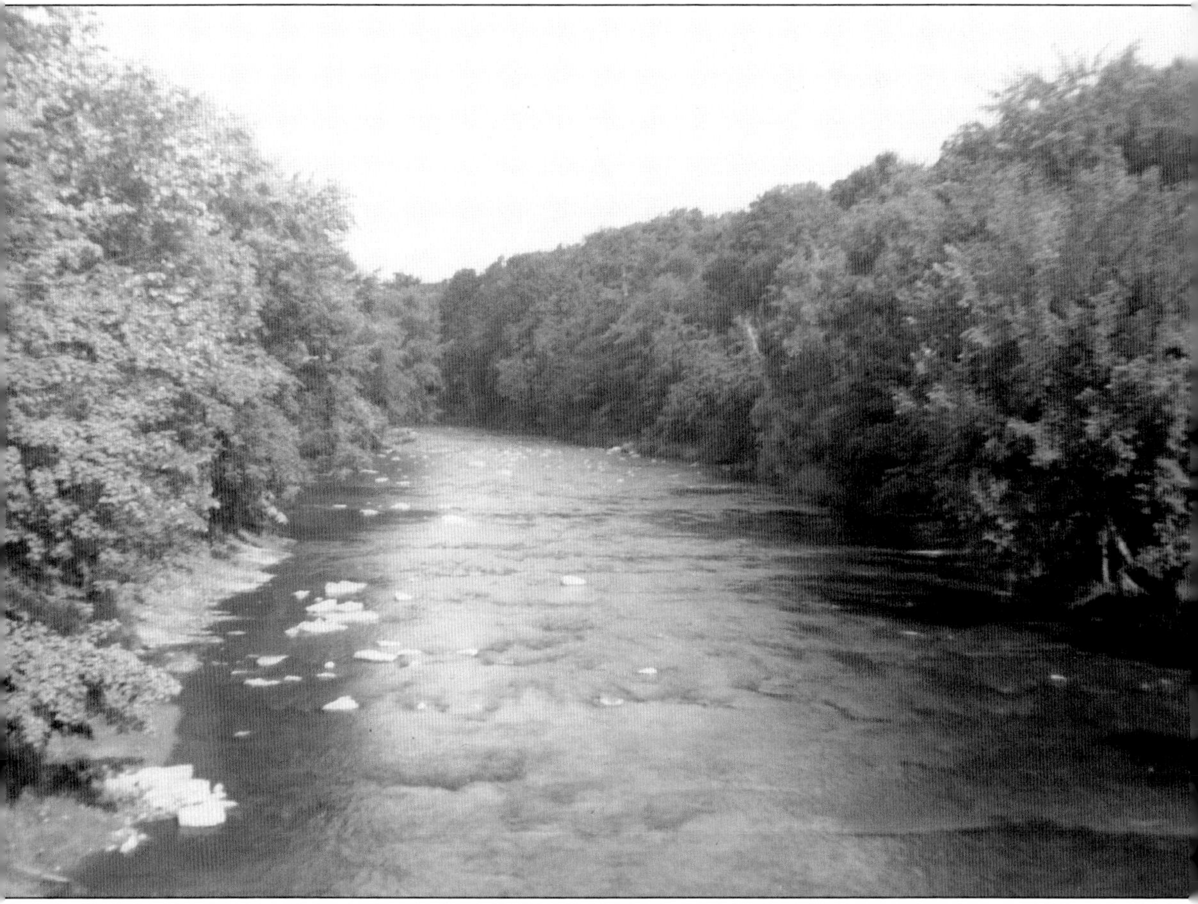

The Nine Mile Creek gets its name from being nine miles long, and most of it is in Marcy.

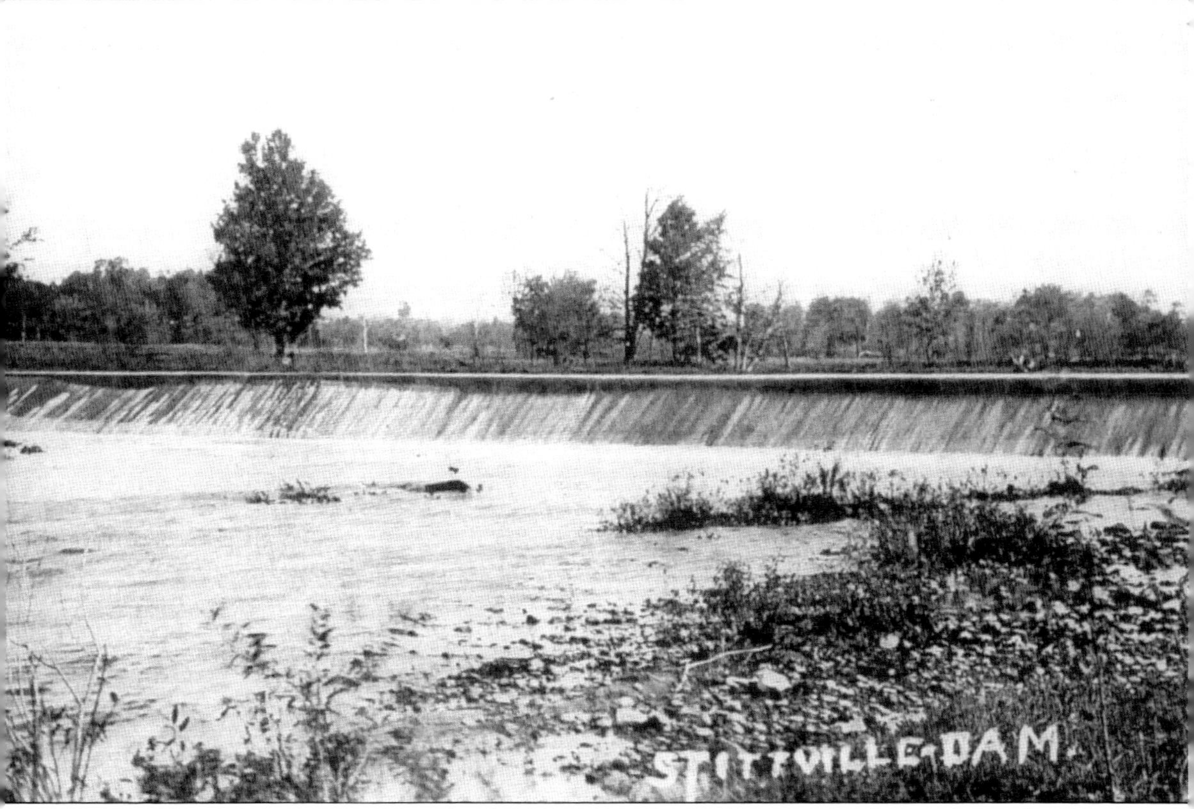

The last 175 years is now water over the dam. It is time to put the events of the past behind and cross over the bridge to the future.